A Concise Companion to
Shakespeare on Screen

Blackwell Concise Companions to Literature and Culture
General Editor: David Bradshaw, University of Oxford

This series offers accessible, innovative approaches to major areas of literary study. Each volume provides an indispensable companion for anyone wishing to gain an authoritative understanding of a given period or movement's intellectual character and contexts.

Chaucer	Edited by Corinne Saunders
English Renaissance Literature	Edited by Donna Hamilton
Shakespeare on Screen	Edited by Diana E. Henderson
The Restoration and Eighteenth Century	Edited by Cynthia Wall
The Victorian Novel	Edited by Francis O'Gorman
Modernism	Edited by David Bradshaw
Postwar American Literature and Culture	Edited by Josephine G. Hendin
Twentieth-Century American Poetry	Edited by Stephen Fredman
Contemporary British Fiction	Edited by James F. English
Feminist Theory	Edited by Mary Eagleton

A Concise Companion to
Shakespeare on Screen

Edited by Diana E. Henderson

Blackwell
Publishing

BLACKWELL PUBLISHING
350 Main Street, Malden, MA 02148-5020, USA
9600 Garsington Road, Oxford OX4 2DQ, UK
550 Swanston Street, Carlton, Victoria 3053, Australia

First published 2006 by Blackwell Publishing Ltd

1   2006

Library of Congress Cataloging-in-Publication Data

A concise companion to Shakespeare on screen / edited by Diana E. Henderson.
    p. cm.—(Blackwell concise companions to literature and culture)
    Includes bibliographical references and index.
    ISBN-13: 978-1-4051-1510-0 (hardcover : alk. paper)
    ISBN-10: 1-4051-1510-6 (hardcover : alk. paper)
    ISBN-13: 978-1-4051-1511-7 (pbk. : alk. paper)
    ISBN-10: 1-4051-1511-4 (pbk. : alk. paper)
    1. Shakespeare, William, 1564–1616—Film and video adaptations.   2. English
drama—Film and video adaptations.   3. Film adaptations.   I. Henderson, Diana E.,
1957–   II. Series.

    PR3093.C65 2006
    791.43'.6—dc22
                                                                    2005006592

A catalogue record for this title is available from the British Library.

Set in 10/12.5pt Meridien
by Graphicraft Limited, Hong Kong
Printed and bound in India
by Replika Press, Pvt. Ltd

The publisher's policy is to use permanent paper from mills that operate
a sustainable forestry policy, and which has been manufactured from pulp
processed using acid-free and elementary chlorine-free practices. Furthermore,
the publisher ensures that the text paper and cover board used have met
acceptable environmental accreditation standards.

For further information on
Blackwell Publishing, visit our website:
www.blackwellpublishing.com

Contents

Contents

Acknowledgments

My thanks to the Blackwell staff for their exemplary work – most especially to Emma Bennett for her warm support and professionalism from start to finish, and to Jennifer Hunt, Karen Wilson, and Brigitte Lee for crucial contributions along the way. My sister Joyce Henderson has once again provided an extraordinarily helpful index, and my contributors have taught me much about collegiality and friendship as well as Shakespeare on screen. Finally, my debt of gratitude – and dedication – to the MIT faculty in comparative media studies, arts, women's studies, and literature, and to Michael Krass, for helping me learn what I needed to know.

Notes on Contributors

Pascale Aebischer is a Lecturer in Renaissance Studies at the School of English, University of Exeter. She is the author of *Shakespeare's Violated Bodies: Stage and Screen Performance* (2004), numerous book and journal articles, and is the principal editor of *Remaking Shakespeare: Performance across Media, Genres and Cultures* (2003).

Mark Thornton Burnett is Professor of Renaissance Studies at Queen's University, Belfast. His most recent book is the co-edited collection *Reconceiving the Renaissance: A Critical Reader* (2005).

Anthony Dawson teaches at University of British Columbia. His most recent books are *The Culture of Playgoing in Shakespeare's England* (2001, with Paul Yachnin) and an edition of *Troilus and Cressida* in the Cambridge series (2003). He has completed a series of articles on text and performance, and is at work on the Arden 3 *Timon of Athens* and a book on memory and Elizabethan theater.

Peter S. Donaldson is a Fellow of the Royal Historical Society, Professor of Literature at MIT, and Director of the Shakespeare Electronic Archive. He is the author of *Machiavelli and Mystery of State* (1988), *Shakespearean Films/Shakespearean Directors* (1990), and numerous essays and multimedia presentations on Shakespeare film. Currently he is working on a book on cross-media Shakespeare.

Anthony R. Guneratne is Associate Professor of Communication at Florida Atlantic University. He has published on issues of postcoloniality in film and literature; the interrelation of film and other media; film history and historiography; and Shakespeare in the cinema. He is completing a book on *Shakespeare, Film Studies, and'the Visual Cultures of Modernity* for Palgrave Macmillan.

Diana E. Henderson is Associate Professor of Literature at MIT, and also teaches in the Comparative Media Studies and Women's Studies Programs. She is the author of *Passion Made Public: Elizabethan Lyric, Gender and Performance* (1995), numerous articles on early modern drama and culture, and *Shake-shifters: The Art of Collaborating with Shakespeare Across Time and Media* (Cornell University Press, 2006).

Barbara Hodgdon, Adjunct Professor of English at the University of Michigan, is the author of *The End Crowns All: Closure and Contradiction in Shakespeare's History* (1991), *The First Part of King Henry the Fourth: Texts and Contexts* (1997), and *The Shakespeare Trade: Performances and Appropriations* (1998). She served as guest editor for a special issue of *Shakespeare Quarterly* on Shakespeare films, is editing the Arden 3 *The Taming of the Shrew*, and co-edited, with William B. Worthen, the *Blackwell Companion to Shakespeare and Performance*.

Douglas Lanier is Associate Professor of English at the University of New Hampshire. He has written *Shakespeare and Modern Popular Culture* (2002), as well as articles on Shakespearean comedy, Shakespeare on film, and Renaissance drama. He is currently working on a study of cultural stratification in early modern British drama.

Kathleen McLuskie is director of the University of Birmingham Shakespeare Institute at Stratford-upon-Avon. She has published widely on feminist and materialist approaches to early modern drama as well as on the performance of Shakespeare's plays on the international stage. She is currently completing a book on *Macbeth* and working on *The Economics of Early Modern Culture*.

Roberta E. Pearson is Professor of Film Studies and Director of the Institute of Film Studies at the University of Nottingham. Her publications include *Eloquent Gestures: The Transformation of Performance Style in the Griffith Biograph Films* (1992), the co-edited collection *Cult Television* (2004), and, with William Uricchio, *Reframing Culture: The Case of the Vitagraph Quality Films* (1993).

Robert Shaughnessy is Professor of Theater at the University of Kent. His publications include *Representing Shakespeare: England, History and the RSC* (1994), *The Shakespeare Effect: A History of Twentieth-Century Performance* (1992), and, as editor, *Shakespeare on Film* (1998) and *Shakespeare in Performance* (2000). He is currently writing the Routledge Critical Guide on Shakespeare and editing *The Cambridge Companion to Shakespeare and Popular Culture*.

William Uricchio is Professor of Comparative Media Studies at MIT and Professor of Comparative Media History at Utrecht University in the Netherlands. He is a Guggenheim, Humboldt, and Fulbright Fellow. His research considers the transformation of media technologies into media practices, in particular their role in (re)constructing representation, knowledge, and publics.

Elsie Walker is co-leader of the Cinema Studies Program at Salisbury University, Maryland, and has published widely on film adaptations of Shakespeare. Her teaching and research interests include processes of adaptation, international cinemas, and soundtracks. She is editor of *Literature/Film Quarterly*.

Bibliographical Note

In order to avoid redundancy, works cited in multiple essays are listed in the Select Bibliography at the end of the volume. Films and videos are listed within the following chronological chart rather than in a separate filmography/videography, for ease of historical contextualization. For most entries, fuller production information is most readily available online through the Internet Movie Database: www.imdb.com/.

Chronology

Year	Historical events	Media events	Shakespeare on screen
1898	Zola's "J'accuse." Spanish–American War		
1899	Dreyfus Affair ends; Boer War begins	Georges Méliès' *L'Affaire Dreyfus*. Marconi sends radiowaves across the English Channel	Film of Herbert Beerbohm Tree's *King John*
1900	Freud publishes *The Interpretation of Dreams*		
1901	Queen Victoria dies; Edward VII king. Theodore Roosevelt elected President. US war in the Philippines ends	Marconi sends radiowaves across the Atlantic	
1902	Boer War ends. Education Act subsidizes secondary education in Britain	Alfred Steiglitz begins publication of the journal *Camera Work*	
1903	Wright Brothers fly first powered airplane at Kitty Hawk	Edwin S. Porter's *The Great Train Robbery* creates a sensation	
1905	St. Petersburg Massacre. Einstein publishes the Special Theory of Relativity	Charles Tait's *The Story of the Kelly Gang*, first feature-length film	

1906	Fessenden's north Atlantic voice broadcast (AM radio)	
1907		Méliès' *Hamlet*; Méliès' *Shakespeare Writing Julius Caesar*
1908	D. W. Griffith begins his career at Biograph Studios	D. W. Griffith's *The Taming of the Shrew*
1910	Edward VII dies; George V becomes king. Union of South Africa	
1911		William Barker's film of Tree's *Henry VIII*; film of F. R. Benson's *Richard III*
1913	Max Reinhardt's *Die Insel der Seligen* and stage production of *A Midsummer Night's Dream*; Parliamentary debates regarding a British national theater	Hanns Heitz Ewers and Stellan Rye's *A Midsummer Night's Dream*
1914	World War I begins	Reinhardt's *Venezianische Nacht*
1915		Griffith's *The Birth of a Nation*
1916	Easter uprising in Ireland	
1917	Russian Revolution. US enters World War I. Balfour declaration	
1918	End of World War I. Formation of independent Irish Parliament. (Limited) women's suffrage in Britain	

Year	Historical events	Media events	Shakespeare on screen
1919	League of Nations established	Shortwave radio invented. RCA established	
1920	Government of Ireland Act. 19th amendment to the US Constitution allows women's suffrage	Robert Wiene's *The Cabinet of Doctor Caligari*	Sven Gade's *Hamlet*
1921	Establishment of Irish Free State; Irish civil war	Newbolt report on "The Teaching of English in England"	
1922	Mussolini's Fascists invited to form government in Italy	40 million cinema tickets sold per week in the US; BBC begins radio broadcasting	
1923	Ceasefire in Ireland	Experimental wireless television broadcasts begin	
1924	Death of Lenin	Leopold and Loeb trial	
1925		Sergei Eisenstein's *The Battleship Potemkin*; Scopes' "Monkey" trial	Hans Neumann's *A Midsummer Night's Dream*
1926		NBC begins radio broadcasting; Alan Crosland's *Don Juan*, the first publicly shown talkie, screened in New York	*Shakespeare's Country*, in *Wonderful Britain* series
1927	Charles Lindbergh makes first non-stop solo trans-Atlantic flight	Cinematograph Films Act passes in UK Parliament	

1928	Amelia Earhart first woman to fly across the Atlantic	Crosland's *The Jazz Singer* (released October 1927) consolidates interest in sound film; GE begins (limited) regular network television broadcasting; *Amos and Andy* begins on radio; completion of the Oxford English Dictionary	Sam Taylor's (Pickfair) *The Taming of the Shrew*
1929	Stock Market Crash, leading to the Great Depression. Stalin to power in the Soviet Union	BBC begins test television broadcasts	
1930		Hays' Production Code formalized	
1931		James Whale's *Frankenstein*; CBS begins regular television broadcasting	
1932	Franklin Roosevelt elected President	Opening of the new Shakespeare Memorial Theatre at Stratford; BBC first broadcast to the Empire (forerunner of the world service); Herbert Kalmus perfects 3-color Technicolor process; Lindbergh baby kidnapping	
1933	Hilter and Nazi party to power in Germany		
1934	Beginning of the Long March in China	Breen office enforcement of Hays' Production Code; F.D.R. begins his radio "fireside chats"	

Year	Historical events	Media events	Shakespeare on screen
1935	Establishment of the WPA (US)	*Fibber, McGee and Molly* begins 15-year radio run; Germany begins regularly daily television broadcasting (until 1944)	Max Reinhardt and William Dieterle's *A Midsummer Night's Dream*
1936	George V dies; Edward VIII's abdication. George VI becomes king. Beginning of the Spanish Civil War	BBC begins regular television broadcasting (until 1939); the Berlin Olympic Games; Berlin begins cable television	George Cukor's *Romeo and Juliet*; Paul Czinner's *As You Like It*
1937	Sino-Japanese war	Tyrone Guthrie's Old Vic *Hamlet* starring Laurence Olivier; Amelia Earhart's disappearance	
1938	Kristallnacht	80 million cinema tickets sold per week in US; second Cinematograph Films Act passes in UK Parliament	
1939	Spanish Civil War ends with Franco in power. Germany invades Poland; beginning of World War II	Victor Fleming (et al.)'s *Gone With the Wind*; BBC television closed for duration of the war	
1940		Cukor's *The Philadelphia Story*	
1941	Bombing of Pearl Harbor; US enters World War II. Genocidal policies of the Holocaust begun in Germany	Orson Welles' *Citizen Kane*; Federal Communications Commission issues first commercial television station licenses in US	

1944		*Laurence Olivier's Henry V*
1945	End of war in Europe. Death of Roosevelt. United Nations established	
1946	US drops atomic bombs on Hiroshima and Nagasaki; Japan surrenders. Ho Chi Minh leads offensive against French in Vietnam	Michael Powell and Emeric Pressberger's *A Matter of Life and Death*; Olivier's King Lear stage performance at the Old Vic; formation of the British Arts Council
1947	Indian independence and partition	Dalton duty on US films (UK) — *Cukor's A Double Life*
1948	State of Israel established	Anglo-American Film Agreement; Powell and Pressberger's *The Red Shoes* and David Lean's *Oliver Twist*; Ed Sullivan's *The Toast of the Town* begins, becomes *The Ed Sullivan Show* in 1955, and goes on to be the longest-running variety television show in history (running until 1971) — Olivier's *Hamlet*; Orson Welles' *Macbeth*
1949	Fall of Chiang Kai-Shek and establishment of the People's Republic of China under Mao Tse-Tung; China invades Tibet	Renewed Parliamentary debates regarding British national theater; MIT introduces "Whirlwind," the first real-time computer
1950	Korean War begins: UN resolution to assist South Korean government	

Year	Historical events	Media events	Shakespeare on screen
1951		CBS temporarily begins color television broadcasts; stopped due to the Korean War; video tape invented	
1952	George VI dies; Elizabeth II becomes queen. Mau Mau uprising begins	Gene Kelly and Stanley Donen's *Singin' in the Rain*	Welles' *Othello*
1953	End of the Korean War. Death of Stalin	*The Robe*, first Hollywood Cinemascope film, released; coronation of Queen Elizabeth II televised	George Sidney's *Kiss Me, Kate*
1954	French defeat at Dien Bien Phu; Vietnamese independence from France negotiated, split of North and South Vietnam	Akira Kurosawa's *The Seven Samurai*; the Army–McCarthy hearings televised; François Truffaut's "A Certain Tendency in French Cinema"	
1955			Sergei Yutkevich's *Othello*; Olivier's *Richard III*
1956	Suez crisis. Hungarian revolution	John Osborne's *Look Back in Anger* on stage at the Royal Court, London	
1957	European Economic Community (Common Market) established. Soviet Union launches Sputnik I	Ingmar Bergman's *The Seventh Seal*	Kurosawa's *Throne of Blood* (*The Castle of the Spider's Web*)
1958	Creation of NASA	Tony Richardson's film of *Look Back in Anger*	

1959	Fidel Castro to power in Cuba		Kurosawa's *The Bad Sleep Well*
1960	Sixteen newly independent African states join the UN	Karel Reisz's *Saturday Night and Sunday Morning*; John Sturges' *The Magnificent Seven*; Resolution 42 of British Trade Unions Conference leads to Centre Fortytwo; Peter Hall's formation of the modern Royal Shakespeare Company	
1961	US-sponsored Bay of Pigs invasion of Cuba	Telstar used to broadcast trans-Atlantic television; Bernstein and Sondheim's *West Side Story* on Broadway; Richardson's *A Taste of Honey*	
1962	Cuban Missile Crisis. India–China conflict	Richardson's *The Loneliness of the Long Distance Runner*	
1963	President Kennedy assassinated		
1964	Harold Wilson's Labour government begins (UK). Civil Rights Act signed by US President Johnson	English translation of Jan Kott's *Shakespeare Our Contemporary*; The Beatles appear on *The Ed Sullivan Show*	Grigori Kozintsev's *Hamlet*; Gielgud's *Hamlet* (rehearsal footage)
1965	President Johnson sends US troops to Vietnam. Second Kashmir War		Stuart Burge's *Othello*; Welles' *Chimes at Midnight*; James Ivory's *Shakespeare Wallah*
1966	Cultural Revolution in China. Escalation of the war in Vietnam	*Star Trek* begins its first season	

Year	Historical events	Media events	Shakespeare on screen
1967	Six-day war in the Middle East. Decriminalization of homosexuality in UK		Franco Zeffirelli's *The Taming of the Shrew*
1968	Martin Luther King and Robert Kennedy assassinated. Civil rights campaign begins in Northern Ireland. Tet offensive in Vietnam. Richard Nixon elected President	20 million cinema tickets sold per week in US	Zeffirelli's *Romeo and Juliet*; Peter Hall's *A Midsummer Night's Dream*
1969	End of the Cultural Revolution. Woodstock festival	John Schlesinger's *Midnight Cowboy*	Richardson's *Hamlet*; Kozintsev's *King Lear*
1970	Edward Heath's Conservative government to power in UK		
1971	India–Pakistan war leads to independent Bangladesh. People's Republic of China seated at the UN	First microprocessor chip developed	Peter Brook's *King Lear*; Roman Polanski's *The Tragedy of Macbeth*
1972	Bloody Sunday in Northern Ireland; "The Troubles" lead to direct British rule. Nixon to China	HBO launched on cable television	
1973	Britain enters the European Community	IBM introduces Ethernet	
1974	Watergate scandal leads to resignation of President Nixon	First small computers developed	

1975	US pulls out of Vietnam, resulting in reunification under communist rule	Bill Gates and Paul Allen start up Microsoft; Steven Spielberg's first "blockbuster," *Jaws*	
1976	Death of Mao	US extends copyright protection to 50 years	
1977		George Lucas' *Star Wars*	
1978	UK "Winter of Discontent" begins, with high unemployment and labor strikes	Michael Cimino's *The Deer Hunter*; Hal Ashby's *Coming Home*	
1979	Margaret Thatcher becomes first female Prime Minister of Great Britain. Sandinista revolution in Nicaragua		Welles' *Filming Othello*
1980	Ronald Reagan elected President. War in El Salvador begins	CNN begins operation	Derek Jarman's *The Tempest*
1981		IBM begins selling personal computers	
1982	Falklands War between UK and Argentina	Ted Kotcheff's *First Blood* [Rambo I]	Paul Mazursky's *Tempest*
1983		Compact discs introduced	
1984	UK miners' strike begins	Pat O'Connor's *Cal*; Apple introduces first Macintosh computer	
1985	Mikhail Gorbachev to power in the Soviet Union	*EastEnders* begins run on BBC	Kurosawa's *Ran*

Year	Historical events	Media events	Shakespeare on screen
1986	Soviet policies of *glasnost* and *perestroika*		
1987	Beginning of the Palestinian intifadah	Oliver Stone's *Wall Street*	
1989	Fall of the Berlin Wall. Soviets complete their troop withdrawal from Afghanistan	Peter Weir's *Dead Poets Society*; first HDTV standards established (digital v. analogue); invention of the World Wide Web	Kenneth Branagh's *Henry V*
1990	Nelson Mandela released from prison in South Africa. Thatcher falls from power, replaced by John Major. Iraq invades Kuwait	Michael Almereyda's *Twister*	Zeffirelli's *Hamlet*
1991	The First Gulf War. Maastricht Treaty, leading to the creation of the EU. Boris Yeltsin becomes President of Russia; dissolution of the Soviet Union	HTML mark-up language created	Peter Greenaway's *Prospero's Books*; William Reilly's *Men of Respect*; Gus Van Sant's *My Own Private Idaho*
1992	UK Stock Market crisis, "Black Wednesday." El Salvador peace agreement. Bosnia/Herzegovenia declare independence; armed resistance by Bosnian Serbs. Bill Clinton elected President	Almereyda's *Another Girl, Another Planet*; Sadie Benning's *It Wasn't Love*	Christine Edzard's *As You Like It*
1993	Oslo Accords between Israel and the PLO signed, ends first intifadah	First versions of DVDs developed; pentium chip introduced	Branagh's *Much Ado About Nothing*; John McTiernan's *The Last Action Hero*

1994	Genocidal massacres in Rwanda. Mandela elected President of South Africa	DIRECTV	Penny Marshall's *Renaissance Man*
1995	Dayton Agreement regarding Bosnian independence signed	O. J. Simpson's 37-week murder trial; Amazon.com online	Oliver Parker's *Othello*; Loncraine's *Richard III*; Branagh's *In the Bleak Midwinter/A Midwinter's Tale* (US 1996)
1996		Kyle Cassidy's *Toy Soldiers*; DISH Network; first DVD players on sale in Japan	Branagh's *Hamlet*; Al Pacino's *Looking for Richard*; Baz Luhrmann's *William Shakespeare's Romeo + Juliet*; Adrian Noble's *A Midsummer Night's Dream*; Trevor Nunn's *Twelfth Night*; Lloyd Kaufman's *Tromeo and Juliet*
1997	Tony Blair's "New" Labour government returned to power. Hong Kong returned to China	Death of Diana, Princess of Wales	Jocelyn Morehouse's *A Thousand Acres*; Richard Eyre's *King Lear*; Jeremy Freeston's *Macbeth*
1998	"Good Friday" peace agreement and referendum in Northern Ireland. Fighting in Kosovo	Bill Viola retrospective at the Whitney Museum; *Shakespeare in Love* wins Best Picture Oscar	John Madden's *Shakespeare in Love*; Michael Bogdanov's *Macbeth*
1999	NATO attacks Serbia	Zeffirelli's *Tea With Mussolini*	Julie Taymor's *Titus*; Michael Hoffman's *William Shakespeare's A Midsummer Night's Dream*; Gil Junger's *10 Things I Hate About You*; Dunne's *Titus Andronicus*; Raja Gosnell's *Never Been Kissed*; BFI release of *Silent Shakespeare*

Year	Historical events	Media events	Shakespeare on screen
2000	George W. Bush becomes President	Mary Harron's *American Psycho*	Michael Almereyda's *Hamlet*; Branagh's *Love's Labor's Lost*; Kristian Levring's *The King is Alive*; Cheah Chee Kong's *Chicken Rice War*; Campbell Scott and Eric Simonson's *Hamlet* (DVD release 2001)
2001	"9/11": Al-Qaeda attack on NYC World Trade Center towers and the Pentagon. US removes Taliban from power in Afghanistan		Tim Blake Nelson's *O*; Edzard's *The Children's Midsummer Night's Dream*; *The Glass House*; Tommy O'Haver's *Get Over It*; Klaus Knoesel's *Rave Macbeth*; Gregory Doran's *Macbeth*; Billy Morrissette's *Scotland, PA*
2002			BBC's *Great Britons*, Shakespeare episode; James Gavin Bedford's *The Street King*
2003	US-led invasion of Iraq		Michael Wood's *In Search of Shakespeare* (BBC); Gary Hardwick's *Deliver Us from Eva*
2004	Massacres in Darfur region of Sudan. Massive earthquake and tsunami in the Indian Ocean	Michael Moore's *Fahrenheit 911*; Mel Gibson's *The Passion of the Christ*	
2005			Michael Radford's *The Merchant of Venice*; Stephen Cavanagh's *Hamlet* completed

INTRODUCTION

Through a Camera, Darkly

Diana E. Henderson

We live in a screen era like never before: big screens, small screens, computer screens vie for our attention. My memory of the past years will be haunted by screen images that both capture and fail to capture the magnitude of world events: still images of torture at Abu Ghraib prison televised; beheadings broadcast on the Internet; devastating footage within Michael Moore's *Fahrenheit 911* projected in packed movie halls; and, dwarfing everything in the sheer scale of inexplicable destruction, the moments when more than 226,000 souls were swept to their deaths by the Indian Ocean, captured on digital cameras and videotapes. Then, going on with my life amidst such unfathomable suffering and loss, I see Michael Radford's *The Merchant of Venice* and turn back to Shakespeare on screen.

The art of the camera is all about perspective, but it is difficult not to sound glib when invoking the word here, seeking a proper perspective to introduce this *Companion* within its historical moment. It would be easier just to bracket the world and get on to the excellent essays that follow, which demonstrate the rich variety of possible roads into the study and interpretation of Shakespeare on screen. Yet they too refuse the ease of bracketing history, of ignoring either their own critical location or that of the screen events they analyze. At a time when education is increasingly driven by the logic of the international marketplace and the role of the humanities is much in debate, we cannot afford that luxury of ignorance – nor does it strike me as either ethically desirable or intellectually productive that we should.

It is not coincidental, then, that a number of essays examine, from different perspectives, recent films that place Shakespeare's words in contemporary contexts, films that wrestle self-consciously with what his stories "do" in our times; it may also not be coincidental that so many of the contributors have chosen to focus upon tragedy.

Tragedy in art has the compensation of giving shape and meaning to suffering, and in the aftermath of many recent horrors, a similar desire to find meaning came to the fore: most cynically in the pressure to shape news stories for commercial broadcast so that they ended with rays of hope, but also in the more troubling invocations of (competing) religions to "justify" others' deaths. Undoubtedly, the unprecedented outpouring of disaster relief after the tsunami confirmed what media-watchers and relief workers have said for years: that, be it good or ill, television cameras have become crucial in creating political change, social action, and communal responsibility. Blurring the line with fiction, screen images evoke powerful emotional responses, and challenge those who theorize the inauthenticity or absence of collective experience among putatively passive viewers of mass media.

Never has it been so urgent and important, then, that we as students, consumers, and producers of screen images comprehend and convey the skills needed to analyze and interpret them well. And just as Shakespeare's plays, over the centuries, have provided occasions for thought and argument about human society, character, and experience – and at the same time have provided great pleasure – so too Shakespeare on screen presents a rich territory for developing these skills as well as taking delight. For those interested in literary adaptations, the (relative) familiarity of Shakespeare's words and stories within English-speaking culture allows greater attention to the formal and sensory components of screen media: because so many of his plays have provided the basic narratives for multiple films and television shows, one can contrast how words, themes, and images function in different visual and conceptual contexts. For those interested in the role of Shakespeare's works in conserving or challenging societal values, screen representations again demonstrate the wide range of possibilities, and testify to changes in dominant attitudes towards authorship, gender, war, and national identity (to name a few enduringly current topics addressed herein) over the past eleven decades. The wider reach and potentially democratic possibilities of screen media broaden access to Shakespeare, but also raise questions about the appropriateness of reiterating centuries-old and often dated political or moral assumptions. The complex play between mediation and immediacy, past and present, aesthetics and politics, imagination and realism: all these and more can be explored through the study of Shakespeare on screen.

The essays here seek meaning in a variety of locations. But humility about truth claims is also in order, even if the consequences of our over- or mis-interpretations pale when compared to those of public policymakers. Within the scholarly field, some have voiced skepticism about the appropriateness of seeking "deep" meanings in popular entertainments, reminding us that a joke can be just that. Such reasonable critiques are never amiss in academia, where we sometimes do underrate the pleasures of mindlessness, sensory stimulation, and making money. But conversely, it does not follow that all films aiming to amuse and amass capital (monetary, personal, or cultural) lack other dimensions, including ones worthy of critical interpretation. If nothing else, the destructive behavior of those who claim a personal hotline to God's will should make us wary of asserting single, definitive interpretations of an event's significance, be the event artistic or commercial, the "reading" symbolic or sociological. Moreover, films such as Radford's *Merchant* serve as reminders that the demise of more "traditional" forms of adaptation has been greatly exaggerated. For all the critical interest in recent films such as Almereyda's *Hamlet* or Taymor's *Titus* that demonstrate overtly postmodern techniques and aesthetics (see DONALDSON and AEBISCHER in this volume), the producers and audiences for Shakespeare on screen are a more eclectic lot. No single theory, perspective, or judgment will suffice to describe this ever-growing phenomenon.

Such a recognition in no way disables or undermines our project of describing accurately and contextualizing carefully what we see, hear, think, and feel. The humanities have always aspired to distinguish between the trivial and the significant in analyzing human creations, and this continues to be an important, if difficult, endeavor. From its origins, theater, and especially Elizabethan theater, has defied easy categorizations, be they of genre, taste, morality, reality, or value. Like our modern screen media, Shakespeare's plays mix crassness with subtlety, the visceral with the intellectual, schlock with art. Only with the rise of English as a nineteenth-century academic discipline did Shakespeare (arguably) become associated first and foremost with words on a page – and even as that mode of interpretation developed, so did the technologies that have led to "his" further relocation (meanwhile, back on the stage, the plays continued to hold their own). The contributors to this volume, based in Film Studies, Communication, Comparative Media Studies, and Theater programs as well as English and Renaissance Studies departments, bring a diversity of professional perspectives to bear, and recognize that economics, marketing, and performance conditions can "mean" just as much as poetry and philosophy – nor does one angle preclude another.

Thus, while there has been a wealth of valuable analysis of screen Shakespeare recently, this volume is distinguished both by its interdisciplinarity and by its explicit goal of introducing the newcomer to the range of interesting questions this subject prompts. A single volume can no longer claim even to ask all those questions, any more than it can "cover" all the forms and manifestations of Shakespeare on screen. This *Companion*, for example, does not discuss animation, nor does it contain close analyses of the myriad televised versions of Shakespeare's plays. One explanation is pragmatic. Even so influential and delightful a series as the BBC's 1960s *An Age of Kings* dramatizations remains unavailable in the mass market (despite the appearance of Sean Connery as Hotspur and Judi Dench as Princess Katherine of France); because one aim of the volume has been to encourage the reader to compare the critical essay with his or her own close "reading," an effort has been made to match these analyses to readily viewable "texts."

But just as importantly, the contributors were asked to model different critical approaches, rather than attempt a survey or taxonomy. This organizational structure instead provides the vocabulary and resources to help readers apply various methodologies to productions of their own choosing: the insights of Pearson and Uricchio addressing televisuality in the representation of Shakespeare as a biographical figure, for example, could fruitfully be employed to analyze the 1950s Hallmark or 1980s BBC/Time-Life television series of Shakespeare "plays." Awareness of the technical ambiguities surrounding *King John*, the earliest extent segment of silent screen Shakespeare (discussed by Guneratne), might be applied to the earliest Shakespeare "talkie," the 1929 Pickfair *The Taming of the Shrew*. Shaughnessy's analysis of the continuing interrelationship between theatricality and British national cinema could provide a model for exploring the place of Shakespeare in other nations' film history, where questions of literal and cultural translation further complicate the picture (which also in part accounts for the largely Anglo-American focus of this collection). Additionally, the overlapping – and sometimes contesting – analyses of Loncraine's *Richard III* (WALKER, HODGDON) or the *Macbeth* spinoff *Scotland, PA*

(BURNETT, LANIER) demonstrate current spaces of critical debate, drama-
tizing the reason that such work goes on: even with seemingly "post-
hermeneutic" screen events, the process of reading, practiced carefully
and critically, is not exhausted by a single interpreter. Now that we
have advanced beyond the "first generation" of screen Shakespeare
criticism, we can also benefit by reapplying and remembering connections to the literary and theatrical, as Dawson and Shaughnessy
attest. Through lively discussion and debate, we all learn more.

Such learning is the most fundamental aim of the *Concise Companion*. In keeping with the recent wave of spinoffs and parodies as well
as more "traditional" encounters between Shakespeare and visually
based media, these essays move the scholarly field outward as well as
onward: they suggest a variety of fruitful ways to locate the Shakespearean subset of screen representations within wider historical, political, artistic, economic, and technological contexts. Simultaneously,
this volume as a whole demonstrates and upholds the different skills
and emphases basic to current humanities inquiry, which may vary
with one's sub-discipline but which include: careful attention to textual specifics; archival and field-specific research; making connections
between and applying insights to various artifacts in order to test (the
limits of) their validity; and analyzing the multiple layers of interpretation encouraged by human creations, especially collaborative works
so deeply affected by cultural and economic conditions.

We may debate the relative difference between our past and present
experiences: I, for example, do not find the experience of watching
the DVD/VCR of a film any more "dislocating" than I found the
experience of watching old musicals rerun on 1960s television, and
hence could not thereupon make an extreme claim about a "post-
historical" shift such as Richard Burt discusses in introducing *Shakespeare, The Movie, II* (Boose and Burt 2003). (Dis)location has been
the very stuff of intellectual and artistic debate – about media, about
"modernity" – since the moving picture era began. Nevertheless, Burt's
remarks force me to refine my distinctions between, say, the Hollywood satire of *Singin' in the Rain* (1952) and the metatheatricality of
Baz Luhrmann's "Red Curtain" trilogy: theoretical disagreement, in
other words, may stimulate better readings and new comparisons. In
addition to debating and combining methodologies, we should also
bring new technical and statistical resources to bear upon our analyses: the rigorous combination of social science research with human-
istic questions, for example, may help move us beyond the anecdotal
and intuitive when discussing audience reception, ostensible standards

of commercial "success," and the difference digital technologies make. Citation of MORI polls and government reports (by Pearson and Uricchio, and McLuskie respectively) gestures in this direction, but more sustained interdisciplinary studies – perhaps initiated by students reading this book – need to be developed. The essays here provide a snapshot of this moment's "state of the field" in order to advance its forward motion into the future. And questions remain to be addressed.

How different *is* our moment from those when film, and then television, became widely accessible? Is our analytic attention discernibly less than when silent films provided "attractions"? Has the DVD blurred the big/small screen distinction, or does Shakespeare's verbal scale still "fit" the large screen more successfully? Isn't it really (having control over) the temporality of viewing that shifts with the VCR/DVD, rather than our relationship to the temporality of the representation? What would a history of Shakespeare cinematography or visual design on screen reveal? Should we try to discern the different aims of the many participants in a production? How should we regard the recent shift in critical emphasis to mainstream or stylistically "popular" films (versus, say, the arthouse emphasis apparent in three notable *Tempest* films by Derek Jarman, Paul Mazursky, and Peter Greenaway, films that received more scholarly attention a decade ago)? Is this a matter of temporal currency; the pressure of the Next Big Thing; shifting politics or tastes among scholars; and/or a sign of fundamental change in the phenomena under discussion? Is it "conservative" politically to conserve formal dimensions of what has been valued in "high" arts during the past 200 years, or to value aesthetic complexity? Can that approach be supplemented, or should it be replaced at the level of first principles? These are among the questions suggested by the chapters that follow, as they explore the fertile ground created by combining the figure and works of a primarily sixteenth-century playwright with primarily twentieth-century screen technologies.

If we keep the wider world in view, the individual approaches announced here must perforce appear narrowly focused: this is the best way to get a crisp picture, after all. But these approaches are in practice neither exclusive nor discrete, and together they reveal a panorama of possibilities. It is left for the reader to fill in the surrounding spaces, to consider who and what "we" have left out. If this more narrowly conceived "we" is in fact post-historical or post-hermeneutical, we are most certainly not post-Shakespeare on screen, in whichever manifestation we care to seek "him" and his afterlives, effects, and remains. We keep making sense of our subject, and await the next viewing. I am confident that we will continue to discern something meaningful: perhaps a new perspective, a reminder of the world or a counterbalance to its more terrifying realities. Sometimes – let us hope often – we may feel sheer irrational pleasure. For the pictures continue to move, in many and mysterious ways.

Chapter 1

AUTHORSHIP

Getting Back to Shakespeare: Whose Film is it Anyway?

Elsie Walker

Near the beginning of *Looking for Richard* (1996), Al Pacino prepares to deliver the famous first speech from Shakespeare's *Richard III*. Sporting an irreverent baseball cap, the actor/director walks onto an ornate, mock-Elizabethan indoor stage. The camera cuts to show where the audience would be and there is only one member, a man whose face and dress resemble the Chandos Shakespeare portrait. "Shakespeare" disparagingly shakes his head, at which point Pacino sighs, shrugs, and walks off the stage without uttering a word of the play. In this virtually silent scene, Pacino wittily confronts what any Shakespearean film actor or director is up against: the pressure of expectational texts. Coined by Barbara Hodgdon, the phrase refers to the preconceptions about what "should" be done or what Shakespeare *intended*, which people bring to any performance of Shakespeare's work (Hodgdon 1983: 143).

A later sequence in *Looking for Richard* shows Pacino and his friend, Frederic Kimball, visiting Shakespeare's birthplace in Stratford-upon-Avon. They enter the birthplace with the zeal of missionaries, wistfully expecting some kind of epiphany. However, their reverent entrance is interrupted by firemen who burst in unceremoniously, alerted to a false alarm. Pacino and Kimball's attempt to commune with some Shakespearean spirit instead emphasizes the impossibility of immediate contact with the author or the intentions behind his work.

Nevertheless, in *Looking for Richard,* Pacino looks everywhere for tangible ways to bridge the gap between himself and Shakespeare, to "authorize" his production of *Richard III.* He consults dusty tomes, people on the street, other actors and directors, and specifically English academics, and visits the site of the new Globe in London (under construction in 1996) as well as the birthplace. About halfway through the film, Pacino suggests that his acting company seek academic advice on playing Richard's seduction of Lady Anne. Kimball immediately flies into a rage of romantic rhetoric, claiming that actors are the "proud inheritors of the understanding of Shakespeare" and the "truth" of his plays, that actors are more qualified than anyone to determine Shakespeare's meanings. The encounter captures the struggle inherent in making a "Shakespeare film," between the sense of (financial and ideological) obligation to "decode" Shakespeare for a wide audience and the necessary admission of the limitations in any interpretation. Also, it suggests a similar problem to one identified in twentieth-century theatrical performance and criticism by W. B. Worthen: "the value of . . . representation is measured not by the productive meanings it releases or puts into play, but by the 'proximity' it claims to some sense of authorized meaning, to something located in the text or, magically, in 'Shakespeare'" (1997: 37–8). Ultimately, Kimball appears to assume that the truth of Shakespeare's meanings can be found.

Many filmmakers similarly "authorize" and market their productions in terms of "proximity" to a given Shakespearean work – the webpages for *Titus Andronicus* directed by Christopher Dunne are littered with grandiose claims about fidelity to the author's original intentions (*Titus* 1998). Branagh claimed authority for his *Hamlet* (1996) by promising the longest version, "more Shakespeare for your money," including the "full" Folio text along with insertions from the Second Quarto (the "How all occasions do inform" speech). He promised, without irony, to present "for the first time, the full unabridged text of *Shakespeare's Hamlet*," "the most fully authentic version of the play" (Murphy 2000: 13) in which he saw an "all-embracing survey of life" (Branagh 1996: xiv). In their attempts to somehow recover *the* text, Branagh, Dunne, and Pacino arguably continue the legacy of "bardolatry" – the "romantic ideology of the timeless and universal Author" and the "timeless text which obscures the historicity of his plays and thereby contains any present political charge they might have carried" (Felperin 1991: 129). The term was coined by Bernard Shaw in 1901 for the idealization of Shakespeare in the later eighteenth and nineteenth centuries, although it is still in currency today.

Just as these directors attempt to represent the "true" or "full" Shakespearean text, many Shakespearean film scholars are wont to talk about films "true to the spirit" of Shakespeare. This "spirit" is, finally, impossible to locate. Nevertheless, the assumption that there are identifiable, singular authorial intentions behind the plays has, until comparatively recently, dominated Shakespearean film (and television) scholarship.

Shakespeare film criticism has been "preoccupied with what gets 'lost in the translation'" (Lehmann 2001: 62). The first Shakespeare "film," Sir Herbert Beerbohm Tree's *King John* (1899), is almost as old as cinema itself (see GUNERATNE). Yet for decades, one-reel adaptations were regarded as mere entertainment for the masses without artistic credibility (even though early film companies set the trend of using Shakespearean subjects to achieve prestige). Despite widespread praise for and interest in some later Shakespeare films, especially those directed by Laurence Olivier (the 1944 *Henry V* and the 1948 *Hamlet*) and Orson Welles (retrospectively, the 1952 *Othello*), many professional and academic critics still responded in a positivist fashion in terms of loss, calculating each film's relative "faithfulness" to *the* Shakespearean text, establishing simplistic taxonomies about the nature of the stage and cinema, and different degrees of adaptation. In particular, they wrote of cinema as a primarily "literal" visual medium incommensurate with Shakespeare's more complex writing. The *"tension* between text and image is one of the strongest motifs in critical *evaluations* of Shakespeare on screen" along with the *tension* between (rather than possibilities in combining) "theatricality" and "visual media" (Simone 1998: 233). Critics such as James Agee and Normand Berlin focused on cuts, the percentage of Shakespearean lines included, evaluating according to degrees of fidelity and/or distortion (in terms of how well the visuals served the language). There was also a prevalent concern that the powerful, primarily visual, "realist" nature of film would displace the stylized integrity of Shakespeare's plays. This concern with the distortion of original texts and the fear that "Shakespeare" and "film" were inherently incommensurate prevailed until the late 1970s, and continued beyond (see Sinyard 1986: 2–3).

Nevertheless, academic studies by Robert Hamilton Ball (1968), Roger Manvell (1971), and Jack J. Jorgens (1977) paved the way for fundamental shifts in Shakespeare-on-screen criticism. Over the last decade critics have moved from "positivism to hermeneutics," "from Victorian conservatism to modernist expansiveness to postmodernist permissiveness." The preoccupation with "what gets lost" in the translation from stage-play to film has given way "to a more open and adventurous foray," "discovering that which is unique and special about each movie" in both aesthetic and sociological terms (Rothwell 2001: 82–3).

Recent writing considers the ideological and cultural work, the various realities that Shakespeare films represent: in *Shakespeare, Cinema and Society* (1989), John Collick provides a Marxist analysis of the social significance of films produced in Europe, Russia, and Japan; *Shakespeare, Film, Fin de Siècle* (2000), edited by Burnett and Wray, analyzes how Shakespeare films of the 1990s confront "millennial anxieties"; *Shakespeare on Film* (1998), edited by Shaughnessy, ranges from formalist analyses to Marxist, psychoanalytic, poststructuralist, feminist, and queer readings of diverse (popular and "arthouse") films; Michael Anderegg (1999) provides a comprehensive, historical account of Orson Welles' productions; *Shakespeare the Movie* (1997), edited by Boose and Burt, establishes cultural, industrial, and aesthetic contexts for the consideration of Shakespeare adapted to film, television, and video; *Spectacular Shakespeare* (2002), edited by Lehmann and Starks, considers their ideological resonance at the multiplex and in the classroom. And yet, surprisingly, in his recent survey of Shakespeare-on-screen criticism, Kenneth Rothwell argues that for most critics the key question remains, "Is it Shakespeare?" (2001: 259).

Arguments about the importance of truly "getting back to Shakespeare" do persist. Daniel Rosenthal's survey focuses on "how 'faithfully' [each film] has treated its source play" (2000: 8), and argues that "with cinema the only restrictions are imposed by the size of the budget and viewers do not expect to have to exercise their imaginations" (2000: 10). The premise here is again that cinema is a "realist" mode of representation prompting a straightforward, passive response. Rosenthal's arguments echo Catherine Belsey's influential 1983 essay (reprinted in Shaughnessy 1998), "Shakespeare on Film: A Question of Perspective," which presents an essentialist argument about the limitations of cinema. Belsey claims that the film medium is inherently conservative because the cinematic frame, like the nineteenth-century proscenium arch stage, reduces the multiplicity of potential meanings to a single, unified point of view which is imposed on the passive viewer. Whereas the Shakespearean text is "interrogative," full of questions, representative of and subject to multiple perspectives, the Shakespearean film is a "classic realist" text which presents unified, selective, and limiting meanings to an audience without permitting interpretive flexibility (Belsey 1983: 155–6). Her article is filled with assumptions about the filmic medium that have not been adequately addressed in (even the most recent) Shakespearean film scholarship: the assumption not only that singular, authoritative messages are presented in films, but also that films prompt determinable responses.

While Kathy Howlett's *Framing Shakespeare on Film* (2000) is a *defense* of films which "deviate" from the Shakespearean source, her approach is nevertheless, like Rosenthal's, prescriptive. She begins by citing Franco Zeffirelli's *Hamlet* (1990) featuring the prince as "Western film hero" and Akira Kurosawa's *Ran* (1985) with King Lear as "a great lord of the Japanese feudal empire." Although the Shakespearean play seems "transformed beyond recognition," Howlett argues that "Shakespeare is still centrally in these films," the "essential concepts remain as one finds them in Shakespeare's text" (2000: 1, 2–3; see also 19). In *Shakespeare in the Movies*, Douglas Brode adopts an even more Romantic approach, evaluating films according to Shakespeare's "personal vision" and "authorial intention" (2000: 225). The implicit assumption is that Shakespeare is a precursor of Andrew Sarris' *auteur* figure – "the film artist who, through the force of his powerful personality and aesthetic preoccupations, is able to overcome all barriers to the expression of his vision" (Lehmann 2001: 62).

My goal is not to provide a comprehensive survey of critical debates, but to illustrate that problems of fidelity remain: the desire and sense that it might be possible to "get back to Shakespeare," to represent his work authoritatively, persists. Such criticism impedes a thorough appreciation and understanding of the diverse cultural and historical contexts in and mediums through which Shakespeare is understood. However, rather than just offer a reaction against fidelity arguments, I want to address what's at stake in the process of claiming Shakespeare in more specific, contemporary terms. I'd like to consider the "textual" work that recent films represent.

Two theoretical points are worth reinforcing before turning to the films themselves. I do not mean to suggest that particular films prompt determinate responses any more than do their Shakespearean sources. The fixedness of a film interpretation *and* its conceivable reception is as illusory as the fixedness of any textual material. Douglas Lanier points out the dangers of approaching films like "stable artifacts rather than contingent, unstable, ephemeral experiences" (1996: 203). Films are, to an extent, "remade" rather than pinned down in each interpretive text about them. Even a self-consciously subjective understanding of a film cannot be described "accurately": in written description, the direct experience of watching and hearing a film is lost. Thus there is some value in borrowing William Worthen's approach to analyzing stage productions "as though they participated in textuality" when considering the theoretical work these films perform (Worthen 1997: 183). In critical practice, however, the once determinable Shakespearean text has often been replaced by the knowable resonance of the film text – the implicit assumption being that the signifying potential of a film is determinable.

Secondly, the resonance of Shakespeare films is most often discussed in accordance with claims about the director. It is standard in Shakespearean film criticism always to mention directors: simply providing a film title and date is not enough to establish which production of a given play is under consideration. But critics have gone further by focusing primarily on the input of the director, often privileging *auteurs* (like Olivier, Welles, Kurosawa, Kozintsev, Branagh) who fulfill the "author-function" as, in Worthen's words, "stand-ins for Shakespeare" (1997: 60). Howlett, for example, is primarily concerned with how the "the director's aesthetic awareness . . . frames questions of identification and definition in the Shakespeare film," following Peter Donaldson's precedent of locating meaning as "an aspect of the director's subjective and personal experience" (Howlett 2000: 3, 6). Without discounting Donaldson's scholarly contribution – he has, perhaps more than any other critic, demonstrated the psychological complexity and resonance of *auteur*-based readings – I suggest that such readings are inevitably limiting if taken as automatically most authoritative.

The *auteur*, like the Author, is the figure who is seemingly "outside" and "antecedes" the text, the figure bringing coherence and unity to a production "through his biography, the determination of his individual perspective, the analysis of his social position, and the revelation of his basic design" (Foucault 1988: 197, 204). Of course such a view must be projected onto the given production; the identification of authorial (directorial) intentions that delimit the meaning/s of a text is an inescapably subjective exercise. We might reasonably identify resemblances between different films involving the same director, and the way a director discusses "Shakespeare" may be an important index to understanding the attitudes and assumptions that governed a

13

film's making. Nevertheless, whilst directors have a key role in any film's development, the filmmaking process can only be understood as a highly collaborative one (see HENDERSON).

Tying a production to an "originator" (whether author, director, or indeed star) is, to adapt Margreta de Grazia's words, to "confin[e] it to the perimeters of a single consciousness. . . . Tying the quotation to its originator, tying the work to its author are modes of denying and curbing discursive possibility" (1991: 68). The ways in which directors speak of staying "true" to Shakespeare point to the ideological work their productions represent. Film directors outside the English-speaking North Atlantic orbit have long taken the lead in self-consciously appropriating Shakespearean texts for their own cultural purposes. When, in the 1960s, Grigori Kozintsev asked Boris Pasternak to translate *Hamlet* into Russian, Pasternak produced a screenplay which he advised Kozintsev to cut: "Cut, abbreviate, and slice again, as much as you want. The more you discard the better. I always regard half the text of any play, of even the most immortal and classic work of genius, as a diffused remark that the author wrote in order to acquaint actors as thoroughly as possible with the heart of the action to be played. . . . Dispose of the text with complete freedom; it is your right" (Kozintsev 1967: 214–15). Akira Kurosawa did not even attempt to translate Shakespeare's language "straight" into Japanese, but used his understanding of the plays' overall structure and thematic concerns as a template for his screenplays (see DAWSON). Since the Shakespearean text was immediately translated, these directors generally avoided simple questions of fidelity or betrayal.

By contrast, the desire to reproduce "the Shakespearean text" is evident in the way English-speaking directors talk. These directors, like critics, speak of "getting back to" Shakespeare in order to authorize their productions: they establish straightforward correlations between author and playtext, director and film, playtext and screenplay, early modern and postmodern contexts of understanding. I want to explore their reasons for this way of speaking, drawing on films by Branagh and Pacino, before turning to four recent films that work differently. Richard Loncraine's *Richard III* (1995), Baz Luhrmann's *William Shakespeare's Romeo + Juliet* (1996), Julie Taymor's *Titus* (1999), and Michael Almereyda's *Hamlet* (2000) do, *despite what the directors say*, represent a more complex, playful, and/or painful confrontation with Shakespeare and with what Jean Howard calls "the radical otherness of the past" (1992: 25). These films, I argue, represent a profoundly nostalgic desire to claim the truth and authenticity attached to Shakespeare's language. At the same time, each film recontextualizes, claiming the power of the words in a highly self-conscious way.

Additionally, there has been a recent burst of adaptations dispensing with the language almost entirely, in favor of modern scenarios which parallel Shakespeare's plot and thematic structures (often themselves derived from other sources). Such films as *Get Over It* (2001, loosely based on *A Midsummer Night's Dream*), *O* (2001, based on *Othello*), *10 Things I Hate About You* (1999, based on *The Taming of the Shrew*), and *Never Been Kissed* (1999, loosely based on *As You Like It*) are witty adaptations in which the nostalgic desire to get back to Shakespeare is not obviously played out (see LANIER). Indeed, the Shakespearean sources are seldom mentioned in their promotional material.

Conversely, every film which does incorporate the historically remote Shakespearean text may be immediately understood as negotiating a "direct" relationship with the past; indeed, Burnett and Wray attribute the recent Shakespeare film "Renaissance" in part to *fin-de-siècle* nostalgia (2000: 3). Some take place in fictionalized historical settings: a forest in Tuscany at the end of the nineteenth century for Michael Hoffman's *A Midsummer Night's Dream* (1999); nineteenth-century England for Branagh's *Hamlet* ("starring" gorgeous Blenheim Palace, birthplace of Winston Churchill). These "period" productions appear to "preserve the 'historical' character of the Shakespearean original," and arguably "use history as a metaphor for the recovery of authentically Shakespearean meanings" (Worthen 1997: 67). The promotional materials and theatrical trailers foreground the adaptation of "classic" text matched with high production values. In such cases the safely distant evocations of a bygone era and the revered, "timeless" text provide an antidote for the anxieties and disruptions of the present – reusing *the* old text satisfies a need for continuity and togetherness in a world where such ideas are problematized or "lost." Branagh's *Love's Labor's Lost* (2000), Shakespeare done in the style of a "classic" 1940s Hollywood musical, is a particularly utopian, though unwittingly disconcerting, vision. Ladies in diaphanous gowns and men in tuxedos dance in Oxford University-style, studio-set courtyards and study rooms. The work of the Author at the center of the canon is located in enclosed, elitist grounds enjoyed by a privileged few. The framing of Branagh's film with black-and-white footage also signals that, here, "Shakespeare" is located in a romanticized past. Towards the end of the film (set loosely during World War II) there is the brief intrusion of a de-Nazified battle. But the war does not seriously threaten the quaint fun of this film: a brief "break" in the Shakespearean narrative and a few grainy images of brave troops and lonely ladies are quickly followed by their reunion.

Love's Labor's Lost fits what Fredric Jameson defines as the "nostalgia film": an "attempt to appropriate a missing past." Such films do not include old-fashioned "'representation' of historical content, but instead represent the 'past' through stylistic connotation," "conveying 'pastness' by the glossy qualities of the image." They attempt to "blur" their contemporaneity "and make it possible for the viewer to receive the narrative as though it were set ... beyond real historical time" (Jameson 1991: 19, 21). In discussing such "moonlit impression[s] of the past," Patrick Wright argues that once history is presented abstractly, "the political tensions which must necessarily inform it are purged: the residual product is a unifying spectacle, the settling of all disputes" (1985: 69). Branagh's *Love's Labor's Lost* is such a utopian vision, featuring "color-blind casting" and accent mixing, an inauthentic past "authorized" by a transhistorical, transcultural text.

The documentary-style *Looking for Richard* similarly attempts to access a fuller, unifying, nonexistent past (despite Pacino's sometimes describing this attempt in an ironic or self-disparaging way; see HODGDON). Though set in the present, the film follows (most particularly) Pacino's romantic quest to "access" the perceived idealism of Shakespeare's early modern language. The academics, actors, and people on the street interviewed by Pacino and Kimball repeatedly espouse reverent regard for the sanctity and "truth" of Shakespeare's words. The film focuses primarily upon rehearsals of *Richard III* and discussions led by Pacino. The actor playing Hastings, Kevin Conway, argues: "In a contemporary play, somebody would say, 'hey you, go over there and get that thing and bring it back to me.' That would be the line. Shakespeare says, 'Be Mercury, set feathers to thy heels, / And fly like thought from them, to me again.'" Those lines, from *King John* 4.2.174–5, excerpt the King's speech instructing Philip the Bastard to visit and win back the loyalty of Lords Bigot and Salisbury (who have been swayed to rebel by rumors that John ordered the murder of his nephew Arthur). Without presuming these lines' ultimate meaning, I would argue that Conway has not only quoted them out of context, but also provided an eccentric paraphrase. In the context of this film, however, such particularities are irrelevant. The words of *the* Poet/Author, regardless of context, are upheld as evidence of a time when words were more beautiful, more carefully chosen. An African-American man on the street argues that Shake-speare's words are more potent, considered, and emotionally "true" than the way people speak today:

> We should speak like Shakespeare. . . . We have no feelings. That's why it's easy for us to get a gun and shoot each other. . . . If we were taught to feel we wouldn't be so violent. . . . If we . . . have no feelings then we say things to each other that don't mean anything. But if we *felt* what we said – we'd say less and mean more.

Pacino and Kimball appear transfixed by this speech and agree emphatically (chiming in several times off-camera). The man then turns to ask a businessman for change, and the camera lingers for a moment before a cut. The poignancy of the moment, the revelation that the most impassioned speech comes from the mouth of a beggar, appears to confirm the filmmakers' belief that Shakespeare speaks to everyone at the precise moment that Pacino's quest is thrown into relief as luxurious. Later, Vanessa Redgrave argues that in Shake-speare's language everything – the aesthetic, intellectual, emotional, and personal – is integrated in a truthful whole: "the music and the thoughts and the concepts and the feelings have not been divorced from the words. And in England you've had centuries in which words have been totally divorced from truth." In this film, "everyone" (from the penniless, African-American man to the distinguished, white ac-tress) understands and defends the restorative power of Shakespeare's language. They likewise argue that we have somehow lost touch with the power of that language which is necessary to our survival.

As Chase and Shaw argue:

> We should not suspend our critical faculty and overlook the ahistorical assumptions behind the simple dualism of modern fractured conscious-ness and the integrated consciousness of times past. . . . If our con-sciousness is fragmented, there must have been a time when it was integrated; if society is now bureaucratized and impersonal, it must have previously been personal and particular. The syntax and structure of these ideas makes them superficially attractive but this appeal is no warrant for their veracity. (1989: 8)

Similarly, in a provocative essay entitled "Nostalgia Tells It Like It Wasn't," David Lowenthal argues that "the past as reconstructed is always more coherent than when it happened," and that it is wrong to assume there exists some "*non*-nostalgic reading of the past that is, by contrast, honest; or authentically 'true'" (1989: 30). *Looking for Richard* attempts to recover the alleged certainties of the past, evincing a partial "recognition, and at the same time an elision, of the fact that all that is solid, 'the cloud-capped towers, the gorgeous palaces,' has melted into air" (Chase and Shaw 1989: 8). As Susan Bennett writes, "it is conspicuous how often Shakespeare performs the role which links the psychic experience of nostalgia to the possibility of reviving an authentic, naturally better, and material past" (1996: 7). Ironically (but perhaps not surprisingly), both *Looking for Richard* and *Love's Labor's Lost* emerge at a time when we confront the impossibility of authentic contact with the past. Jameson argues that in our present "we are condemned to seek History by way of our own pop images [or] simulacra of that history, which itself remains forever out of reach" (Jameson 1991: 25).

With such arguments in mind, it is perhaps easy to dismiss the words of the man on the street or Vanessa Redgrave in *Looking for Richard*. Nevertheless, the desire to harness or rediscover the power of Shakespeare's words implicitly, ironically suggests the fear that they recede from us. This becomes more resonant considering that even those making the most self-consciously postmodern Shakespeare films speak of the restorative power of the endlessly enduring, immediate, and relevant Shakespearean text. Ian McKellen, the star of Loncraine's *Richard III*, was inspired by the 1958 film version directed by and starring Laurence Olivier – it confirmed McKellen's "sense that Shakespeare was for everybody" (McKellen and Loncraine 1996: 37). Similarly, *Romeo and Juliet* is, for Luhrmann, an "archetypal" story which must and will be told over and over again. Luhrmann's "MTV style" film was immediately controversial for challenging "acceptable," "authentic" representations of Shakespeare but the notion of "getting back to Shakespeare" is everywhere in Luhrmann's own discussions. He denies significant historical and cultural differences by likening Elizabethan theater audiences to modern film audiences, describing the enduring resonance of a play for "everybody from the streets-sweeper to the Queen" (an idea that is ironically literalized in Madden's *Shakespeare in Love*; 1998).[1] Luhrmann does not pretend his film is "definitive" – he expects his interpretation to be "replaced" soon – but the play itself will endure as "myth": "As Benjamin Britten said, if a story is true there will be many different productions in different places and it will survive forever.... Any adaptation is right if it reveals the heart of the story and engages and awakens the audience to the material."

Similarly, Julie Taymor directed *Titus* because she believes that Shakespeare's play is the most powerful "dissertation on violence" for all time: for Taymor, Shakespeare speaks "directly" to a twentieth-century audience (2000a: 174). She also argues that the generic complexities of his plays anticipate the juxtaposition of disparate elements in modern films (Lindroth 2001: 113). The eclecticism of Taymor's *Titus* has affinities with both Elizabethan theater practice and postmodern playfulness. This eclecticism may be read as "a sign of the play's fragmented or disconnected discourse" and its "intermittent relation to contemporary modes of understanding," but Taymor wanted (to adapt Worthen's words) to signal "the universality and coherence of the [play as a] basic myth" – the signs of specific histories are subordinate to the authority of the text (Worthen 1997: 68). Almereyda, inspired by Jan Kott, likewise argues that *Hamlet* can be made to speak to the "present moment" without sacrificing the integrity of the play (Almereyda 2000: viii, ix). Thus these directors lay claim to an authentic encounter with a timeless Shakespeare, who captured fundamental forms of human relations, individual and collective action.

Despite what these directors say, however, the films themselves do not point to an "authorial," "single position which is the place of the coherence of meaning" (to quote Belsey's description of the classic realist text; 1980: 92). And rather than representing a past "forever out of reach," they demand to be understood in contemporary contexts. Luhrmann's *Romeo + Juliet*, featuring ubiquitous guns, has particular resonance in America; Loncraine's *Richard III* is a parable of twentieth-century fascism which resonates with the rising popularity of the British National Party during the 1990s; some of Taymor's bloody *Titus* was shot in war-torn Croatia two months before war broke out in Kosovo; and Almereyda's anti-capitalist *Hamlet* was released soon after the first large-scale anti-globalization demonstrations occurred. None of these films places Shakespeare in the museum of distant history. Instead, his language is self-consciously recontextualized for present purposes. I want to explore briefly how such films problematize notions of a coherent text and timeless meaning, employing anti-illusionist devices to undermine a sense of spatial (as well as narrative) coherence. In other words, they might be understood as inviting interrogative responses in precisely those ways Belsey disallows.

Loncraine's *Richard III* is dominated by the parodic incorporation of "period" details, sending up the reconstruction of history associated with heritage films (Loehlin 1997), and indeed the very notion that history or "Shakespeare" can be authentically represented. Items from the 1940s are seductively photographed in close-up: from genuine "Abdullah" cigarettes (a rare packet was bought especially) to cars and costuming (McKellen and Loncraine 1996: 48). Patrick Wright describes British "historical" dramas which play out their

> stories in reconstructed interiors packed with period objects, all arranged in that slightly obsessive manner which speaks of a present yearning for a time when things at least had the dignity of an indisputable place in an ordered world . . . the aura of overwhelming Romance – the sense of deep psychological investment and compensatory meaning – that permeates and gives lustre to the national past. (1985: 168)

By contrast, in Loncraine's *Richard III*, the aestheticizing of the past is made sinister by the explicit allusions to Nazism, and the Nazi way of manipulating history, in the portrayal of Richard's rise to power. Thus recalling the past does not automatically mean sentimental nostalgia or the recovery of lost meaning and order associated with "Shakespeare." McKellen asked for the playwright's initials to be placed on the dance-band's music stands in the opening scene at "The Victory Ball" (1996: 58). Yet the first words of the film (after ten minutes have elapsed) are the big-band song setting of Christopher Marlowe's "The Passionate Shepherd to his Nymph" – so the author's initials are aurally paired with verses that are not his own. The initials of *the* Author, ornately embroidered in red and gold, are part homage, part parody of any attempt at an authentic representation of the Author's work (compare LANIER).

Similarly, the recasting of Shakespeare's "sword" and "longsword" as gun trademarks in Luhrmann's ironically titled *William Shakespeare's Romeo + Juliet* marks its derivative relationship to an "original" at the precise moment that it marks its distance from the conditions under which that play was produced (Worthen 1998: 1104). Several scholars, including James Loehlin, assume that the film's title is "a gesture to bardic authority" (2000: 121).[2] I argue that the film is a more self-conscious recontextualization than this assumption suggests. It aggressively foregrounds the processes by which it "updates" Shakespeare, relocating stage language within a cinematic world: from the billboards featuring Shakespearean lines as slogans ("Prospero's finest whiskey: the stuff dreams are made of"; "I am thy Pistol and thy Friend") to the dominance of a decrepit stage (located beside a pool hall called "The Globe").

Taymor's *Titus* is an equally playful collage featuring heterogeneous film iconography, an international cast, and a hybrid *mise-en-scène* emphasizing temporal and cultural differences rather than homogeneity. Instead of "re-creating Rome, 400 A.D.," Taymor wanted to evoke an ancient world of ritual, mausoleums, and orgies alongside elements of modern America. Tanks, horses and carriages, limousines, bows and arrows, machine guns, and electric Olympics-style torches appear in close-up. There is no synthesizing stability in *Titus* – different peoples, architectures, "texts," and cultures coexist rather than blend. And whilst Taymor speaks of the enduring, unifying resonance of Shakespeare's words, those words are continually "upstaged" by savage spectacles: this is in keeping with much twentieth-century criticism which emphasizes the clash between Shakespeare's figurative, sometimes absurdly ornate language and the horrific, relentless violence of the play. The film's final moments show young Lucius carrying Aaron's baby away from the other characters and the Coliseum, walking slowly towards a painted sunrise, as if reaching beyond the action of the film, the play, and the words which don't work anymore (see AEBISCHER).

The difficulty of preserving "Shakespeare" is perhaps most painfully explored in Almereyda's *Hamlet*. There is little time in this film for the uninterrupted contemplation of Hamlet's speeches: telephones, fax machines, door buzzers, and a bombardment of visual information (surveillance cameras, television screens showing explosions and rapidly edited montages) cut short almost every key speech. The frequently whispered and cut-off dialogue, the absence of non-musical sounds except for voices suggesting spaces in a vacuum evoke a world closing in. The film is dominated by slogans, trademarks, and prices which "speak louder" than Shakespeare – the privileging of individual subjectivity attributed to Hamlet's speeches seems out of place, naive, and indulgent in the context of a late capitalist world driven by money and faceless masters.

Each film foregrounds the clash between early modern text and postmodern *mise-en-scène*. Because the viewer is offered a variety of possible subject positions, narrative and ideological coherence is further disrupted. As noted, pinning down the "perspective" of any film is problematic. But these Shakespeare films emphasize the point by demystifying the process of filming "reality": to recontextualize the words of Linda Hutcheon, "what they represent is self-consciously shown to be highly filtered by the discursive and aesthetic assumptions of the camera-holder."[3] Loncraine's *Richard III*, for example,

21

highlights the conventions of cinematic "realism" by sometimes disobeying them. The film potentially, to paraphrase Graham Holderness, interrogates the ideologies which underpin an apparently unmediated presentation (the kind of "straightforward" representation that Belsey associates with "classic realist" works).[4] McKellen as Richard makes several direct addresses to camera, breaking the "fourth wall" convention of film performances (itself derived from nineteenth-century theater). The music which punctuates his victories (composed by Trevor Jones), and the consistently distancing camerawork – the apparent objectivity of which could be "read" as Richard's own detached viewpoint – reinforce Richard's "directorial" control disconcertingly, prompting us to seek another perspective beyond the limits of the frame (see HODGDON, LANIER).

Luhrmann likewise wanted to avoid making *Romeo + Juliet* a conventionally "naturalistic," "window-on-reality" film. He says he directed *Strictly Ballroom* (1992), *Romeo + Juliet*, and *Moulin Rouge* (2001) in the "red-curtain style," that is, as "theatricalized," "audience-participation cinema." Each film world is both self-consciously stylized and "realistic" in different ways. His comments about the "heightened creative" world of *Moulin Rouge* also seem pertinent to *Romeo + Juliet*: "we use devices that awaken the audience to the fact that they are watching a movie . . . most of the naturalistic cinema that's been the vogue for years puts the audience to sleep and asks it to look at reality through a keyhole. We're doing the exact reverse" (Fuller 2001: 7). Luhrmann's *Romeo + Juliet* features different camerawork styles – from the "distorted out-of-control close-ups" and "super-macro slam zooms" for the "action movie" beginning (Pearce and Luhrmann 1996: 9), to the more conventional, lingering shots of Romeo and Juliet when they are alone. By foregrounding various ways of filming "reality," the film avoids privileging a particular point of view. The camera often seems transfixed by Romeo and Juliet, and the method of filming perhaps beguiles us into idealizing the fantasy of escapism that they represent. However, in the final scene, after a series of tight close-ups throughout Romeo and Juliet's death speeches, the camera pulls dramatically away from the lovers' deathbed giving a painterly bird's eye view of their lifeless bodies surrounded by a multitude of candles, neon crosses, and rose petals. The movement away from the lovers, accompanied by the climactic ending of Wagner's *Liebestod*, draws attention to the scene's Romanticism in a self-conscious, almost parodic, way, emphasizing the "excess" and the dangerous appeal of that sacrificial vision.

Taymor likewise wanted to emphasize the subjectivity of reality presented in *Titus*, to disrupt the "safe space" of illusionist cinema by featuring editing *discontinuity*, subjecting her audience to spatial and temporal confusion. Taymor and her editor Françoise Bonnot did not attempt to shoot every character and scene "with the obligatory master shot, medium two shots, singles and reverses" (2000a: 182). For one thing, Taymor did not have the time and money to cover every scene extensively. But she also wanted to disobey conventional shooting and editing practices: in the scene where Lavinia and Bassanius are attacked by Tamora's sons, for example, Taymor favored a chaotic series of rapid, disconnected shots. She asked her camerawork team to match Lavinia and Bassanius' sense of panic with unsteady, unnerving shooting and she had the editor splice the shots without "perfect" continuity – saying, "I wanted the audience to feel like the attacked" (Taymor 2000b). In Almereyda's *Hamlet*, some scenes and speech snippets are shown as the central character's video diaries, black-and-white disjointed sequences which Hamlet edits on his computer screen (see DONALDSON). Each case reveals the process of manipulating reality for particular emotional and aesthetic effects: by highlighting the subjectivity of representation, the films (not unlike Brecht's epic theater) provoke complex responses hovering between detachment and engagement.

These Shakespeare films include many allusions to popular films, and draw from diverse generic film templates to engage and "awaken" cine-literate audiences. Their explicit intertextuality "sits well with the postmodern interrogation of the supposed integrity and coherence of all textual announcements" (Burnett and Wray 2000: 5). The films also implicitly decentralize Shakespeare the author "as the unique and isolated source of meaning" as well as the notion of the printed book as a fixed entity (Murphy 2000: 19). Of course no film, no "text" exists in a cultural vacuum and so will be, intentionally or not, a "woven fabric" of quotations (Barthes 1977: 159): within every film there will be references or moments reminiscent of other films. For instance, Collick examines how Reinhardt's *A Midsummer Night's Dream* (1935) draws on nightmarish elements of contemporary animated cartoons (1989: 80–106), and Branagh's films are often "read" in relation to those of Olivier and the wider Hollywood "intertext" (i.e., the "quotation" from *The Magnificent Seven* near the beginning of *Much Ado About Nothing*, 1993). It is "standard Hollywood practice" to incorporate (or appear to incorporate) diverse generic elements. As Rick Altman demonstrates, studios, producers, and directors aim for an inclusive product to draw a wide audience (1999: 141). This Holly-wood practice is parodied in *Shakespeare in Love* when Henslowe com-missions Shakespeare to write a "crowd-tickler" play incorporating various generic elements: "mistaken identities, a shipwreck, a pirate king, a bit with a dog, and love triumphant."

Genre mixing is often connected with the "bricolage, pastiche, and intertextuality" at "the very heart of the postmodern style," although, Altman observes, generic ambiguity in film is not a new (or solely postmodern) phenomenon. Movies are usually connected to a single, specific genre only retrospectively and, besides, genre boundaries are difficult to define: "What western is not at some points a melodrama? What musical can do totally without romance?" (1999: 141). He adds, however, that until the so-called "postmodern era" "attention was rarely drawn to the disparities among the genres" combined in many films, and argues that recent, postmodern films "often use intertextual references and conscious highlighting of genre conventions to stress genre *conflict*" (1999: 141, my emphasis). Loncraine's *Richard III*, Luhrmann's *Romeo + Juliet*, Taymor's *Titus*, and Almereyda's *Hamlet* are set apart from many other Shakespeare films by the highly self-conscious way in which they accentuate generic "clashes" and work against the "safe" familiarity of their widely disseminated Shakespear-ean sources.

Romeo + Juliet, for example, begins with a montage summarizing the action, accompanied by Craig Armstrong's "O Verona" (a musical parody of Carl Orff's "O Fortuna" from *Carmina Burana*), followed by a television-style "introduction" of the principal characters (each turn-ing towards the camera in close-up along with a name caption), fol-lowed in turn by a parody of westerns and action movies in the first Capulet/Montague showdown sequence. The close-up slow-motion and freeze-frame shots of Tybalt lighting, smoking, and extinguishing his cigarette and the extreme close-ups of his silver-heeled boots "quote shots of Clint Eastwood in *A Fistful of Dollars* and Charles Bronson in *Once Upon a Time in the West*"; the fight music alludes to Ennio Morricone's familiar western scores (guitar chords, eerie whistling, and male chorus), and the subsequent fast editing, changing camera speeds, and slow-motion shots of Tybalt leaping into the air while firing two guns at once are a parody of, or homage to, the action movies directed by John Woo (Loehlin 2000: 126). The cheeky allu-sions lose predominance in the scenes focusing on Romeo and Juliet – explicit parody gives way to more "serious" romance designed to engage the spectator less self-consciously. This effectively highlights the unsustainable idealism of Romeo and Juliet's speeches: within an aggressive, postmodern context, their sweetness and absolutes have no place. The Shakespearean text is used to make a statement about the difficulty of speaking about truth and love in a world of irony, surfaces, and commercialization.

As James Loehlin details, Loncraine's *Richard III* is similarly eclectic, combining the *mise-en-scène* of Merchant–Ivory productions with the narrative template of 1950s gangster movies: the strangeness of this mixture is part of what makes the film original. Taymor's *Titus* likewise brings disparate styles together: in the first sequence (scripted by Taymor), a "clown" crashes through the wall of a regular boy's kitchen and drags him into the Coliseum where much of the action is based. This "prologue" alludes to both Loncraine's *Richard III* (where Richard crashes through Prince Edward's study) and *The Last Action Hero* (1993), in which a boy becomes subsumed within an action movie starring Arnold Schwarzenegger as a modern-day anti-Hamlet. By contrast, Taymor's final scene, with its bright colors, *tableaux vivants*, and horrendous subject matter, surely borrows from Peter Greenaway's *The Cook, The Thief, His Wife and Her Lover* (1989); in both films, nasty events are portrayed in a stylish way. The mix of diverse filmic iconography newly illuminates the disconcerting mixture of tone in *Titus Andronicus* for a cine-literate audience.

The explicit film quotations and allusions within Almereyda's *Hamlet* also create generic confusion, problematizing any talk of originals or single sources, inviting plural readings. Hamlet's own *film* (instead of play) is a montage of different film clips: *The Mousetrap* opens with a rose unfurling with time-lapse cinematography (as in Scorsese's *The Age of Innocence* credit sequence), cuts to Golden Age television images of a boy with his parents, to "Monty Pythonesque" cartoon images of the ear poisoning, to porn clips, to a shot of an audience emphatically clapping, to various images of death. In this climactic film-within-the-film, words are dispensed with altogether. Almereyda's treatment of a familiar scene prompts a new response, demanding that the audience (both within and outside the film world) piece the story of *The Mousetrap* together by assimilating the cinematic montage (the images evoke the text, rather than the other way around). In all previous *Hamlet* films, *The Mousetrap* takes place on a stage (within the given film world), whereas this *Mousetrap* can only be understood cinematically. Paradoxically, the sequence of quotations that is *The Mousetrap* in Almereyda's *Hamlet* is therein original (see SHAUGHNESSY, DONALDSON).

This *Mousetrap*, made from a pile of Blockbuster videos, is perhaps also a meditation on the Hollywood filmmaking industry as a network of endlessly recyclable material, an industry in which the same stories are told/adapted with "regulated difference," to use Steve Neale's phrase (1990: 64), where it is difficult for individual voices – the "voice" of Almereyda the independent director, the voice of Hamlet, of Ethan Hawke in the lead – to make themselves heard. Hawke makes several false starts at the "To be or not to be" speech – the most famous Shakespearean "soundbite" sounds trite, then haunting when it is repeated. Such famous lines and whole speeches apparently cannot be delivered "whole" without a sense of embarrassment or loss (whether metaphysical or temporal). In Ethan Hawke's words, explaining the exclusion of the "alas, poor Yorick" speech, "How do you find a skull in a modern day cemetery?" (Anderson 2000). Hawke finally delivers "To be" in the action aisles of a Blockbuster video store. Clichéd action sequences are displayed on television screens: explosions and bodies thrown in the air, guns firing, the invincible hero of *Crow II* walking through flames and waving at the camera, visually mocking Hamlet's indecision. Hamlet begins the speech in voiceover and then begins speaking out loud in the videostore, as if addressing his words to the stories of mainstream Hollywood heroism that surround him. Hamlet's efforts to emulate such heroism are inescapably parodic: in his maniacal multiple shooting of Claudius during the final scene, swords are replaced by a gun, drama becomes action movie, and Hamlet is finally more like Jules from *Pulp Fiction* than Olivier's or Branagh's sweet Prince.[5]

Much of the meaning of these films lies not within themselves but in their relationships with other texts: they do not attempt to be original in the narrow sense but instead participate in a postmodern free-for-all. The knowledge that all work is allusive and/or intertextual is celebrated and exploited. Materials from both "high" and "low" (popular) culture sources are not simply quoted but incorporated into the film's very substance, dissolving the fixedness of each frame, shifting "Shakespeare" and the revered texts into a democratic, postmodern arena of playful recycling. In Jameson's words, "they no longer 'quote' such texts as Joyce might have done . . . they incorporate them, to the point where the line between high art and commercial forms seems incredibly difficult to draw" (1996: 186). The sequentially ordered sections of these films are, to borrow from Linda Hutcheon's description of postmodern novels, "disrupted by a particularly dense network of interconnections and intertexts, and each enacts or performs

. . . the paradoxes of continuity and disconnection, of totalizing interpretation and the impossibility of final meaning" (1989: 14–15).

Richard III, Romeo + Juliet, Titus, and *Hamlet* obviously are not
"unmediated," nostalgic evocations of the past. Instead, each is an
engaging riff on the multiplicity of cultural referents that come into
play whenever we encounter Shakespeare. As Hutcheon points out,
postmodernism is usually defined in terms of "negativized rhetoric,"
"discontinuity, dislocation, decentering, indeterminacy, and anti-
totalization" (1989: 3). But these films demonstrate the "positives" of
postmodernism she identifies: the recognition of cultural and temporal
differences, the freedom that comes with realizing there is no "final"
text, the democratization of art (mixing "high" and "low" elements),
the use of parody and playfulness to challenge the "authority" and
"authenticity" of a "revered" text in the process of reclaiming that
text for a wide, contemporary audience. Shakespearean sources are
used to raise, rather than provide an antidote to, anxieties. The illusions
of consensus, all-embracing perspectives, and final truths are revealed
as such in the cultural eclecticism of these films. While filmmakers
and critics continue to invoke Shakespeare's timelessness to "authorize"
productions, the films themselves represent a much less straightforward, parodic, and sometimes painful process.

We could use these productions to explore the complex significance
of the sign "Shakespeare" further: he may read as subversive and/or
conservative, queer and/or straight, timeless and/or time-bound, threatening and/or under threat, elite and/or popular. Clearly, the desire to
"get back to the truth of Shakespeare" represented in much Shakespeare film criticism is a desire that may be easily dismissed as stulti-
fying and out of step with developments in both Shakespearean and
film scholarship. Yet these films convey the paradoxes of all that is
involved and at stake in attempting to get back to Shakespeare. Seen
thus, the process may be understood as reactionary, conservative,
romantic, limiting, earnest, doomed to failure – and, at the same time,
ironic, playful, subversive, moving, inspired . . . and open-ended.

Notes

1 Luhrmann explained this to me in an interview on July 9, 2000 at the
   House of Iona (the Bazmark headquarters) in Sydney, Australia. The other
   quotations in this paragraph also come from that interview.
2 In fact, in a subsequent radio interview with Kim Hill, Luhrmann revealed
   that he gave the film that title so that even when audiences saw the

wordless images and music of the preview they would still know to expect Shakespearean dialogue. "Nine to Noon" show, *National Radio*: Wellington (New Zealand), February 4, 1997.

3   I quote Hutcheon's description of "postmodern" photographs as obviously subjective instead of "neutral representations" or "technological windows on the world" (1989: 7).

4   Holderness (1998: 75) directly challenges Belsey's assertion of cinema's inherent conservatism. As Shaughnessy notes, Holderness provided an important challenge to the prevalent assumption when his essay first appeared in 1985 (a view that is "still particularly dominant within new historicism") that "Shakespeare is an inevitably conservative and reactionary cultural force" (1998: 11).

5   The parodic (self-conscious, contestory) "language" of these films is different from the "straight," "dead language" of pastiche that, for Fredric Jameson, dominates postmodern work (especially "nostalgia films"). For Jameson, postmodern texts are trapped into recalling texts of the past because it is no longer possible to make a new, "unique" statement: "With the collapse of the high-modernist ideology of style – what is unique and unmistakable as your own fingerprints . . . the producers of culture have nowhere to turn but to the past: imitation of dead styles, speech through all the masks and voices stored up in the imaginary museum of a now global culture" (1991: 17–18). Therefore, Jameson argues, where modernist artists used parody, postmodern artists are forced to use pastiche. I do not understand these postmodern films as somehow "haunted" by dead forms, but as collages of older forms which have been recontextualized, defamiliarized, "made new" for the use of the present.

References and Further Reading

Agee, James (1945). "*Henry V.*" In Gerald Mast and Marshall Cohen (eds.), *Film Theory and Criticism*, 1st edn. London: Oxford University Press, 1974: 333–6.

Altman, Rick (1999). *Film/Genre*. London: BFI Publishing.

Anderson, Jeffrey M. (2000). "Brushing Up Shakespeare: A Conversation with Michael Almereyda and Ethan Hawke." www.combustiblecelluloid.com/inthawke.shtml.

Barthes, Roland (1977). *Image/Music/Text*, ed. and trans. Stephen Heath. London: Fontana.

Belsey, Catherine (1980). *Critical Practice*. London and New York: Methuen.

—— (1983). "Shakespeare on Film: A Question of Perspective." *Literature/Film Quarterly* 11.3: 152–8.

Bennett, Susan (1996). *Performing Nostalgia: Shifting Shakespeare and the Contemporary Past*. London and New York: Routledge.

Berlin, Normand (1977). "Peter Brook's Interpretation of *King Lear*: 'Nothing Will Come of Nothing.'" *Literature/Film Quarterly* 5.4: 299–303.

Brode, Douglas (2000). *Shakespeare in the Movies: From the Silent Era to Shakespeare in Love*. New York: Oxford University Press.

Chase, Malcolm, and Christopher Shaw (1989). "The Dimensions of Nostalgia." In Malcolm Chase and Christopher Shaw (eds.), *The Imagined Past: History and Nostalgia*. Manchester and New York: Manchester University Press: 1–17.

De Grazia, Margreta (1991). "Shakespeare in Quotation Marks." In Marsden, ed.: 57–71.

Felperin, Howard (1991). "Bardolatory Then and Now." In Marsden, ed.: 129–43.

Foucault, Michael (1988). "What is an Author?" In David Lodge (ed.), *Modern Criticism and Theory: A Reader*. London and New York: Longman: 197–210.

Fuller, Graham (2001). "Baz Knows the Score." *The Observer*, August 19, Review section: 7.

Hodgdon, Barbara (1983). "Two *King Lears*: Uncovering the Filmtext." *Literature/Film Quarterly* 11: 143–51.

Holderness, Graham (1985). "Radical Potentiality and Institutional Closure." In Jonathan Dollimore and Alan Sinfield (eds.), *Political Shakespeare: New Essays in Cultural Materialism*. Manchester: Manchester University Press: 182–200. Repr. in Shaughnessy 1998: 71–82.

Howard, Jean E. (1992). "The New Historicism in Renaissance Studies." In Richard Wilson and Richard Dutton (eds.), *New Historicism and Renaissance Drama*. London and New York: Routledge: 19–32.

Hutcheon, Linda (1989). *The Politics of Postmodernism*. London and New York: Routledge.

Jameson, Fredric (1991). *Postmodernism, or, The Cultural Logic of Late Capitalism*. London and New York: Verso.

—— (1996). "Postmodernism and Consumer Society." In John Belton (ed.), *Movies and Mass Culture*. New Brunswick, NJ: Rutgers University Press: 185–202.

Lanier, Douglas (1996). "Drowning the Book: *Prospero's Books* and the Textual Shakespeare." In Bulman 1996: 187–209.

Lehmann, Courtney (2001). "Book Reviews: Brave New Bard." *Cinéaste* 26.1: 62–6.

Lindroth, Mary (2001). "'Some Device of Further Misery': Taymor's *Titus*." *Literature/Film Quarterly* 29.2: 107–15.

Loehlin, James N. (2000). "'These Violent Delights have Violent Ends': Baz Luhrmann's Millenial Shakespeare." In Burnett and Wray, eds.: 121–36.

Lowenthal, David (1989). "Nostalgia Tells It Like It Wasn't." In Malcolm Chase and Christopher Shaw (eds.), *The Imagined Past: History and Nostalgia*. Manchester and New York: Manchester University Press: 18–32.

Marsden, Jean I., ed. (1991). *The Appropriation of Shakespeare: Reconstructions of the Works and the Myth*. London and New York: Harvester Wheatsheaf.

Murphy, Andrew (2000). "The Book on the Screen: Shakespeare Films and Textual Culture." In Burnett and Wray, eds.: 10–25.

Neale, Steve (1990). "Questions of Genre." *Screen* 31.1: 45–67.

Pearce, Craig, and Baz Luhrmann (1996). *William Shakespeare's "Romeo + Juliet": The Contemporary Film, The Classic Play*. London: Hodder Children's Books.

Rosenthal, Daniel (2000). *Shakespeare on Screen*. London: Hamlyn.

Rothwell, Kenneth (2001). "How the Twentieth Century Saw the Shakespeare Film: 'Is it Shakespeare?'" *Literature/Film Quarterly* 29.2: 82–95.

Simone, R. Thomas (1998). Reviews of *Shakespeare and the Moving Image: The Plays on Film and Television*, ed. Anthony Davies and Stanley Wells, and *Screen Shakespeare*, ed. Michael Skovmand. *Shakespeare Quarterly* 49.2: 232–5.

Sinyard, Neil (1986). *Filming Literature: The Art of Screen Adaptation*. London and Sydney: Croom Helm.

Taymor, Julie (2000b). Director's commentary. *Titus* DVD. Twentieth Century Fox Home Entertainment.

"*Titus Andronicus*: William Shakespeare's Savage Epic of Brutal Revenge" (1998). Joel Redner Productions. Official website. May 13; home1.gte.net/titus98/tawsite8.hml.

Worthen, W. B. (1998). "Drama, Performativity, and Performance." *PMLA* 113.5: 1093–107.

Wright, Patrick (1985). *On Living in an Old Country*. London: Verso.

Chapter 2

CINEMA STUDIES

"Thou Dost Usurp Authority": Beerbohm Tree, Reinhardt, Olivier, Welles, and the Politics of Adapting Shakespeare

Anthony R. Guneratne

Even with the earliest documented performances, the political dimensions of Elizabethan theater, and of Shakespeare's plays in particular, elicited powerful responses. His works engaged issues that preoccupied Renaissance political thinkers from Guicciardini and Machiavelli to Montaigne and Grotius. Yet it was not as political theorist, but as part owner and manager of a theatrical troupe, that the dramatist played an oblique, if for him no doubt alarming, role in Tudor intrigue: the most salient evidence of an Elizabethan play's effect remains the vigorous exception taken by the queen and her ministers to the timing of a revival, widely believed to have been a suitably modified version of Shakespeare's *Richard II*. On February 8, 1601, the day after its command performance at the Globe, those who had commissioned the performance (the most prominent participants in the Essex rebellion) were arrested for treason and the players sought for questioning. The queen's personal objection to the episode was later recorded by William Lambarde, Keeper of the Rolls: "I am Richard, know ye not that," she is supposed to have said, adding, rather curiously, that "this tragedie was 40^{tie} times played in open streets and houses" (Schoenbaum 1999: 44, 49).

It may then come as little surprise that modern adaptations of Shakespeare often assume a political edge, even attempting to shape public policy by "speaking" in specific ways to their various audiences. Given that any restaging or adaptation is, by its nature, an ideological gesture expressive of an attitude to a textual residue, I limit my argument here to a few films that had explicitly political dimensions for their intended audiences. In addition, the four examples chosen – cinematic interpretations of *King John*, *A Midsummer Night's Dream*, *Henry V*, and *Othello* – were the product of collaborations in which theater directors of note, all (arguably like Shakespeare) at one time managers of their own companies and thus capable of determining even the minutiae of *mise-en-scène* and performance style, played a dominant role.

I do not, however, propose to treat them all in the same detail: the carefully worked-out and much-discussed texts that are among the major films of Max Reinhardt, Laurence Olivier, and Orson Welles here appear as supplements to a discussion of Herbert Beerbohm Tree's 1899 *King John*, a scrap of film scarcely a minute long. There have been carefully reasoned attempts to reconstruct – or, more properly, reconstitute – *King John*, and part of my purpose is to indicate why these efforts have yet to provide a sufficiently thoroughgoing historical contextualization of that recently rediscovered "relic," whose status as progenitor of a long and growing tradition has led to a clash of two perspectives (one assertively of the "film studies" mold, the other emanating from literary studies and theater history). An instructive instance of the mobilization of star power for a medium that was still in its infancy, Tree's brief but vivid reenactment of the poisoned monarch's agonizing demise is also an outstanding example of the challenges faced by cultural historians attempting to answer fundamental questions about early cinema, and about Renaissance politics restaged in that medium in such a way as to address contemporary concerns. The minute we have of *King John* allows us to make connections among forms of political power (Renaissance autocracy versus appeals to public opinion in the age of mass media), forms of textual authority (what makes a text's author the author? what is the "text" that confers authority?), the interactions of communicative media (how does intermediation, particularly in the relation between images and words, work?), film criticism, and the material facts of film history.

Whose Text?

That Tree should be credited with the first attempt to adapt a theatrical performance to the new medium of cinema could potentially have been a source of dispute. Contrary to the early literature on the film (see Ball 1952: 228–9), the surviving scene is not a recreation of its stage equivalent; it flattened the *mise-en-scène*, bringing the backdrop suggestive of Swinstead Abbey into focus and requiring the actors to be grouped tightly around a throne placed just before it and a blossoming tree (the latter being one of Sir Herbert's scenic trademarks). Such rearrangement was probably suggested by the seasoned camera operator William Laurie Dickson or his assistants. It was Dickson who realized Thomas Edison's dream of inventing a device that could record images that would synchronize with his sound recordings; but upon falling out with Edison over claims to this Kinetograph's paternity, he co-founded the rival American Mutoscope and Biograph Company, and returned to Britain to help establish a branch there. It may thus have been his idea to use another experimental technology pioneered by the British division of Biograph to create publicity materials for one of Tree's stage productions at Her Majesty's Theatre. As the eminent film historian Luke McKernan (who has taken an especial interest in this *King John*) points out, the film premiered on the same night as the theatrical production, at London's Palace Theatre, a variety theater that was Biograph's main exhibition venue, where the gigantic screen size drew enthusiastic audiences (McKernan and Terris 1994: 82).

Shot at 40 frames per second on large-format (68mm) stock, the Biograph technology could serve equally well to record short scenes in "real" time on celluloid or as a considerable number of still photographs on Mutoscope flip-cards. Indeed, the similarity of the methods used to create the short film, the Mutoscope cards, and the illustrations for the theatrical program souvenir (lavishly supplied with still photographs) resulted in a misleading statement by G. W. Smedley, Chairman of the British Mutoscope and Biograph Company (reported in the *Westminster Gazette*, September 21, 1899). Smedley was either less technologically sophisticated than Dickson, or was misquoted to the effect that "10,000 series of King John pictures were posted from London last night, and were now 'unreeling' before the public gaze at their destinations" (4). McKernan notes that were the "pictures" instead "frames," as seems clearer later in the interview, the boast would not indicate 10,000 separate prints but something that at 40 frames a second lasted a little over four minutes (1993b: 50).

No recent commentator has described the rediscovered fragment as W. K. L. Dickson's *King John*, however, despite his probable participation; and they are correct, if not entirely fair, to grant Tree the major share of the film's authorship. One imagines that if Dickson and his team could have exerted the power of choice in selecting subject matter, they would have opted for a play more familiar to potential audiences, or they would have chosen to film an "attraction" (the term given by Tom Gunning and other historians of early cinema to a visually striking and self-explanatory event), as indeed Dickson had done when working for Edison. And we know that a far more flamboyant production of *A Midsummer Night's Dream* – also designed by Percy Anderson, and by common consent his visual masterpiece – went into rehearsal at Her Majesty's not long after the same actors who were to don the ethereal costumes of Shakespeare's "fairy" play trudged to Dickson's studio by the Thames, garbed in stage armor and heavy cloaks, to commit scenes of *King John* to film (Kachur 1991: 48–9).

The choice of *King John* was thus unlikely to have been casual, and was almost certainly determined by Tree, who was in sole charge of all aspects of production at Her Majesty's, the sumptuous theater Charles Phipps had completed barely two years earlier. An advertisement for the stage opening reveals Tree's relationship to his source: not only had he "improved" Shakespeare's play by condensing its highlights into three acts, but also added panoramic *tableaux vivants* of the French and English armies confronting each other at Angiers and of the signing of the Magna Carta – the latter not even mentioned by Shakespeare but conforming to the theatrical dictates of an increasingly historicist approach to staging Renaissance plays (Orgel 2003: 56). The first major historian of Shakespeare on film, Robert Hamilton Ball, remarks on Tree's selection with incredulity (1952: 228); but some of the mysteries surrounding the surviving footage may well be explained by Tree's conflicting motivations, and by his particular vision of the cinema as medium. Even the next Shakespeare film in which he acted (timed to coincide with his 1911 stage production of *Henry VIII*, in which he played Wolsey) was for him a means of publicity and exploitation – not to mention the £1,000 his star power could command. By 1911 the cinema was a highly formalized international industry, and a contractual agreement that prints of the *Henry VIII* film be burned after a short run at movie theaters (from February

27 to April 3, 1911) indicates a prerogative available only to a "personality" of Tree's unquestioned eminence. What the seasoned film director Will Barker might have felt about the arrangement was not recorded since he died just as he was about to communicate with Ball (1952: 232). For many reasons, then, the question of why Tree chose *King John* as his first filmed Shakespeare production, and the progenitor of a thriving tradition, is not a trivial one.

"Tickling Commodity"

In his anticipatory *Shakespeare on Silent Film*, Ball employed many of the evidentiary techniques for reconstructing lost films that historians were to rediscover during the late twentieth-century resurgence of interest in early cinema. Even so, he begins his monumental work with a rare flight of fancy that deserves to be quoted:

> If [Bernard] Shaw stood at his window contemplating Cleopatra's needle and glanced obliquely elsewhere, he saw . . . groups of people in elaborate and antiquated costumes who walked and gestured in a strangely theatrical manner. . . . Two individuals were in charge. . . . The name of the first man has vanished, but what he was operating was a motion picture camera. The second man Shaw might have recognized – he had indeed known him for some years. It was Herbert Beerbohm Tree, and he wore the crown of King John. This was the first Shakespearean film. . . . It is improbable that much of the film was photographed. Perhaps the site on the embankment gives a clue. Here was greenery and the Thames, an approximation to Runnymede. The tableau of the granting of the Magna Charta needed no words, only pantomime for its effect. This may have been all. If so, it is ironic that the first film of a performance of a Shakespeare play was of a scene which Shakespeare did not include. (1968: 21–3)

It was only much later that Dickson's vanished name resurfaced, but shortly after his book appeared Ball received a letter from one of the actors, Lt. Col. C. C. S. O'Mahony (who played Arthur under the stage name Charles Sefton), and published a correction. Lamenting once more that the film no longer exists, Ball suggests that, if it did, the scene we would witness would be "in fact that in which King John incites Hubert into agreeing to kill Prince Arthur" (1973: 455), the only one described by O'Mahony.

There the matter rested for two decades until theater historian B. A. Kachur resolved to revisit this primal Shakespearean scene. Sifting through a wider spectrum of evidence than Ball, Kachur pointed out that the filming need not have occurred outdoors and that at least part would have taken place in the Biograph studio located by the Adelphi embankment of the Thames. Taking Tree's claim that the film was a photographic "transcript" of the stage play to mean that it was a digest of Tree's three-act version, Kachur surmises that the film might well have been a compilation of five or more scenes, each some three to four minutes, which, when assembled, might have been up to 20 minutes in length (1991: 55). The following year Kachur argued convincingly that many elements of Tree's stage revival derived from its topicality, its connection to the impending declaration of war in South Africa.

If these political elements were initially obscure to the general public, they could not have been after the demonstrations of one spectator: Colonial Secretary Joseph Chamberlain, the most active proponent of the war, stepped forward to bow to the audience from the royal box at Her Majesty's, and proceeded to applaud passages about English military prowess (Kachur 1992: 30). Tree, too, played up the patriotic angle by commending the closing speech (lit by a glowing sunset with the orchestra playing) in which Louis Waller's Faulconbridge uttered a "resounding cry of British victory." According to Tree, it was "possibly the most beautifully patriotic speech to be found in all of Shakespeare's works" (Kachur 1992: 30).

Despite Kachur's insight into the nationalistic impulses of Tree's adaptation, a correction of her attempt to reconstitute the film was not long in coming, albeit in a circuitous way. It began with McKernan's sensational confirmation in the *Shakespeare Bulletin* that *King John* had been rediscovered: "One can never say with finality that a film is lost," wrote McKernan, who assumed that the minute-long fragment, found during an inventory at the Nederlands Filmmuseum, represented Tree's entire film (1993a: 35). He may have based his assumption on a statement in the Palace Theatre's program of November 6, which announced "A Scene 'King John' – now playing at Her Majesty's Theatre" (1993a: 36). McKernan soon offered a correction based on Kachur's observation that four frames reproduced in the 1899 London news magazine the *Sketch* were extracted from scenes that had been filmed, although McKernan preferred to think of them as representing three scenes rather than four (1993b: 49). Moreover, he demonstrated that the 5,000-foot film that Kachur's 20-minute version would indicate was technically impossible, and that films of 1899 were not constructed sequentially from shots in an integrated form as we presently understand film narrative. *"King John* was a news event, and the Biograph film a report on that event" (1993b: 50).

Although McKernan now admitted that only a fragment of the film was represented by the known extant material, the three scenes he describes are not those he settles on in his next attempt at reconstituting the film. In *Walking Shadows* he repeats his assertion that the film was not a good "record" of either the stage production or Shakespeare's play, and that it was adapted to the screen to "provide what amounted to an advertisement for Tree's production, or better still a news report, for the Biograph company were making their reputation with actuality coverage" (McKernan and Terris 1994: 2–3). He also identifies the four scenes suggested by the *Sketch* stills: "The Battlefield Near Angiers" (where John attempts to persuade Hubert to kill the captive Arthur), "The French King's Tent" (where Constance laments Arthur's fate), and John's final agony and Prince Henry's coronation in "The Orchard of Swinstead Abbey" (McKernan and Terris 1994: 82). Of these, only the third has been rediscovered.

While the matter of the actual *King John* film seen by the audiences in September 1899 remains far from resolved, what is striking about this series of amendments and self-corrections (each couched in a tone of confidence, at times even certainty) is the same desire to recover a lost object, the same passion for getting to the truth of that object, that Orgel in *The Authentic Shakespeare* (2002) ascribes to theater criticism and literary scholarship associated with Shakespeare (see also WALKER). This is not to contend that such a search is fruitless: despite being couched in combative terms, McKernan's emphasis on the technology of filmmaking and the film's generic context (i.e., the publicity news bulletin), as well as his ability to examine a rediscovered text from an archival standpoint, affords insights that are at variance with Kachur's, but no less significant in mapping the cultural history of a Victorian performance ethos than is the latter's emphasis on the sociopolitical dimensions of both the theatrical and cinematic versions of Tree's *King John*.

But what of the work of the literary scholar who initiated the study he dubbed "Shakespeare on film"? His was the first of the retractions, and no one has yet invented a Shakespeare film with Ball's verve. Whether substantial or not, it is to Ball's intuition that I propose to return, by way of three films that do exist, at the conclusion.

Performing Power

Let us continue to broaden our frame of reference and consider more ambiguities connected to the power of performance, and by extension to the power exerted over textual traces. Tree, at once autocrat and populist, readily modified his theatrical conceptions to the exigencies of the moment. The night on which *King John* opened should have coincided with the close of the most celebrated *fin-de-siècle* legal scandal of the nineteenth century. The latter had provoked the most famous of French newspaper op-ed articles (novelist Emile Zola's "J'accuse") and incited riots in the streets of Paris. News of the release of the pardoned prisoner, Alfred Dreyfus, briefly displaced the imminent Boer War from the headlines even in England, and the events of the case continued to resonate for some time as the disgraced army captain fought to clear his name. Georges Méliès, who made the earliest multi-scene adaptation of a Shakespeare play (*Hamlet*, 1907), and who ventured a special-effects-dominated precursor of *Shakespeare in Love* (showing the poet struggling to dramatize challenging material in *Shakespeare Writing Julius Caesar*, 1907), turned the Dreyfus controversy into the screen's first multi-scene biopic, *L'Affaire Dreyfus* (1899).

While Tree might have regarded the solitary scene in which he occupied centerstage the most worthy of display and preservation, in this context King John's granting of the charter of judicial rights, the director's only dramaturgical innovation, held more resonance for his contemporaries. The chance survival of Tree's death scene provides compelling evidence that any historical record embedded in film remains (or masks) a multivalent negotiation of the "message" embodied by the principal actors, director, its producers, and perhaps even its critics and spectators. Admittedly, some of the uncertainties resulting from such a division of labor, and hence of artistic intent, diminish when the director doubles as actor-manager. It is therefore no coincidence that Shakespeare films are very often the result of directors selectively transposing their creative energies from one medium to another: Kenneth Branagh is perhaps the outstanding example of a contemporary filmmaker who has continued Tree's now firmly rooted tradition.

Yet it could be argued that this very tradition complicates the attribution of responsibility for the *King John* film to Tree. Orson Welles, serving as a chronological mid-point between Tree and Branagh, associated his claim to film authorship not with his control of staging but with his mastery of cinematic technique. In a 1954 discussion at Oxford University, he defended his most recent Shakespearean film (against a largely hostile reaction among anglophone critics who felt he had done violence to Shakespeare's authorial prerogatives), with the argument that: "*Othello*, whether successful or not, is about as close to Shakespeare's play as was Verdi's opera. I think Verdi and Boito were perfectly entitled to change Shakespeare in adapting him to another art form; and assuming that film is an art form, I took the line that you can adapt a classic as freely and vigorously for the cinema." Cinema, according to Welles, is a visual medium, and he remains a master of the camera (1954: 121).

Nevertheless, Welles' conception of authorial autonomy was sharply at odds with the demands of the industrial mechanism that facilitated his technical virtuosity, that same studio system whose apogee is often taken to be *Citizen Kane* (1941) and which discarded him scarcely two years after the completion of his *chef d'oeuvre*. Whereas Tree thrived in an era when he could impose his authority on the technological apparatus of film production, Welles' authority derived from his resistance to Hollywood's "system." That within the discipline of film studies Welles' defiance defines a particular paradigm of artistic vision is largely a historical accident, yet one that has obscured the variety of authorial negotiations within studio systems. The examples provided by Max Reinhardt and Laurence Olivier, who faced very different political contexts and studio demands than those facing either Tree or Welles, remain just as revealing about the process of adaptation and authorship in the cinema.

On Auteurship and Authority

The notion of a "degree" of authorship was quite late in coming to film studies, but had its origins with the group of critics whose guiding figure was André Bazin (it was Bazin who argued that the excellence of Hollywood's films derived not from the creative activity of an individual, except in rare instances, but from the "genius of the system"). They promulgated a certain vision of art in the cinema – one that gained ascendancy in the post-World War II European festival circuit – which reacted against Hollywood's industrial dominance even before achieving international recognition with François Truffaut's 1954 polemic, "A Certain Tendency in French Cinema." Truffaut reviled France's "Tradition of Quality," wherein the government sought an antidote to Hollywood by funding adaptations of French literary classics (generally scripted by the indefatigable pairing of Jean Aurenche and Pierre Bost, whom Truffaut treated with ferocious contempt). This article became a rallying-point for the critics in the *Cahiers du Cinéma*, whose number included the most prominent of France's next generation of filmmakers.

Although proposed initially as a *politique des auteurs* (a politics or policy of authorship, by which they sought to contest the ideologies inherent in a model of industrialized mass production), the approach to filmmaking advocated by these critics achieved prominence in the English-speaking world through the efforts of Andrew Sarris. He proposed an *"auteur theory"* whose main purpose was to encourage certain forms of superior filmmaking – even within the studio system – by creating a hierarchy of important films and directors. The American version of the *politique des auteurs* emphasized the power exerted over the finished product, a necessary concomitant being a certain stylistic elegance. In this respect it diverged from the European tradition: for the *Cahiers* critics, the *auteur*'s claim of responsibility for the finished product was even more a political than an aesthetic gesture.

Within both traditions, to be a Shakespearean *auteur* represents something of a contradiction, although that appears not to have troubled Truffaut or more recent *auteur* critics. Clearly, a stage director who had exerted control over all aspects of production, from the movement of the actors to set design, would play an even more determinative role in the visual aspect of a film than do the vast majority of directors, thus fulfilling the central tenet of the *politique des auteurs*. On the other hand, the initial position articulated by Truffaut would suggest that the material should in all instances bear the imprint of the "author's" hand, thus precluding adaptation from consideration as *auteur* filmmaking.

The "solution" adopted by Truffaut, and indeed many of the *Cahiers* filmmakers, consisted of preserving their own narrative and visual styles as transcendent marks of the *auteur*. They interpreted their adapted text as a form of counter-text, one in dialogue with the original – as was outstandingly the case with Orson Welles' "Shakespeare." Welles, in fact, is perhaps the crucial figure in the drama of American *auteur* criticism. Precisely because he was canonized by Bazin and embraced by Truffaut, he became an object of ridicule for such influential American critics as Pauline Kael. Welles' Shakespeare, in particular, elicited vigorous denunciations among anglophone critics for the very reason that, unlike Laurence Olivier who seemed respectful of the traditions that informed Shakespearean performance, Welles was regarded as too much the *auteur*, imposing his aesthetic vision on Shakespeare's sacrosanct text. For Welles to persist in this vision of Shakespearean adaptation, when he was well aware that it defied Hollywood's production system, exemplified the folly of genius to some and to others a heroic last stand against the Hollywood machine.

Within the disciplinary context of film studies, then, the starting point for analysis of screen Shakespeare would logically be with the *politique des auteurs*, and the implications of that authorship for a rearticulated text: indeed, filmmakers such as Peter Greenaway have shown a sensitivity to such issues, and *Prospero's Books* (1991) is a prolonged meditation on the subject. The *politique* brings into focus the empowerment (the freedom to adapt into different contexts) afforded by texts enjoying the wide cultural circulation and currency of Shakespeare's, and the simultaneous constraint placed on filmmakers whose creative latitude is necessarily limited by the weight of Shakespearean tradition.

There are, of course, those who approach film adaptation from outside this narrow disciplinary framework. Historians of early cinema have at times resolutely resisted the encroachments of critical approaches and theories they regard as subjective and damaging to the discipline in compromising the veracity of data, while students of theater history (and cultural historians in general) have emphasized the social dimensions of films as communicative texts. In fact, few better examples of such contending perspectives can be found than in the attempts of Ball, Kachur, and McKernan to reconstitute the fragmentary *King John* from the flotsam and jetsam of surviving evidence. Yet synthesizing these perspectives can also be fruitful, as becomes evident when we consider the fates of the descendents of *King John*.

"Doing Thee Injuries"

A different sort of archival rediscovery might help us better contextualize a later, much-adjusted version of Shakespeare. In the 1935 Warner Brothers production of *A Midsummer Night's Dream*, political content became in effect textualized apoliticism, the conscious suppression of certain discursive formations in order to produce a work of "high art" responding specifically to new kinds of Hollywood censorship introduced in 1934.

41

In 1998 Russell Jackson reported the chance discovery in the Birmingham Public Library of a shooting script of this *Dream* dated December 6, 1934 and marked "final" beneath the identificatory "Script of the film produced by M. Reinhardt for Warner Brothers" (1998: 41). Jackson makes careful note of several scenes not included in the released film, including an opening montage showing Theseus' defeat and subjugation of Hippolyta, narrative intrusions by Bottom's "virago" wife, and the use of a color film technique to "paint" love-in-idleness, the western flower "now purple with love's wound." Jackson ventures that "like most 'final draft' shooting scripts, prepared just before principal photography, this one includes elements that did not find their way either onto celluloid or into the cinema. The omission of any element of this script from the released film does not necessarily indicate any disagreement, artistic failure, or exertion of pressure from the 'front office'" (1998: 40). Shortly thereafter Michael Jensen, having come across the movie's tie-in book written by Helen Davidson and illustrated with frame blow-ups taken from scenes that had been shot, argued that some of the omissions must have occurred at the editing stage, since five of the photographs are from three "missing" scenes (2000: 37).

If we permit ourselves to textualize an "absence," then these missing scenes represent a facet of Bazin's "genius of the system," revealing the power exerted by studios such as Warner Brothers in shaping its product. If some of the scenes were indeed shot, the decision to discard them (and thereby jettison some of the sexual politics preserved in the final shooting script) would have rested not only with the directors but also with Jack Warner who, while flaunting the claim that he had never read a book, experimented with courting audiences of successful stage-plays, pored over his directors' dailies together with production head Hal Wallis, and maintained rights over the final edits of even the most "literary" of his films (Zierold 1969: 253–5). That the studio's conception of *A Midsummer Night's Dream* diverged from the tradition familiar to, and in part even created by, Reinhardt could nowhere be more evident than in Davidson's book: published by the Five Star Library, which specialized in movie tie-in books for children, the small-format work with text and photographs on alternating pages bore a picture of an animated, juvenile Puck (Mickey Rooney) on the cover.

Reinhardt was no stranger to filmmaking. His early works *Die Insel der Seligen* (1913) and *Venezianische Nacht* (1914) emphasized elements of fantasy, but other German films of *A Midsummer Night's Dream* from the 1910s and 1920s, with which he must have been familiar, emphasized the play's sexual symbolism, particularly that of the fairies who became associated with the forest spirits of Central European folklore. In 1913 Hanns Heinz Ewers and Stellan Rye directed the first major German film based on this play for Deutsche-Bioscop (Lippmann 1964: 19); Ball suggests the film transposed Ewer and Rye's risqué modern-dress stage version designed to rival Reinhardt's Deutsches Theater production of the same year (1968: 176–7). The better-known 1925 Hans Neumann film seems saturated by Expressionist influences, including stylized performances (the fairy-folk, for instance, were well-known dancers, Oberon being played by a Russian ballerina known as "Tamara"). Expressionist designer Erno Metzner created the costumes (partly reproduced in Lippmann 1964: 22), and Alfred Henschke, "well known . . . for his association with expressionism" (Ball 1968: 297), designed parodic intertitles that apparently took up more time than the film images themselves (Lippmann 1964: 22).

As Gary Williams points out in his magisterial performance history of Shakespeare's play, Reinhardt's numerous stagings of *A Midsummer Night's Dream* (including 587 performances in Germany alone) evolved through a succession of styles. The most influential German theater director of his generation, Reinhardt's contribution to the development of monumental stage design and lighting, overwrought *schrei* acting, stylized Expressionist set design and costuming, and even the intimate *kammerspiel* had a greater impact on German Expressionist filmmaking than the work of any individual film director (indeed, directors F. W. Murnau and Fritz Lang were deeply indebted to Reinhardt, and many prominent actors began their careers with him at Berlin's Deutsches Theater). Although initially espousing a "fundamentally neoromantic," "playful" conception in his productions between 1905 and 1927 (Williams 1997: 166–74), Reinhardt's vision of the play darkened as the Weimar Republic foundered and Hitler's faction rose to prominence: his theaters were among the first such "Jewish" establishments expropriated by the Nazis, and in 1934 he emigrated to the United States. That summer Reinhardt restaged the vast outdoor productions from Florence (1933) and London (1934) at the Hollywood Bowl. In Bottom's terrified reaction to his transformation and in the sinister, black-clad Oberon carrying off the First Fairy on his shoulders as her fingers flutter in a shaft of light (an effect repeated in the 1935 film), Williams sees "the first dark theatrical images in the performance history of the play," characteristic of the troubled twentieth century (1997: 176).

For the most part the film followed the theatrical version. The studio, perhaps seeing potential in two of the stage stars, Olivia de Haviland (as Hermia) and Mickey Rooney (as Puck), and with a former Reinhardt student, Wilhelm (William) Dieterle, already under contract as a director, decided on this production as the basis for its "prestige film" of the year. They augmented the personnel with a notable Austrian composer, Erich Wolfgang Korngold (who would make a crucial contribution to American film music, but was in this instance required to retain most of Mendelssohn, whose music was by now proscribed in Germany), and the principal choreographer of the Ballet Russe, Bronislava Nijinskaya. Reinhardt and Dieterle were both given directing credit, and their version underlines some of the more sinister elements (see Williams 1997: 175–89). Nevertheless, even while emphasizing the forest as a place of danger and providing a visual allegory of the conquest of the light by the powers of darkness in the mid-European hinterlands, the film (as revealed by Jackson and Jensen) muted what in the United States proved the culturally riskier theme of sexual conquest.

Reinhardt's participation lent the studio cultural prestige, a fact not lost on Hal Wallis on the eve of Hollywood's implementing its most restrictive form of self-censorship up to that point with the Production Code of 1934, drafted under the authority of Will Hays and enforced by the Breen office. But Warner Brothers was principally investing in Shakespeare's authority as playwright, rather than Reinhardt's as stage director, and did not expect to recover the outlay for cultural capital in hard cash at the box office. Although Shakespeare had much less to do with the film than with the 1601 Globe performance, his authorship had undergone a remarkable transformation over the course of three centuries. If he was wanted now, it was not for treason but as a genius and icon of respectability. Nick Roddick points out that for the studio their adaptation's most significant result might have been a reply by Hays to an enthusiastic letter by the President of the Shakespeare Association of America: Hays predicts that the film would inaugurate "a new epoch in the popular and universal appreciation of Shakespeare" (1983: 233). Contrary to the still commonly voiced critical opinion that lukewarm box-office receipts might have tempered Warners' enthusiasm, Roddick maintains that: "*A Midsummer Night's Dream* did not, of course, spark off a Shakespeare cycle of any kind, at Warners or anywhere else. Reinhardt was at one stage supposed to do a second picture for Warner Brothers but nothing came of the plan: the company's respectability established, the impetus for prestige production moved elsewhere" (1983: 233).

"Once More Unto the Breach"

It was not prestige or moral rectitude but a wartime requirement for morale-boosting propaganda that provided the impetus for Olivier's *Henry V*. While *King John* might have contained "the most beautifully patriotic speech to be found in all of Shakespeare's works," it is *Henry V* whose plot most suits a message of national unity against a common foe, however duplicitous a character Shakespeare's Henry might be. Thus, emphasizing Olivier's distortion of Shakespeare's play anachronistically ignores its *raison d'être* (see Davies 1988: 27). As Harry Geduld points out, rather than merely disguising political expediency (as has been claimed about Olivier's rendering of the Archbishop's Salic Law interpretation), the comedy provides modern audiences a view of Renaissance theatrical practice (what Mikhail Bakhtin might have called carnivalesque interruptions of religious authority figures by the groundlings), while simultaneously serving as the culmination of a series of gaffes, artificial conventions (the use of boy actors), and histrionics (the bombast of the Chorus) which underline "the shortcoming of the theatre as a medium for presenting a dramatic epic"; it thus prepares the film's spectators for the eventual abandonment of the theatrical space of Shakespeare's "wooden O" for the cinematic one of the "vasty fields of France" (Geduld 1973: 27–9). Davies likewise observes that Olivier's artistic ambitions went beyond merely adapting theatrical conventions to the historical situation, for his film is a "treatise on the differences between cinema and theatre as media for the expression of drama" (1988: 26).

The circumstances that permitted Olivier to exert control were extraordinary, particularly considering his lack of experience as a filmmaker. Except in the ephemeral case of Welles at RKO in 1940, such a situation could never have occurred in Hollywood's closed cartel, where film production followed a strict industrial model whose efficient operation depended on the vigilance of the studio head. Nor could Olivier have achieved his vision without the unstinting support of Filippo Del Giudice, the head of Two Cities Films. Dallas Bower, who had conceived of a patriotic adaptation of the play as early as 1938, heard Olivier's radio broadcasts of Henry's "Harfleur" and "St. Crispin's Day" speeches in May 1942, and persuaded Del Giudice to take on the project. Del Giudice not only acquiesced to Olivier being executive producer and lead actor, but also insisted that he direct the film after William Wyler, Carol Reed (Beerbohm Tree's illegitimate son), and Terence Young turned down the project. From this point onwards Olivier took charge of all production matters, choosing the art directors and selecting William Walton to compose the music. He also cast all the roles, a prerogative shared by only one other contemporary director of Shakespeare adaptations, Orson Welles. "It was Olivier's inspiration rather than teamwork that was to determine the quality of the film," writes Geduld (1973: 16): Olivier had become an *auteur* by accident. He gained renown as a filmmaker, creating one of the acknowledged masterpieces of the Technicolor film process, before winning comparable acclaim as a theater director. Ironically, while the Reinhardt–Dieterle *Midsummer Night's Dream* was an equivocal success with audiences and critics, yet served its purpose for the studio, Olivier's *Henry V* was a resounding success, yet forced his studio into near bankruptcy. As production costs escalated and the major backer withdrew, Del Giudice opted to become a subsidiary of the giant Rank Organization rather than halt the film (Geduld 1973: 21–2).

Spared the fiscal concerns that were to dog Orson Welles, Olivier was free to explore the potentialities of a filmic vocabulary expressive of a certain aesthetic and a particular ideology – patriotism to some, jingoism to others. The choice of medieval and Renaissance illustrations as visual models, ranging from the Limbourgs to Uccello to English miniatures, made Henry and his troops bright, dynamic, red-hued harbingers of the Renaissance, while their French combatants remain trapped in the pale blues and flat perspectives of medieval art. Moreover, the chance discovery of a technique for "normalizing" Renaissance dialogue through contrast with reverse tracking shots drawing the camera away during heightened speeches, proved fortuitous (Geduld 1973: 18).

Elaborate cross-cutting later in the film also serves an ideological function, although its lack of allegorical specificity has drawn criticism (see Durgnat 1970: 109). While elements of the French court disapprove of Katharine and Henry's impending matrimony, the preparatory sequences before the couple meet imply her acquiescence and his gallant magnanimity. Durgnat points out that it might have been France as much as Germany that had to be won over: D-Day was in the offing, the need for international collaboration paramount, and France became an ally by the time of the film's completion.

Moreover, the propaganda message was no fuzzier than that of *Casablanca* (1940; albeit that film's promise of a "beautiful friendship" was not couched in matrimonial terms).

To most commentators, Olivier as *auteur* simplified Shakespeare's King Henry. Nevertheless, Olivier's control over most aspects of filming and his assumption of the mantle of Shakespearean leading man paradoxically seemed to assure proximity to authorial intentions. James Agee, for instance, apologized for not being Tory, monarchist, Catholic, a medievalist, an Englishman, or a supporter of war, but admitted the film made him want to be them all. He sees the author through the *auteur* as if through a magnifying lens: "I was persuaded, and in part still am, that every time and place has since been in decline, save one, in which one Englishman used language better than anyone has before or since, or ever shall; and that nearly the best that our time can say for itself is that some of us are still capable of paying homage to the fact" (Geduld 1973: 69).

"Nothing Extenuate"

Predictably, Orson Welles' artisanal adaptations initially suffered in comparison to Olivier's polished creations. Michael Anderegg remarks perceptively that "Welles's Shakespeare films are part of a counter tradition of Shakespeare, what might be thought of as 'Shakespeare from the Provinces,' a tradition that included amateur and school productions, abbreviated texts, [and] almost any Shakespeare taking place outside the theater capitals of London . . . and New York"; thus critics familiar with the bolder experimental productions in "venues such as the Deutsches Theater (Berlin), the Piccolo Teatro (Milan), and the Théâtre de Soleil (Vincennes)" found Welles more congenial than did their Anglo-American counterparts (1999: 67–9).

The almost concurrent appearance in 1948 of Olivier's "classical" *Hamlet* and Welles' visually expressionist, pluri-generic *Macbeth* provoked an exemplary outburst from *Life* magazine: having granted Olivier a pensive, in-costume portrait-bust cover on March 15, the October 11 edition proceeded to ridicule Welles' pretensions. Suggesting he somehow had advance knowledge that Olivier's film had won the Silver Lion at the Venice Film Festival, *Life* imputed Welles' hubris in claiming his film's superiority (even after withdrawing it) was the bravado of a Hollywood has-been (Anderegg 1999: 74). In Welles' documentary *Filming Othello* (1979), he makes the no less

47

improbable claim that he withdrew the film at the insistence of the US State Department.

Filming Othello is, Anderegg observes, one of a series of competing texts about the making of his 1951–4 *Othello*, at least five of which Welles edited himself. This documentary, staged as part personal essay and part conversation using two of the actors, Micheál MacLiammóir and Hilton Edwards, revisits the tortuous production of the film. In the process the triumvirate invoke MacLiammóir's published diary account of the filming, *Put Money in Thy Purse*, even as they speculate about yet another, more perfect film. Welles' next film after *F for Fake* (1973) – a systematic deconstruction of documentary form – *Filming Othello* turns out to be another wry joke about authorship. Early on, Welles indicates that he is not to be trusted, quoting critic Jack Jorgens and then paraphrasing him in a way that creates ambiguity as to where the citation ends and plagiarism begins (Anderegg 1999: 101).

There is, however, an autumnal poignancy to the good cheer of *Filming Othello*, for it commemorates one of the supreme struggles of independent filmmaking. When his Italian producer Montatori Scalera unexpectedly withdrew from the project, Welles saved the film by taking acting jobs, borrowing equipment, filming actors draped in towels while awaiting costumes, and taking reverse shots and consecutive sequences months apart in locations as disparate as Mogador, Safi, Venice, Viterbo, and Rome. Bazin's brood had yet to fledge the eggs of *auteur* criticism, but the first Palme d'Or awarded to an African entry at Cannes (*Othello* representing Morocco in 1952) was as much a celebration of genius outside the system as it was of Welles' obvious mastery of his medium.

Paola Quarenghi notes that much of the initial criticism of *Othello* seems "surpassingly unjustified," particularly in holding Welles to Olivier's model – even Bazin considered Welles' performance insufficiently elevated (2002: 119). She notes, too, the irony that Olivier's later Old Vic performance filmed by Stuart Burge (1965) revealed all too clearly the actor's studious attempts to recreate an authentic African by observing black denizens of London streets, an "external" construction of character that is today decidedly out of critical fashion (2002: 123–4). In marked contrast, Welles "plays a light-complexioned Moor and consistently underplays racial difference" (Donaldson 1990: 97), suppressing instances of melodrama beloved of stage actors (Naremore 1989: 182). Kathy Howlett, concentrating on Iago's perverse mechanism of control through sight, notes that what appears to be film's sadistic male gaze (as described by Laura Mulvey) is an extension of Vittore Carpaccio's object fetishism in the quattrocento frescoes Welles used as a visual model (2000: 64–91). In keeping with his penchant for polysemy, Welles' Carpaccioesque spaniel (to which Howlett devotes considerable attention) also references Jan van Eyck's near-contemporary *Arnolfini Betrothal*, where it functions iconographically as a symbol of fidelity in perhaps the most famous marriage painting of the Western tradition. Van Eyck's concave mirror, with its unmistakable frame, serves as the scene of the perverse marriage and exchange of vows between Othello and Iago; it denotes the moment at which Othello sees himself as irredeemably other, racially as well as sexually betrayed (see also Donaldson 1990: 93–126 on Welles' mirror imagery). As in the painting, the artist-witness, van Eyck–Iago, remains visible as a diminished background figure who nevertheless must be the author of the spectacle. The dog that in van Eyck bears witness to marital faith, in the film is exquisitely placed to observe the disintegration of the various "marriages" contracted by Iago.

This extraordinary formal control and the striking use of a technology as metaphor distinguishes *Othello* even from the rest of Welles' *oeuvre*. Much has been made of Welles' use of film stock to achieve high-contrast black-and-white images using low-key lighting. What has not been noted is that the quality of light actually changes, as do the textures of the musical accompaniment. The moon-dappled night and brilliant daylight of Venice give way to the increasingly dim, echoing interior mazes of Cyprus. *Othello* does not begin as a film noir; it becomes one as Iago begins to steal the light from the other characters. In the early island scenes, the lack of interior light is offset by Othello's flowing white robe; by the time he bursts through a door on his final visit to Desdemona's bedchamber, he has become a silhouette (indeed, as he walks towards the camera his cloak smothers it in jet black). When his hand is placed on Desdemona's blonde hair before he smothers her, it seems blacker than it has ever been: white Iago's inner blackness finally engulfs Othello, which is to say, more prosaically, that it is not Othello's skin but the light his environment casts on him that blackens him.

Could such a commentary on race relations – a topic Welles addressed not only on film but in speeches, on the radio, and in the theater – have been made within the confines of a studio? Anderegg observes that when Paul Robeson, the first African-American Othello of the twentieth century to perform in New York, was photographed embracing his blonde Desdemona, Uta Hagen, the images printed by the ever-present *Life* magazine provoked a "strong racist reaction." He adds that "when news of Welles's *Othello* plans were made known, the Breen office informed one possible backer that it would not pass on the film were Othello to be played as a black man, even if that black man was a white actor in blackface" (1999: 110). Meanwhile, in Welles' Venice one is left wondering what Brabantio's fuss is about, for the stern protagonist who responds to the senate with sarcasm could almost pass for white; yet on the craggy island not far from his ancestral home, Othello – to borrow the title Naremore gives his book on film noir – grows darker than night.

"If You Prick Us"

Among the first entertainment media to exploit the leisure capital of non-elites, the English Renaissance theater was nevertheless of great political consequence for aspiring gentlemen (such as theater share-holders) and aristocratic patrons. With the advent of mass media in the nineteenth century, the phenomenon that philosophers of social change such as Oskar Negt and Alexander Kluge have referred to as a dynamic popular public sphere, countervailing a static bourgeois public sphere, began to make itself felt. When Zola published "J'accuse" in the January 13, 1898 issue of *L'Aurore*, quadrupling sales of the newspaper that day, he was forced to flee Paris for London to evade charges of defamation brought by authorities he named as complicit in the wrongful conviction. But the heat of popular opinion he generated compelled their reopening of the case; had his words not had a social effect beyond his own control, he would have remained in exile.

Precisely by being transculturally and transtemporally significant texts, Shakespeare's plays offer the cultural historian valuable insights about the changing role of media in society, about questions of authority vis-à-vis technologies of communication and performance practices, and about the process of intermediation, the symbiotic interaction of media. Whether what is adapted of Shakespeare is his words, his appeal to a common cultural foundation, or his prestige, what survives as source material is, as Orgel observes, vivified only in the process of cultural inflection.

No less revealing than the socially specific reshaping of discourse is the study of the movement of "Shakespeare" from one medium to another, and in this regard the fragmentary *King John* remains of exceptional significance. Although McKernan is correct to argue that the spectacle granted the audience at the Palace Theatre on September 20, 1899 was a news bulletin, it was both more (having a wider range of significance than imparting news) and less (in that it was not quite a film in the way we conceive of cinema). At least to one of its contemporaries it remained 10,000 still photographs strung together to simulate a moving picture. To the reporter from the *Sketch* who noted the actors heading off to be "biographed," those who performed the deed were "shrewd" suppliers of "Animated Photographs" (Sept. 20, 1899: 3). Then again, another reporter, perhaps with fatal consequence to that moving picture if Tree read the news, wrote: "Why pay half a guinea for a stall at Her Majesty's when you can see the play round the corner for a penny?" (*Westminster Gazette*, Sept. 21, 1899: 4). Could this be why the only rediscovered scene depicts Tree occupying the center of the frame, deadly serious in his regal suffering and writhing, while those around him look amused at the outset and then all but inert (i.e., impressive as spectacle but a poor substitute for theatrical action)? To imagine that performance in the theater and performance before cameras were conceived of as generically different, or that a clear sense of separation existed between still photography and moving photography, would be anachronistic media chauvinism.

Who, then, is not to say that what Jacques Derrida calls the "trace" still survives of the film Ball imagined, an absence invoked by what is there? The review of the opening night in *The Times* suggested that far from being presented as allegories for the overthrow of the monarchy, Shakespeare's history plays might well be made to move a little faster in a new age: "Mr. Tree's aim has been so to regroup and recast the scenes as to accelerate the action of the play without impairing anything of its truth and spirit. This is a proper aim, for rapidity is of the very essence of a 'chronicle play' – which should have something of the kaleidoscope, or rather of the kinematograph" (Sept. 21, 1899: 4). And of the scene that Shakespeare forgot to include, a certain E. F. S., writing for the *Sketch*, has this to say: "At present the Dreyfus case is really quite a King Charles's head with most of us, and I could not keep it out of my mind when glancing at a copy of the famous charter which Mr. Beerbohm Tree will be granting nightly, for many days to come, I hope at Her Majesty's Theatre. 'None shall be condemned on rumors or suspicions, but only on evidence of witnesses.' It does seem quaint that even by now France is not sufficiently civilized to have a law of justice deemed fundamental on July 15, 1215" (Sept. 27, 1899: 412). What Emile Zola, then in England and soon to take up residence at the Queen's Hotel in the south of London, where he reportedly devoted his waking hours to his passion for still photography, might have thought of the scene, does not appear to have been recorded.

Acknowledgments

Special thanks to those without whom this work would not have been possible: Betsy Walsh and the rest of my adopted family at the Folger Shakespeare Library, David Frasier, Professors Harry Geduld, Patricia Parker, Diana Henderson, and Richard Vela, and my Dantesque muse and translator, Stephanie Beatrice Hamels.

References and Further Reading

Ball, Robert Hamilton (1952). "The Shakespeare Film as Record: Sir Herbert Beerbohm Tree." *Shakespeare Quarterly* 3.3: 227–36.

—— (1973). "Tree's King John Film: An Addendum." *Shakespeare Quarterly* 24.4: 455–9.

Durgnat, Raymond (1970). *A Mirror for England: British Movies from Austerity to Affluence.* London: Faber and Faber.

Freedland, Michael (1983). *The Warner Brothers.* New York: St. Martin's Press.

Geduld, Harry M. (1973). *Filmguide to Henry V.* Bloomington: Indiana University Press.

Greenblatt, Stephen (2001). "Racial Memory and Literary History." *PMLA* 116.1: 48–63.

Jackson, Russell (1998). "Surprising Find in British Archive: A Shooting Script for the Reinhardt–Dieterle *Dream*: The War with the Amazons, Bottom's Wife, and Other 'Missing' Scenes." *Shakespeare Bulletin* 16.4: 39–41.

Jensen, Michael P. (2000). "Fragments of a *Dream*: Photos of Three Scenes Missing from the Reinhardt–Dieterle *Dream*." *Shakespeare Bulletin* 18.4: 37–8.

Kachur, B. A. (1991). "The First Shakespeare Film: A Reconsideration and Reconstruction of Tree's *King John*." *Theatre Survey* 32: 43–63.

—— (1992). "Shakespeare Politicized: Beerbohm Tree's *King John* and the Boer War." *Theatre History Studies* 12: 25–44.

Lippmann, Max, ed. (1964). *Shakespeare im Film.* Wiesbaden: Deutsches Institut für Filmkunde.

McKernan, Luke (1993a). "Beerbohm Tree's King John Rediscovered: The First Shakespeare Film, September 1899." *Shakespeare Bulletin* (Winter): 35–6.

—— (1993b). "Shakespeare on Film: Further Notes on Beerbohm Tree's *King John.*" *Shakespeare Bulletin* (Spring): 49–50.

Naremore, James (1989). *The Magic World of Orson Welles.* Rev. edn. Dallas: Southern Methodist University Press.

Orgel, Stephen (2002). *The Authentic Shakespeare.* New York: Routledge.

—— (2003). *Imagining Shakespeare: A History of Texts and Visions.* Houndmills: Palgrave Macmillan.

Quarenghi, Paola (2002). *Shakespeare e gli inganni del cinema.* Rome: Bulzoni Editore.

Roddick, Nick (1983). *A New Deal in Entertainment: Warner Brothers in the 1930s.* London: BFI Publishing.

Schoenbaum, Samuel (1999). "Richard II and the Realities of Power." In Kirby Farrell (ed.), *Critical Essays on Shakespeare's Richard II.* New York: G. K. Hall: 41–57.

Welles, Orson (1954). Interview: "The Third Audience." *Sight and Sound* 23: 120–2.

Williams, Gary (1997). *Our Midnight Revels: A Midsummer Night's Dream in the Theatre.* Iowa City: University of Iowa Press.

Zierold, Norman (1969). *The Moguls.* New York: Coward-McCann.

Chapter 3

THEATRICALITY

Stage, Screen, and Nation: *Hamlet* and the Space of History

Robert Shaughnessy

Released in 2000, Michael Almereyda's *Hamlet* has been well received as a coherent and persuasive transposition of the Shakespearean text into the milieu of urban postmodernity. Fast-paced, youth-oriented, and relentlessly contemporary, Almereyda's treatment is part of the wave of Shakespearean films, initiated by Baz Lurhmann's *William Shakespeare's Romeo + Juliet* (1996), which have sundered the genre's long-standing affiliations to period costume drama and historical epic; in this instance, by setting the play in Manhattan, styling Ethan Hawke's Prince as an upper-middle-class dropout and amateur filmmaker, and rendering its action in terms of corporate intrigue and the micro-politics of the WASP post-nuclear family (see also WALKER, DONALDSON). Two innovations in particular interest me here. First, the domain of the film's action is neither military nor political but economic. Envisaging a metropolitan scene in which, in the context of American-led globalization, the classic European nation-state has become irrelevant and even meaningless, Almereyda makes Denmark over as the Denmark Corporation, a mysterious, smartly logoed transnational; an incarnation of business culture familiar from *Wall Street* (1987) and *American Psycho* (2000), it provides a comprehensible generic location for corruption, violence, and paranoid plotting, and for the protagonist's alienated impotence and eventual defeat. The fable's potential universality (like the export value of American movies

as a whole) rests upon the capacity of "New York" to act more globally, to represent a state of mind and a generalized urban experience
(see BURNETT).

The second of Almereyda's innovations to concern me is that there
is, in this film, no performance of *The Mousetrap*. Its place is taken by
what has been called "one of Almereyda's more daring departures
from Shakespeare's text" (Lanier 2002a: 174): *The Mousetrap* as "a film
by Hamlet," an experimental, confrontational home video assembled
from clips from old films and television shows (a silent *Cleopatra*,
1950s sitcoms, cartoons, the notorious porn flick *Deep Throat* [1972],
etc.), screened in Claudius' private movie theater. Announced by title
graphics which mimic those of the film in which it is embedded, *The
Mousetrap* is as much an attack upon media culture as an attempt to
expose Claudius; more radically, it is a self-reflexive device which, by
encouraging the identification of Hamlet the disaffected *auteur* with
Almereyda himself, proposes a qualified, and pessimistic, critique of
the film's own location within the corporate media apparatus. Despite
its championing of the independent *auteur* as urban guerrilla, the film
is, Lanier points out, all too aware of the difficulty of "fashioning and
occupying a space outside . . . 'the phantom empire of film,'" and of
"imagining a specifically filmic mode of resistance"; ultimately, the
best escape it can offer is "the privileging of a private subjective space
– 'our thoughts' – that remains inviolably 'ours'" (2002: 175, 177,
179).

At one, relatively straightforward, level, the effectiveness of
Almereyda's substitution of the screen for the stage lies in its reinvention
of the play's metatheatricality as cinematic self-reflexiveness; evading
the stagy literalism that has dogged the Shakespearean cinematic tradition, Almereyda's *Mousetrap* provides an analogy for *The Murder of
Gonzago* rather than a *mise-en-scène* enactment of it. Code-switching is
central to the film, in that it is implicated within its politics of resistance and accommodation, and its tactics of negotiation between
private, corporate, and cultural space. Lanier's spatial terminology is
both significant and suggestive in alluding to one of the film's central
problematics: its absence, indeed negation, of both public and performance space. There is no space in the film which is not privatized,
and there is, in a literal sense, no place for theater either within the
transnational realm of the Denmark Corporation or Almereyda's hip
aesthetic. In this respect, the two aspects of the film I have foregrounded are cognate: just as "Denmark" as a marker of both nationhood and geographical location is deterritorialized, emptied of history,

and recirculated as a free-floating corporate signifier, the transposition of *The Mousetrap* from theater to film jettisons the appurtenances of both performance (rehearsal, Hamlet's scripted intervention, negotiations between prince and players, theatrical gossip) and dramaturgy (narrative, rhetoric, and characterization), in favor of a montage technique whose *raison d'être* is its bourgeois-baiting capacity for scandal, its potential to antagonize and expose. The chief lesson of Hamlet's trawl through the archive of film history (which at another remove tropes a relationship not only with the broader performance histories of the play, of theater, and of media culture but also with history itself) is that the potency and value of the past lie in its potential to be recycled, fairly indiscriminately, as kitsch.

Theatricality's disappearance (or, in this instance, determined erasure) is seemingly in tune with current thinking about Shakespeare on film. In much recent criticism, the terminology of theater and performance rarely features; Shakespearean film studies, like this turn-of-the-twenty-first-century film, has become fully cinematized, so that the plays' theatrical origins, potentialities, and histories of performance have come to seem embarrassing or irrelevant. Lanier, for example, frames his discussion with the statement that the "one overarching aim of recent Shakespeare films has been to definitively establish the screen image – and thus the cultural industries that make and market that image – as the principal vehicle for sustaining Shakespeare's cultural authority in a posttheatrical, postliterary age," which has involved "uncoupling Shakespeare from an increasingly debilitating association with the theater" (2002: 161–2). His evaluation of Almereyda's investment in the "post-theatrical" prompts an interrogation of the "ascendancy" of "metaperformative criticism" which has been facilitated by the imprecision of performance as a category: rather than encompassing film and theater within the same rubric (and employing theater to read film and vice versa), Lanier urges us to attend to "the specific qualities of Shakespeare film *as film* – of film as a distinctive medium but, more important, of film as a distinctive and pervasive cultural industry" (2002: 180).[1] Richard Burt takes the "post-theatrical" agenda a stage further, suggesting that the digitalization of screen media now means that even the experience of "theatrical" viewing of Shakespeare films in darkened dream palaces is obsolete, the DVD redefining a "horizon of expectation" which is "composed of multiple viewing possibilities that reframe the initial theatrical viewing ... in media that are often old and new (DVDs textualize film, for example by dividing scenes up into chapters) and that are both increasingly integrated – such as the computer as home theater – and dispersed – such as cell phones and portable DVD players" (Boose and Burt 2003: 4). In Burt's view, this has created the conditions for a "post-historical" culture of film reception; in the context of multimedia proliferation and reconfiguration, the moment of a film's production cannot be privileged as an arbiter of how it is to be read. Digitalization, moreover, interfaces with globalization, as cinema mutates into post-national, pan-national, and transnational forms: the proliferation of formats moving across the nation-state's increasingly porous boundaries (Boose and Burt 2003: 5–6).[2]

Theater, in this context, has become a cinematic anachronism, albeit one which retains a powerful nostalgic charge, as manifested in the recent spate of theatrically centered Shakespeare movies which includes *In the Bleak Midwinter* (or *A Midwinter's Tale*; dir. Branagh, 1996), *Looking for Richard* (dir. Pacino, 1996), *Shakespeare in Love* (dir. Madden, 1998), *A Midsummer Night's Dream* (dir. Noble, 1996), and *The Children's Midsummer Night's Dream* (dir. Edzard, 2001). During the formative stages of Shakespearean film criticism, however, the theater represented the point of departure for analysis and evaluation; indeed, the major project of the first generation of Shakespearean film scholars was to legitimize the canon of Shakespearean film as something other than second-order performance.

In the first full-length critical study of Shakespeare and the cinema (1977), Jack J. Jorgens proposed a three-part scheme for locating and formally categorizing various Shakespearean films. The three basic modes are – in ascending order of significance, legitimacy and efficacy – the theatrical, the realist, and the filmic. Each mode is defined in terms of the treatment of *mise-en-scène*, and of the degree of reverence, caution, or literalism with which it regards both the literary text and the theatrical medium taken to be the text's natural provenance. The "theatrical" film (Jorgens' examples include Burge's 1965 National Theatre *Othello*, Gielgud's 1964 rehearsal record of *Hamlet* on Broadway, and Tony Richardson's 1969 Roundhouse version of the same play) is characterized by "[l]engthy takes in medium or long shot" which "stress the durational quality of time"; a tendency to treat the cinema frame as "a kind of portable proscenium arch" in which "meaning is generated through the words and gestures of the actors"; and a performance style "more demonstrative, articulate, and continuous than actors are usually permitted in films" (1977: 7–8). Tied to the documentation of stage production, the theatrical Shakespearean film is, for Jorgens, not quite of the medium it claims to inhabit: "[i]t has the look and feel of a performance worked out for a static theatrical space and a live audience" (1977: 7). Films of this type usually combine limited circumstances of production and distribution with distinctly high-art aspirations, in that they require relatively developed skills of tolerance, attentiveness, and cultural competence.

Jorgens' categorization of adaptations was intended, in part, as a means of tracing a "great tradition" of Shakespearean films; this canonical work was consolidated at the end of the 1980s by Anthony Davies, whose *Filming Shakespeare's Plays* (1988) refined Jorgens' readings of Kurosawa, Brook, Welles, and Olivier within a discourse of cinematic analysis which, whilst asserting film's autonomy from theater, nonetheless returns repeatedly to the relationship between the media. A lengthy opening chapter is devoted to identifying distinctions between "theatrical" and "cinematic" space (1988: 5–25), yet the series of case studies concludes with a reiteration of the reciprocity and interdependence of screen and stage, in that the worth of the "classic" Shakespearean films lies in their capacity to "meet the challenge of reconciling theatrical resonance and centripetality with the fluidity, the discontinuity and the centrifugality of cinematic space" (1988: 184). Theater is not only a formal point of reference; it is a crucial (if unacknowledged) means of arbitrating the competing claims to cultural authority of Shakespeare (assumed to exist as an enduring literary-theatrical construct, traditionally termed the "undisputed literary classics" that constitute the *oeuvre* of "the world's greatest dramatist" [1988: 1, 187]) and film (assumed to consist of a minority Shakespearean cinema of the avant-garde).

But Davies' study appeared at the moment at which theoretically and culturally conscious cinema scholarship began to call the security of these assumptions into question; it also coincided with the emergence of the new wave of populist Shakespearean filmmaking (inaugurated by Kenneth Branagh's *Henry V*, and encompassing the films of Almereyda, Edzard, Loncraine, Lurhmann, Parker, and Taymor). This new wave marks its generic location through a self-consciously referential cinematic vocabulary which aspires to appeal to both art-house and multiplex (see WALKER). To continue the preoccupation with film's primary relation to theater, or to sustain the theatrical identity of the plays as a privileged or authoritative point of origin, seems redundant or counterintuitive: for increasing numbers of spectators (and critics), Shakespeare films are read in relation to other films (Shakespearean and otherwise), rather than to – and even instead of – literary or theatrical versions of the text. Separating considerations of theatrical performativity from those of cinematic affect is a logical critical response to the current configuration of Shakespearean film, in which theatricality survives predominantly in an embedded, quoted, or parodied form, as well as a sign of the increasing sophistication and self-sufficiency of a Shakespearean film studies sub-discipline which is theoretically and methodologically attuned to the specificities of the cinematic medium.

Even so, and Almereyda notwithstanding, neither the Shakespearean cinema nor its critics seem quite ready to let go of theater just yet. Even the most hyperkinetically filmic of Shakespearean films, Lurhmann's *William Shakespeare's Romeo + Juliet*, seems to value the ghosts of live performance. As Peter Donaldson demonstrates, the burned-out shell of Sycamore Grove, occupying a liminal space between land and sea, nature and culture, city and wilderness, can be read as both a derelict movie theater and an abandoned playhouse (the duality/indeterminacy is suggestive); it is "a site for fragmentary and improvised alternatives to the powerful media-intensive culture of the center . . . a free space for satire and poetry, slower rhythms, older media" (2002: 70).

Donaldson's sense of the positive, oppositional potential of what could be regarded as an obsolete, retrograde form calls to mind Raymond Williams' account of cultural practice. Williams envisages the *dominant* culture of a society (its "central system of practices, meanings and values" [1980: 38]) as produced through the dynamic, selective, and creative incorporation of *emergent* and *residual* cultures, the former defined as "new meanings and values, new practices, new significances and experiences" (1980: 41), the latter as those elements which "cannot be verified or cannot be expressed in terms of the dominant culture" (1980: 40). Examples of residual culture include "certain religious values" and "notions derived from a rural past, which have a very significant popularity" (1980: 40–1); importantly, he thinks of it not just as the repository of anachronistic, obsolete practices and beliefs but as a potential area of resistance to dominant culture, manifested as "a reaching back to those meanings and values which were created in real societies in the past, and which still seem to have some significance because they represent areas of human experience, aspiration and achievement, which the dominant culture under-values or opposes, or even cannot recognise" (1980: 42). I would suggest that live performance, even – and perhaps especially – in a predominantly mediatized culture, remains a key site for the articulation of the residual values, experiences, and practices to which both Donaldson and Williams refer; and that these are most powerfully realized in those characteristics of theater that screen media are incapable of reproducing.

As Peggy Phelan has asserted, in a much-cited (and contested) formulation, the "ontology" of performance is one of "representation without reproduction": its "only life is in the present," and this unique commitment to the moment in which it "becomes itself through disappearance" is a space of resistance and critique, since "only rarely in this culture is the 'now' to which performance addresses its deepest questions valued" (Phelan 1993: 146). Unique, unrepeatable, and ephemeral, the theatrical event is implicated within a temporal ethics in which the pleasure of participation is shadowed by mourning for its inevitable loss. The *now* of performance is as irreducible, and irreproducible, as the *here* in which it takes place: located within space, amidst an audience, in a specific neighborhood which it may or may not acknowledge, theater always happens within circumstances which, as far as the visual and aural record of filmed performance is concerned, are at best on the periphery of vision. Yet perhaps it is precisely this "other" quality, which stubbornly cannot be accommodated to a culture in which space, time, communality, and ordinary mortality have been digitally eradicated, that constitutes theater's continuing appeal; incapable of being fully assimilated into the screen media, filmed performance inhabits a space elsewhere, an awkward, recalcitrant, unruly enclave within film's "phantom empire" wherein its dominant values may be called into question. As one of cinematic realism's discontents, the persistence of the theatrical has more to say to the emergent (or filmic) practices of the avant-garde than has yet been acknowledged.[3]

The idea that Shakespearean film history can be approvingly tracked as a progressive movement away from the theater continues to enjoy a widespread currency: according to one fairly typical recent account, the early years of "silent" Shakespearean film were characterized by efforts to establish the medium's autonomy, "to break out of the prison house of the proscenium stage on nearby Broadway and make a film that did not look as if it had been photographed with a camera nailed to the floor in the sixth-row orchestra" (Rothwell 1999: 7–8). This account reiterates a long-standing antipathy to theater within film criticism and practice. For the early film theorists, traces of theatricality compromised the aesthetic independence and purity of the medium; as the authors of a recent study of the relationship between

cinema and theater point out: "The contaminating art . . . is the theatre, and early film aestheticians' predominant demarcation dispute
was with the aesthetics of theatre, or with 'theatricality' in films and
film-making traditions" (Brewster and Jacobs 1997: 5). That body of
film criticism which has been concerned to legitimize and naturalize
film art has aligned itself sympathetically with the industry's own
practices; Brewster and Jacobs argue that this has led film scholarship
to emphasize those aspects of cinematic vocabulary (montage, continuity editing, non-demonstrative acting) which most spectacularly
fulfill the medium's technological and industrial ambitions. In the
process, the theatricality of early cinema (and, by implication, of its
successors) has been misrepresented and underestimated; meanwhile,
the stage itself has been – and continues to be – characterized not
only as the more progressive medium's unwanted parent, but also as
its antithetical other. Theater, conceived as static, histrionic, and viewed
from a fixed and singular perspective, is also undynamic, antiquated,
elitist, old-world; cinema, conversely, is mobile, dynamic, progressive,
and popular.

Observing that "the Film d'Art obsession with theatrical models
distracted continental cinéastes from the main challenge of envision-
ing Shakespeare in cinematic tropes" (1999: 5), Rothwell explicitly
voices the general perception that there is a link between filmic
vocabularies and American versus European (or, more usually, British) national identities. John Collick has shown that, in the early
years of the twentieth century especially, and in keeping with nascent
efforts to establish a British national cinema, theatricality was consciously embraced and foregrounded by British filmmakers as a means
of differentiating cinematic Shakespeare from its American competitors. William Barker's 1911 record of Herbert Beerbohm Tree's
stage production of *Henry VIII* established the principle that "cost,
exclusiveness and high dramatic art became associated with cinematic
quality," and that these values could be opposed to those of "the
mass-production techniques used by the American cinema industry
to churn out large numbers of cheaply-produced movies" (1989: 41–
2). In the films that followed (notably the 1911 record of F. R. Benson's
Shakespeare Memorial Theatre production of *Richard III*), mannered
and demonstrative acting, two-dimensional sets, formalized blocking,
and resolutely static camerawork formally articulate "a deliberate
attempt to make the theatrical methodology explicit" (1989: 43); Collick
concludes that, in their efforts to resist "the gradual encroachment
of American melodramatic narratives into the country's cinemas,"

British filmmakers sought a solution in "a unique and distinctive national film idiom," Shakespeare defined as "uniquely English, high-class culture" (1989: 45–6). It was an idiom which was to prove remarkably persistent in twentieth-century British screen Shakespeare.

As the most frequently filmed of Shakespeare's plays, *Hamlet* focuses the problematic relation between theater and film in a particularly acute form. Instantly recognizable within popular culture as emblematic of high (elitist, outmoded) theatrical culture, the play has provided cinematic source material for any number of derivatives, spinoffs, and spoofs. Moreover, its screen history has been more closely connected with stage tradition than most, in that a significant proportion of the film and television versions originated in theatrical performances (Johnston Forbes-Robertson [1913], Laurence Olivier [1948], Maurice Evans [1953], John Neville [1959], Christopher Plummer [1964], Richard Burton [1964], Nicol Williamson [1969], Kenneth Branagh [1996], Campbell Scott [2000], Adrian Lester [2001]; see HENDERSON). Implicated within a long tradition of cinematic commemoration as well (enhanced, in the case of Olivier's and Kozintsev's films, by monochrome cinematography, and in Branagh's by a postmodern stylistic pastiche of "classic" British cinema), *Hamlet* on film has often seemed rooted in a past which Shakespearean cinema elsewhere has increasingly sought to disavow. In what follows I focus upon two films of *Hamlet* which have been generally identified – not always supportively – with cinematic "theatricality": Olivier's canonical 1948 version and the 1969 transfer of the Roundhouse production, directed by Tony Richardson. My aim is to suggest ways in which theater may be more nuanced, more historically located, than has previously been conceded, and that in a cultural context of seemingly endless and inescapable mediatization, this may be a positive force.

II

The release of Olivier's second directorial Shakespearean film venture in 1948 was marked by two tie-in publications: a collection of essays, *The Film Hamlet*, edited by Brenda Cross, and what its publishers called a "special commemorative edition" *Hamlet: The Film and the Play*. Handsomely illustrated with stills from the movie, the second of these included the full (conflated) text of the play with cuts indicated by square brackets, augmented with descriptive accounts of the film's *mise-en-scène*, an essay by script editor Alan Dent detailing and defending the alterations, and a foreword by Olivier himself. Written in Olivier's characteristic vein combining bravado with mock humility, it offers a routine defense of the liberties taken with the play, framed in terms of the relative freedoms and constraints inherent in the cinematic and theatrical media. More provocatively, it grounds this project in the director's self-identification with Shakespeare: "my whole aim and purpose has been to make a film of *Hamlet* as Shakespeare himself, were he living now, might make it"; anticipating objections to the interpolated scenes (the sea battle, the drowning of Ophelia), he contends that Shakespeare would have "eagerly welcomed the means to show [such events] more realistically, if they had been to his hand." Breaking with a half-century of revivalist polemic and practice that had sought to revive the essence of Shakespeare through reconstruction of the physical conditions of the early modern playhouse, he declares: "Nothing that we know of Shakespeare suggests that he actually enjoyed being 'cabin'd, cribbed, confin'd' by the rudimentary conditions of the stage for which he wrote." If this remark suggests Olivier had given up on the theater both as a medium for Shakespeare and as his own primary working environment, the foreword's closing paragraph is more conciliatory: "both I and my wife . . . wish to affirm most strongly our faith in the future of British films. To those who fear that we may for a moment have forgotten the stage we say, 'Bear with us, filmgocr and playgoer; we love you both!'"

This address to a theatergoing fanbase upon whom Olivier projects feelings of abandonment and betrayal deserves putting in context. Olivier had started filming *Hamlet* in May 1947, marking the end of a highly successful period at the Old Vic, in which he had played a series of high-profile leads, culminating in his 1946 Lear. At the same time (together with actor Ralph Richardson and former radio producer John Burrell), he was responsible for the artistic direction of the Old Vic Company; and, in particular, for advancing its interests as the prototype for an English National Theatre, an idea which since the end of the nineteenth century had become virtually synonymous with an ideal permanent English theater for Shakespeare. Despite the formation, in 1946, of the Arts Council, whose mandate was to promote and develop the performing arts at the metropolitan, national, and regional levels, this aspiration still appeared unachievable.

As Loren Kruger has documented, the seemingly endless procrastination over the establishment of the English National Theatre was largely due to the antagonistic and contradictory claims made by its various supporters, claims that were deeply rooted in competing understandings of, and loyalties to, nation, culture, and class: "Confronted with the evident divisions of class and region, the advocates of an English national theatre attempt to ground their hope for national unity in the aesthetic realm of a shared English language that might transcend mere political disagreements" (Kruger 1992: 85). Although for many early national theater advocates (including George Bernard Shaw and Harley Granville Barker), engagement with contemporary British and European drama – and models of theatrical organization – was as much (if not more) the objective, Shakespeare, unsurprisingly, featured prominently at the level of cultural and political discussion.

Debated in Parliament in 1913, the idea of a National Theatre attracted the support both of those who stressed its democratic, philanthropic potential ("What we want," declared the speaker of the House, "is education of the world through our Shakespeare . . . our Shakespeare should be popular and educational" [quoted in Kruger 1992: 125]), and of those who saw it as an opportunity to reinforce cultural hegemony and imperial authority. "'From the imperial point of view,' the National Theatre might prevent the English language from 'disintegrating into dialects' and thus . . . might reinforce the cultural as well as political pre-eminence of the exemplary Britains at home" (Kruger 1992: 127). When the subject eventually returned to the House of Commons for a second reading in 1949, what was generally agreed to be a "non-partisan, non-controversial Bill" was debated with a nationalistic fervor that was all the more vigorous because the reality of postwar, post-imperial Britain was rapidly revealing the precariousness of the cultural assumptions upon which it rested. The view of Oliver Lyttleton, Conservative member, trustee of the Shakespeare Memorial Theatre, and chair of the joint council of the Old Vic and National Theatre, was that a state-subsidized national theater would "not only set the standard for the drama but also preserve from pollution the language in which these dramatic works are played. . . . A national theatre in Great Britain would help to keep undefiled the purity of the English language" (*Hansard* 1948–9: 447). Kruger comments: "representing the nation to the nation can no longer be the simple matter it still seemed in 1913: it becomes rather the articulation of the desire to demonstrate, in the face of contradictory information, that the nation is still intact" (1992: 129).

What also needs stressing is the importance in these debates of the links between Shakespeare, nationhood, and theater itself, as medium, institution, and cultural activity. The National Theatre's standing as a citadel of the mother tongue rather obviously defines its defensive role against ethnic contamination, but it also indicates another responsibility: for the preservation of the spoken word's integrity against the onslaught of the industrially produced, ubiquitously circulating visual image. A key factor informing the postwar campaign for the National Theatre was this anxiety about the standing of the British literary-theatrical heritage, which the institution was intended to preserve, within mass culture, of which cinema was now indisputably a central component. Two contributors to the 1949 Parliamentary debate (Lieutenant-Colonel Lipton, the Conservative member for Brixton, and the Labour member for Maldon, Tom Driberg) sought an accommodation when they expressed the hope that the projected National Theatre building might itself accommodate what Driberg described as "a small model cinema with a permanent repertory of good early films." "Shakespearean films," suggested Lipton, prompting Driberg to speculate that "It would be interesting to see Sir Laurence Olivier in *Hamlet* on the stage and then go downstairs and see him in *Hamlet* on the screen" (*Hansard* 1948–9: 484). In general, however, the most enthusiastic supporters of the National Theatre tended to endorse the view of postwar cultural commentators that live performance of the classics needed protection (increasingly, the argument ran, by means of state subsidy) not only from public indifference but also from the corrosive effects of mass media culture and consumer society. Importantly, these were seen by many as synonymous with the culture of the United States, perceived as the malign source of dime novels, popular music, and Hollywood movies.

If the nationality of cinematic discourse is, as I suggested earlier, one aspect of the theater–film binary that has periodically returned to shadow the legitimacy debates around Shakespeare on film, it is a particular concern of Olivier's published apologia for *Hamlet*. As the most important British-made Shakespearean film since Olivier's *Henry V*, *Hamlet*'s significance was connected with its status as a flagship product of the British film industry. The dual declaration of loyalty and love to the "filmgoer and playgoer" rests upon an affirmation of faith in "the future of *British* films" (Dent 1948: n.p., emphasis added), a patriotic salutation which, in its historical context, was both pointed and timely. In sharp contrast to the *laissez-faire* economics of the theater profession during the same period, the British film industry had since the 1920s been protected and cultivated by governmental support.

In 1927, the passing of the Cinematograph Films Act had established a quota principle to the production of British films. By 1936, 20 percent of films shown had to be British, which meant that "All studio scenes had to be shot within the Empire, and not less than 75 percent of the labour costs incurred in a film's production . . . had to be paid to British subjects. . . . The scenario had to be written by a British author" (Street 1997: 7). Nonetheless, American films continued to dominate the market throughout the 1930s and 1940s, leading in 1938 to the second Cinematograph Films Act, which extended the quota principle but also attempted to reach a new accommodation between British filmmaking and American finance, upon which the industry was to become increasingly reliant during the economic downturn of the 1930s and the war years that followed. By the end of the war, it had become abundantly clear that this dependency operated in the context of American determination "to dismantle trade barriers and protective quotas for indigenous film industries" (Street 1997: 14). In 1947 the Dalton duty levied a 75 percent tax on imported American films. This was introduced by a Board of Trade anxious to do something to alleviate Britain's worsening balance of payments, much to the dismay of Hollywood producers but also a number of key British players – including J. Arthur Rank, who "feared that the duty would jeopardize the distribution of British films in America and sabotage his well-publicized deals with American companies." The Motion Picture Association of America retaliated by boycotting the British market, while for nearly a year British filmmakers struggled to meet the demand. Agreement was reached in 1948, the duty removed with the proviso that "American companies could remit no more than $17 million a year, plus a sum equal to the earnings of British films abroad" (Street 1997: 15). Intended to support film production in Britain, the Anglo-American Film Agreement confirmed the vital significance of American finance to postwar British film.

As part of the Rank Organization's output during the period of intense production which also yielded Powell and Pressburger's *The Red Shoes* and David Lean's *Oliver Twist*, Olivier's *Hamlet* offered itself as a statement of national achievement and potential, an attempt to formulate a distinctively British aesthetic of Shakespearean film that emulated but also surpassed the Hollywood version. Seen in this light, the film's negotiation of the languages of theater and cinema is revealed as not just an aesthetic problem but a matter of cultural positioning. It has long been recognized that the film represents Olivier's attempt at a formal reconciliation between screen and stage, producing, as Bernice Kliman sees it, a complex hybrid: "not a filmed play, not precisely a film, but a film-infused play or a play-infused film" which proposes to evade the spatial restrictions of theater through an expansion and extension of *mise-en-scène*; Olivier's Elsinore of staircases, pillars, platforms, and archways, highly reminiscent of the Spartan flexibility of 1930s Old Vic designs, is "the connected space of a stage set, rather than the disjunctive space of a film," but one "too mammoth to fit any known theater" (Kliman 1988: 23, 25). Davies, similarly, identifies "a manipulation of spatial elements, which generate a tension and an oscillation between the theatrical and the cinematic" (1988: 42), the film's penchant for mobile camerawork, lengthy takes, and deep-focus scenic composition establishing the narrative as both continuous and cyclical (beginning and ending at the castle's highest point), and securing an identification of director-*auteur*, protagonist and point-of-view, that maps Elsinore as, primarily, a psychic domain.

This avenue is further explored in Donaldson's exemplary psychoanalytic reading which traces the film's darker purpose as an "Oedipal text" through its manifestly "phallic symbolism of rapier and dagger," but also through its relentlessly inquisitive camera, epitomized in the "repeated dolly-in down the long corridor" to Gertrude's "immense, enigmatic, and vaginally hooded bed" (1990: 31). As Donaldson points out, Olivier's Freudianism (characterized as "robust and readily identifiable, if naïve" [1990: 31]) was initiated by his theatrical partnership with director Tyrone Guthrie at the pre-war Old Vic, in a 1937 production of the play which included consultation with psychoanalyst Ernest Jones as part of the rehearsal process (1990: 32ff.). Film allowed Olivier to manifest (or, as many critics felt, to labour) an interpretation/explanation of play and protagonist that had been merely latent or implied in its theatrical manifestation. Thus the film's "theatrical" handling of space, its patterns of rise and descent, tracking and pursuit, and its melancholy surveillance of vast, empty rooms and staircases, externalize the dynamics of presence and absence, mourning and introspection, identification and cyclical abuse that, for Olivier, define the character of the prince.

As I have argued elsewhere (2002: 94–120), the efficacy of psychoanalysis in the 1937 staging was not confined to the methodologies of character analysis; it was also an attempt, on Guthrie's part at least, to reframe the traditionally pragmatic, anti-theoretical practices of English Shakespearean performance in terms of the European intellectual and theatrical modernist avant-garde. As such, it connected with Guthrie's desire to think Shakespearean staging out of the proscenium box and, in a move which would prove decisive during the postwar period, onto the open stage. Principles of exegesis, disclosure,

67

and flexible sexuality could be applied to a theatrical rhetoric of authenticity, egalitarianism, and community participation; in the Shakespearean cinema, the diagnostic and investigative potential of psychoanalysis, and its preoccupation with dreamwork, allowed aspects of the cinematic avant-garde to be incorporated within a nominally realist framework.

Olivier's *Hamlet* took one of its cues from the Warner Brothers Max Reinhardt and William Dieterle's *A Midsummer Night's Dream* (1935), which had established a stylistic rapprochement between American show business values (the musical spectacular, the toga drama, screwball comedy) and the visions of German Expressionism on the terrain of fantasy (see GUNERATNE); in *Hamlet,* the play-world's reality is skewed by similar subjectivist techniques drawn from the Hollywood genre which enabled an institutional renegotiation of European Expressionism, film noir. It has been recognized that Olivier's treatment of the *Hamlet* narrative in terms of a lone, alienated protagonist at odds with a corrupt system, his techniques of filming, and his film's sexual politics, together provide the classic ingredients of a noir thriller. But it is noir of a particularly British kind: clad in doublet and hose, consensual rather than paranoid, indebted to theater rather than pulp fiction, and ultimately soft-centred rather than hard-boiled.

Olivier's pluralization of the normative codes of Hollywood realism establishes a space in the film for the work of retrospection, fantasy, and memory. If Olivier's interest in threshold space, and the interactions it permits between character and architecture, can be compared to that of Orson Welles in *Citizen Kane* (1941), so too can the regressive temporal structure of his *Hamlet* narrative. It opens with the moment of death clouded by an enigma of motive (the "vicious mole of nature" being the equivalent of Welles' "Rosebud" moment, albeit one immediately explained away as the banal "tragedy of a man who could not make up his mind"), and similarly proceeds through narrative retrospection. Even closer than Welles, however, is the emphatically English magic realism of Michael Powell and Emeric Pressburger, in particular the 1946 fantasy, *A Matter of Life and Death.*

Like Olivier's *Hamlet*, Powell and Pressburger's film (which incorporates an inset rehearsal of *A Midsummer Night's Dream*) is a drama of a protagonist "crawling between heaven and earth," which is played out, unforgettably, upon an immense, emblematic staircase. It begins with a desperate conversation between a doomed RAF bomber pilot, Peter (David Niven), and an American wireless operator, June (Kim Hunter), as he bails out of his burning aeroplane over the English

Channel; after his seemingly miraculous survival, he experiences baroque hallucinations of a heavenly trial to decide his survival, debated in terms of the competing claims of life and death, law and love, articulated through a stylistic contrast between monochrome heaven and Technicolor earth. Peter's heavenly prosecutor is an American: the final scenes in a huge pan-national, transhistorical Greek-style amphitheater emphasize the film's determination to fashion a space for England (personified by a hero who considers himself "Conservative by instinct, Labour by experience") in an American-dominated postwar world. With its vast audience encircling a monumental arena stage, this trial space evokes the ideal configuration of the English national theater that would be realized, some three decades on, in the National's Olivier auditorium; in Olivier's film, it is echoed on a smaller scale in the organization of the court for the performance of *The Mousetrap*, disposed in a ragged circle around a tiered open stage, the site of self-scrutiny, exposure, and judgment, housing a performance which simultaneously quotes the performance styles of Victorian theater and silent film.

In both *A Matter of Life and Death* and Olivier's *Hamlet*, the relationship between theater and cinema mediates the contending claims of the past and modernity, the old world and the new. This liminality reflects what Andrew Higson has described as the capacity of "the classic British films" to "project" Britain, "imagining the nation as a consensual space," characterized by "travel across boundaries, the forming of new relationships, the mixing of different identities, rather than safe enclosure within familiar boundaries" (2000: 45).[4] In Olivier's film, theatricality is a means of organizing and regulating the "centrifugality" (to borrow Davies' term) of cinematic intertextuality and generic hybridity, and to return it to definably English territory; it also serves to do the work of an English national theater, that, in 1948, seemed indefinitely postponed. "Bear with us, filmgoer and playgoer; we love you both!"

III

Reviewing Tony Richardson's *Hamlet* on its American release, the *New York Times* film critic Roger Greenspun reported (December 22, 1969) that it was marketed with an eye for contemporary resonance, citing a newspaper advertisement bearing the tagline "To thine own thing be true" and showing Nicol Williamson's Hamlet "about to nibble the up-slung shoulder of Ophelia." This image (taken from the film's hammock-bound nunnery scene) was also used on the publicity poster, which announced a new work "from the author of *Romeo and Juliet*": appearing in the wake of Franco Zeffirelli's 1968 youth-centered hit film of that play, this was not only "The *Hamlet* of our time . . . For our time" but "the love story of Hamlet and Ophelia." It also carried a puff from *Playboy* which praised Williamson's portrayal of "a caustic, contemporary man . . . a young firebrand who brings the institutions of his elders crumbling around their heads!" Here was a *Hamlet*, ostensibly positioned at a countercultural intersection of free love, generational conflict, and anti-establishment rebellion; yet for Greenspun, an American reviewer of a British film which seemed to him to display the traditional characteristics of filmed Shakespearean performance, the film simply exhibited "a kind of square theatrical ridiculousness." For the film to aspire to radical chic in principle and appear clumsily stagy in practice was quite an achievement, and one which was partly shaped by the theatrical context from which it had emerged.

Richardson's *Hamlet* is a straight-to-film record of an acclaimed production originated at the Roundhouse in London's Camden Town before visiting the United States in the summer of 1969. Commentators on the film usually note that the Roundhouse is a Victorian building originally used as a locomotive engine turning shed, but this hardly does justice either to its architectural distinctiveness or to the cultural context in which it, and the performances it housed, operated. The Roundhouse was a pioneering 1960s example in the British Isles of a "found" space appropriated for performance; as David Wiles points out, "[t]he classical overtones of the space, with its twenty-four iron columns, combined with its industrial origins" contribute to a "spatial logic . . . bound up with Greek democracy, medieval cosmology, circus and railway timetables" (2003: 204, 206). Prior to *Hamlet*, in 1968, the Roundhouse had hosted Peter Brook's collage *Tempest*, prompting Brook to call it "the most exciting playing space in Europe" (Wiles 2003: 204).

Before that, it had served as the metropolitan home of Centre Fortytwo, a broad-based arts organization, funded by the trade union movement, intended to combine top-down provision of the canonical arts with grassroots and community arts work, and aimed (in the words of its founder, the playwright Arnold Wesker) to address "the bus driver, the housewife, the miner and the Teddy Boy" (*Encore*, November 1958). Taking its name from Resolution 42 of the 1960

Trades Union Conference, which had committed the movement "to ensure a greater participation by the trade union movement in all cultural activities," Centre Fortytwo offered a rolling program of regional arts festivals; the prevailing idea was that cultural enrichment would energize political debate. The project was the subject of acrimonious criticism from the beginning, particularly from those on the cultural left who viewed it as a paternalistic attempt to foist bourgeois high culture upon the working classes.

By the end of the decade, Centre Fortytwo's failure left the Roundhouse acting as a venue for hippie gatherings, protest group meetings, rock and jazz performances, and avant-garde theater. Something of the flavour of the place can be gleaned from Irving Wardle's report on *Hamlet*'s first night, which noted the pop singer Marianne Faithfull in the cast (as Ophelia), the folk group the Happy Wanderers "busking in the foyer," and "a police cordon ringing the Roundhouse to protect the Prime Minister's party" (*The Times*, February 18, 1969). In the earlier, more optimistic, days of Prime Minister Harold Wilson's Labour government, a similar group had attended the Roundhouse's official opening.

The Roundhouse still seemed a particularly democratic and inclusive space for a radical theatrical Shakespeare. Certainly this was how Tony Richardson saw it: wishing "to free the theatre from the tyranny of the proscenium arch and the social habits that go with it," he claimed the Roundhouse as "a masterpiece of Victorian architecture which will put the actors back into immediate contact with the audience"; in place of "terrible formality" it "lets actors speak in a room instead of up on an artificial platform" (interview in *The Times* quoted in Manvell 1971: 127–8). Invoking the space's industrial past, Richardson imagines it as "a magical engineering shed, but for theatre." The potent fusion of magic and engineering epitomizes the aspirations of the 1960s British theatrical and cinematic New Wave, welding together fantasy and pragmatism, vision and authenticity. Richardson (who began his directing career in television) was a Royal Court stalwart and director of the screen incarnations of the working-class theatrical breakthroughs *Look Back in Anger* (1958) and *A Taste of Honey* (1961); his *Hamlet* was produced by Woodfall films, the independent production company he had set up to finance the first of these. His desire to hear his Shakespearean actors "speak in a room" was informed by a cross-media poetics of vitality, emotional honesty, immediacy, and authenticity that brought theatrical, televisual, and cinematic realism into close, mutually supportive alignment: "[i]t is

71

absolutely vital," Richardson had declared on the release of *Look Back in Anger*, "to get into British films the same sort of impact and sense of life that what you can call the Angry Young Man cult has had in the theatre" (quoted in Hill 1986: 40).

In the stage version, attention focused upon Nicol Williamson's incendiary performance, played very much in the spirit of 1950s Anger: "ironical, sardonic, witty, high-spirited, mischievous . . . deeply tormented, shaken with violent passion," as Martin Esslin put it, but also "detached, philosophical, remote, tired with life" (*New York Times*, February 28, 1969). Esslin observed that Williamson was of "the generation of actors who came in after the Osborne breakthrough which established non-U English on the English stage as an idiom for central characters." According to Wardle, this was "the first performance I have seen that really escapes the shadow of Gielgud's regionalism," and it did so by imposing the counter-regionalism of a "flailing northern accent," together with "a derisive, rancorous intelligence that looks at the human masquerade of crime and vanity and reduces it to a smoking heap of rubble." Freed from the proscenium arch, scenery and ghosts (represented in this production by Williamson's recorded voice over the tannoy, an effect preserved in the film), the play was stripped bare for this bruising encounter.

The relation of Richardson's film to the stage production is defined by its deployment of a cinematic discourse roughly analogous to its particular theatrical aesthetic of the "empty space," which frames a forensic scrutiny of the detail of Williamson's performance within embedded memories of the Roundhouse building (filming was conducted during the run of the stage show, in, around, and beneath the Roundhouse). Although the film's prevailing impression is of its principals silhouetted against a black void, the limit of its diegetic space is very clearly marked by a material boundary: the signature brickwork which provides the backdrop to the opening title sequence and which is seen periodically throughout. Defining a theatrical domain which traps the action within a claustrophobic circle (the opening shot pans down to an emblematically glowing brazier, suggesting the outer circle of hell), the bricks locate the film within both cinematic and stage history. For the film buff, they may evoke the dripping sewers of Carol Reed's *The Third Man* (1949), the ramparts of Olivier's Elsinore, or film noir's generic lonely streets, but also, more locally, the rain-streaked tenements and industrial wastelands of early 1960s British working-class realist cinema (*Look Back in Anger, A Taste of Honey, Saturday Night and Sunday Morning* [1960], *The Loneliness of the Long*

Distance Runner [1962], etc.). The theater historian, meanwhile, may be reminded of the internal architecture not only of the Roundhouse but also of other modern performance spaces in which exposed brick-work acts as a repository of history and a signifier of the authenticity of found space: the Royal Court (the production was designed by Jocelyn Herbert, a defining force in the Court's minimalist, anti-decorative aesthetic), the Glasgow Tramway, the Almeida Theatre in Islington, Peter Brook's Bouffes du Nord.

Simultaneously redolent of overt theatricality and the quasi-documentary real, the brick walls of the Roundhouse enclose a climate-free, artificially illuminated zone of performance which is both psychologically claustrophobic and socially indeterminate. Neil Taylor has calculated that "close-ups and medium shots account for ninety-six percent" of the film, and that its penchant for lengthy takes means that it has "fewer shots per minute" (1994: 188) than any of the major film versions of the play; the effect is to subject Claudius' court to the dispassionate gaze of the documentarist, but also to re-produce the impression of intimacy and direct encounter attributed to live production (the film's refusal of cinematic expansiveness has prompted speculation that it was intended for television [Kliman 1988: 167]: the evidence is inconclusive). Dominated by close-grouped headshots, the film inhabits a social milieu characterized by its lack of clear boundaries between public and private, or personal and polit-ical, spaces; this is epitomized in Claudius and Gertrude's reception of Rosencrantz, Guildernstern, and Polonius (2.2), in a scene of bargain-basement Fellini-esque decadence, while snacking in a dog-ridden four-poster bed. In such a context, Ophelia's incestuous fiddling with Laertes is among the film's starkest manifestations of a perversity rooted in the violation of personal boundaries.

Richardson's *Hamlet* evinces its cultural context most clearly in its critical, even puritanical, stance towards 1960s permissiveness – and in this respect the much-derided casting of Marianne Faithfull makes sense, implanting within the film an icon of the drug-centered rock-and-roll counterculture celebrated for her sexual adventures. Gener-ally blank and understated for the first part of the film, Faithfull's Ophelia is a vacuous sex object, an establishment playmate who de-generates into a perverted flower child, an acid casualty serving as a focus for Hamlet's (and perhaps the film's) prevailing misogyny. Sardonic, ironic, and swiftly brutal in the style of a New Wave anti-hero, Williamson's Hamlet is a fastidious intellectual, delivering his lines at great speed, usually with palpable contempt for his interlocutors;

in this respect, as in others, the portrayal is a conscious riposte to Olivier's. Despite his neurotic demeanor Williamson is also emphatically and aggressively masculine, nowhere more assertive than when he affords Osric (played as a flamboyant camp stereotype) a good verbal seeing-to. And it is with regard to its treatment of gender and sexuality that characterization, *mise-en-scène*, and the film's cinematic and theatrical vocabularies converge. If Hamlet is a hard man, the brick landscape that provides his immediate environment of enclosure and entrapment makes him so; although he digs impotently with his dagger at the tunnel walls during the "smiling, damned villain" soliloquy, he is of the same material as they. Moreover, the austere anti-design statement that is embodied in the brickwork can be read, in the context of theater history, not only as a clear articulation of the minimalist aesthetic that would become the mainstream of 1970s Shakespearean stage production, but also as a manifestation of the New Wave's determination to eliminate the traces of what it viewed as an effete, frivolous, and extraneous tradition of staging and scene design. As Dan Rebellato argues, the school of direction and design represented by Jocelyn Herbert and Tony Richardson (like the school of acting represented by Williamson) "acted upon its determination to restore sincere, authentic unity to the voices of the national culture" through "the disciplining of meanings on stage" (Rebellato 1999: 99); this was central to the project of remasculinizing and re-heterosexualizing the English theater. In this light, perhaps *Playboy* magazine's endorsement of the film is not so surprising.

Richardson's film of *Hamlet* has been marginalized by Shakespearean film critics as a record – albeit a valuable one – of a stage production that is ultimately compromised by its continued investment in a theatricality which can now appear dated, primitive, and parochial. To those whom Barbara Hodgdon describes as "a generation who may not have seen one of Welles's or Zeffirelli's films – perhaps not even one of Branagh's" (2002: x), Olivier's film, too, seems likely to look increasingly like an obsolete relic of a vanished age of stage and screen history. As I have attempted to demonstrate, however, the theatricality of these films (and of similar canonical and non-canonical film texts), once seen in the light of history, is more complex and nuanced than is often credited; "theatricality," in theses instances, designates a variety of forms of national self-consciousness ranging from the uncertainly post-imperial to the defiantly parochial. There is, it seems to me, considerably more at stake in the prospect of a "post-historical" epoch of "post-theatrical" Shakespearean film than much current film scholarship's endorsement would appear to allow. If one aspect of this moment has been the increasing tendency (within pedagogy and scholarship) to identify the start date of modern Shakespearean film as, at the earliest, 1989 (the year of Branagh's *Henry V*), the limit thus marked effectively confines critical discussion to the cinematic products of a mainstream postmodernism that, for the most part, encourages a predominantly American film idiom to function as a global currency (Almereyda's *Hamlet* is exemplary in this respect). At the very least, the "theatrical" Shakespearean film, particularly the one which is viewed with the advantage of historical and cultural distance, reminds us of the ways in which performed Shakespeare is not like mainstream cinema, and cannot be comfortably assimilated to its generic and representational norms. At most, the anti-cinematic qualities of the form, the demonstrative acting and restricted spatiality that, contrary to the borderless perpetual present of recent Shakespearean cinema, testify to performance's habitation of a particular locale, social milieu, time, and place, may also serve as witness to the limits of the medium which attempts to colonize it. The rest, as the Prince of Denmark nearly said, is history.

Notes

1 Lanier's point is key, but I would also stress its corollary: we need to be attentive to stage performance *as* performance, and not move too readily between media without articulating and theorizing their differences.

2 Burt's proposals are offered by way of introduction to the sequel to the 1997 collection *Shakespeare: The Movie*, edited by Boose and Burt; *Shakespeare: The Movie II* symptomatically drops most essays in the first volume which focused on Shakespeare films released prior to 1989 (the year of Branagh's *Henry V*).

3 Hodgdon explicitly cites Williams' model in her characterization of Olivier's *Henry V*, suggesting that Olivier's mobilization of Shakespearean history to serve a nation at war, "poised between a theatrical and art-house heritage and fully cinematic imagining," provides "a stunning illustration of 'Shakespearean authenticity' conveyed through the power of residual, dominant and emergent visual technologies" (2002: v).

4 Higson proffers the postwar Ealing comedies as example, which often "explore a liminal space on the margins of nation in order to be able to grasp its apparent centre": in *Passport to Pimlico* (1949), "a war-damaged space at the centre of London temporarily becomes a part of the kingdom of Burgundy and leaves the united kingdom" (2000: 45).

Robert Shaughnessy

References and Further Reading

Brewster, Ben, and Lea Jacobs (1997). *Theatre to Cinema: Stage Pictorialism and the Early Feature Film*. Oxford: Oxford University Press.

Dent, Alan (1948). *Hamlet: The Film and the Play*. London: World Film Publications.

Donaldson, Peter S. (2002). "'In Fair Verona': Media, Spectacle, and Performance in *William Shakespeare's Romeo + Juliet*." In Burt ed.: 59–82.

Hansard (1948–9). *Parliamentary Debates (Hansard)*. Fifth Series, vol. 460. London: HMSO.

Higson, Andrew (2000). "The Instability of the National." In Justine Ashby and Andrew Higson (eds.), *British Cinema, Past and Present*. London and New York: Routledge: 35–48.

Hill, John (1986). *Sex, Class and Realism: British Cinema 1956–1963*. London: BFI Publishing.

Hodgdon, Barbara (2002). "From the Editor." *Shakespeare Quarterly* 53.2: iii–x.

Kliman, Bernice W. (1988). *Hamlet: Film, Television and Audio Performance*. London and Toronto: Associated University Presses.

Kruger, Loren (1992). *The National Stage: Theatre and Cultural Legitimation in England, France and America*. Chicago and London: University of Chicago Press.

Phelan, Peggy (1993). *Unmarked: The Politics of Performance*. London and New York: Routledge.

Rebellato, Dan (1999). *1956 And All That: The Making of Modern British Drama*. London: Routledge.

Street, Sarah (1997). *British National Cinema*. London: Routledge.

Taylor, Neil (1994). "The Films of *Hamlet*." In Davies and Wells, eds.: 180–95.

Wiles, David (2003). *A Short History of Western Performance Space*. Cambridge: Cambridge University Press.

Williams, Raymond (1980). "Base and Superstructure in Marxist Cultural Theory." In *Problems in Materialism and Culture*. London: Verso.

Chapter 4

The Artistic Process

Learning from Campbell Scott's *Hamlet*

Diana E. Henderson

What are we talking about when we discuss Shakespeare on screen? Most critical inquiry focuses upon films and videos as completed artifacts invested with cultural and aesthetic meanings – which they of course are, whether the meanings are intended or not. However, in so doing we often move swiftly past the actual artistic space and conditions of production: the process of *making* that motivates and creates an artifact, and is the almost exclusive site of interest for participating artists. As a result, we not only fail to address the concerns of those who produce our "material" but also leave ourselves open to charges of willful, unnecessary misreading and misattribution of cause-and-effect relationships. By exploring some dimensions of the artistic process that went into the making of Campbell Scott's *Hamlet* (2000), I hope to provide a cautionary as well as illuminating example of the concerns preoccupying filmmakers, their views of their own roles, and the ways in which their priorities redirect or even defy the usual forms of scholarly interpretation.

Why this film? In part because it has been overshadowed by the two other *Hamlet* films released within the same five-year time span, those directed by Kenneth Branagh and Michael Almereyda. The reasons for this are both commercial and artistic. Although well reviewed in the *New York Times* when it premiered on the big screen, Scott's *Hamlet* failed to get widespread release of the sort we still call "theatrical"; thus most viewers had to wait for its DVD release by Hallmark Entertainment (in 2001). Moreover, the artistic priorities of its prime mover did not include making major public claims about the film's completeness or interpretive ingenuity. Campbell Scott is known as an actors' actor rather than someone who actively seeks stardom and commercial attention, and his film remains deeply connected to its theatrical roots and interest in Shakespeare's playtext. While featuring as many widely known television and film actors as did Almereyda's version (including not only Scott but Blair Brown, Lisa Gay Hamilton, Jamey Sheridan, and Roscoe Lee Browne), this *Hamlet* did not attempt to be stylistically flashy or meta-filmic. Its production and distribution serve as reminders of the shifting hierarchical distinctions as well as convergence among multimedia arts, with mass market forms increasingly getting the lion's share of critical as well as business attention.

Being overlooked by scholarship, this *Hamlet* also raises the question of what we are documenting in our screen histories and analyses: is it the shape of Shakespeare on screen at a specific historical moment, or an endorsed canonical subset of criticism-friendly (or savageable) "great works"? Now that popular culture methodologies in film studies have assumed a dominance once accorded *auteur* analysis, scholarship on screen Shakespeare tends to focus on works that do double-duty: as this volume attests, films such as Julie Taymor's *Titus* (1999) and Almereyda's *Hamlet* (2000) lend themselves to a variety of sociopolitical arguments as well as artistic (dare one say *auteurist?*) "close reading." Certainly, I shall argue that Scott's *Hamlet* also allows – in more muted fashion – timely commentary and the opportunity for reflection upon what an "American" Shakespeare film looks like and how race matters. But I am not interested in elevating it thereby into that select postmodern subset of repeatedly re-read films (where it would not fit comfortably); instead, I hope to suggest the utility of widening our coverage without ceding the ground to what Richard Burt calls "post-hermeneutic" (a.k.a. sociological) analysis alone. For in this instance at least, the artists did make choices and hoped some of their decisions had effects upon the viewing audience. Most importantly, then, and in keeping with the actual testimony of those involved in this film, I want to highlight a collaborative, rather than *auteurist*, model of understanding Shakespeare on screen – without effacing the labor, agency, and craft of the collaborators.

One more good reason to focus on this *Hamlet*: it involved an exceptionally articulate, reflective group of artists willing to meditate upon their choices after the fact and with a professional scholar. This is no small matter: many excellent performers have grown so skeptical of criticism (be it journalistic or academic) that they no longer see the point of trying to communicate their very different priorities. Some have been damaged by bad reviews, but just as often filmmakers and artists express bafflement at the inaccurate presumptions, arcane selectivity, and sheer irrelevance of much that is written about their work. Having witnessed the kinds of questions (or indeed pronouncements and judgments) that some Shakespeareans pose when they encounter theatrical professionals, I can see their point. Nor is the converse "fan" response (asking indulgently softball questions and expressing delight at any reply approaching a complete sentence) likely to advance fruitful dialogue across professions.

Of course the problem is not one-sided. Some artists are committed to a process that privileges intuition and emotion to the exclusion of conscious analysis – to such an extreme that all premeditation, articulation, and self-situation is deemed mere rationalization, if not an overt impediment to compelling artistry. This defensive anti-intellectualism seems more common in the United States, with its tradition of Method acting and its reigning myth of individual self-creation. Just as importantly, even when artists might be open to retrospective reflection, the conditions of their employment seldom encourage it. Moving from project to project, they need to learn new lines, rent new cameras, design new costumes. Other than the publicity tour – when one trots out a few pithy comments (sometimes quite insightful) – there is little time, reward, or opportunity for artists to reconsider the meanings, much less the wider sociopolitical situation, of their work. Were more scholars overt about their interest and ability to provide a useful supplementary perspective to that of reviewers, general audiences, and other artists, however, this could change for the better, to the benefit of both professions.

In this instance, the director/Hamlet (Campbell Scott), Gertrude (Blair Brown), and costume designer (Michael Krass) were willing to advance the conversation. Furthermore, because each respected the others' different knowledge and perspectives, they encouraged cross-commentary and recognition of group process. When the director also stars as Hamlet the "ownership" certainly veers in one man's direction; but what Scott and his collaborators repeatedly indicated was their sense of being one among many, whose collective energies created an artifact in which choices and messages could seldom if ever be attributed to only one individual. Hence the importance of considering others besides the director or star, and including design as well as acting and directing when we think about so visual a form as film or video. Nevertheless, film remains what Blair Brown calls a "director-centered" medium, even before the post-production editing; from her perspective, it is a "hierarchical collaboration rather than a collective," and requires a strong director to move the process forward. Clearly Scott played that role on this project, his first film as principal director. (On *Big Night*, he says he held a subordinate position to Stanley Tucci, as Eric Simonson did to Scott on this *Hamlet*.) In what follows, I try to convey some sense of what these participants found significant and worth knowing about their *Hamlet*, before comparing this information with my own perceptions as a scholarly viewer.

Putting on a Show

The impetus for this *Hamlet* derived from the theater: as the previous chapters attest, Shakespeare on screen bears traces of the theater well beyond the mere recording of stage productions. Campbell Scott had played Hamlet twice onstage, first at the Old Globe in San Diego (1990), directed by Jack O'Brien, and later at the Huntington Theater in Boston (1996), directed by Eric Simonson. Unlike other major Shakespearean roles he had played (including Angelo in *Measure for Measure* and Pericles), Hamlet was the part that for ten years "wouldn't let me go": Scott continued to wrestle with it, was haunted by it, and wanted to try it again before it was too late. He felt already on the cusp of being too old, and so despite the recent and current competition of other film Hamlets, he went forward on a shoestring budget and with limited time. But he also brought a wealth of stage experience: consciously deciding not to cast anyone else from the two stage productions so as to avoid the effect of a "museum" reconstruction, Scott nevertheless acknowledged his debt to both those casts and to the directorial advice of Simonson (whom he invited to help direct the film) and especially O'Brien. The decision to move the "To be" soliloquy to its earlier First Quarto location, for example, he attributed to O'Brien's precedent; he found it less disruptive to the overall "nunnery" sequence, and felt it worked better as the audience's first direct view of Hamlet post-ghost, registering the deeply disorienting effect of that encounter (visually reinforced in the film by beginning with his head shot sideways, offsetting the lines' familiarity). His overarching conception of the character had been established in live performance, and the film provided the opportunity for further refinement.

Theater also informed the pre-production process, and would have played an even larger role had the initial plans with Hallmark borne fruit. They had envisioned doing a series of Shakespeare plays first onstage, and then thoroughly reworking them for television, re-rehearsing with cameras (along the lines of the Theater in America/ American Playhouse series that once aired on PBS). As with many other ideas, however, financial constraints led to scaling back and altering the format: the contract became one three-hour film of *Hamlet* (there had been some discussions, in 1998, of a miniseries, but these different media formats did not ultimately affect Scott's conception of the film). Nevertheless, and quite unusually for film, Scott was committed to having the cast experience the play in its original form, and thus ran theatrical rehearsals, in narrative sequence, even as he was organizing the pre-production. Blair Brown, a veteran of the PBS series, knew how valuable and rare that experience was, and wished they could have sustained this group process into the actual film shooting (although her simultaneous Broadway run in *Copenhagen* was another complicating factor in the schedule). As it was, some actors joined the rehearsal process only two weeks before their film performance; time, money, and scheduling made it impossible to sustain the theatrical model any longer. It was also exhausting for Scott to attempt two fulltime projects at once (film pre-production plus theatrical direction): although glad to have done it, he says he would never attempt it again – at least not within the limitations of a 29-day shoot. While a month can sometimes be enough time for a modern-day film shoot, it is "not enough for Shakespeare."

The labor of getting the show off the ground was a major part of the experience for all those involved. For Krass, an experienced theatrical designer running a film operation for the first time, this involved learning subtler differences between media – and facing daily crises without a safety net. Just as the actors began with theater-style rehearsals, so Krass did all the fittings before rehearsal (the theatrical norm), surprising film-trained wardrobe assistants used to working week-to-week. But in fact the discipline of doing more in advance was appropriate to the low budget: whereas the industry norm presumes three copies of each outfit to cover problems and retakes, Krass could not afford that luxury, nor did the shooting schedule allow shopping time or major design changes in process. When a lady-in-waiting was replaced mid-shoot with someone of a substantially different build, he had to rely on a well-draped shawl to cover the gap at the back of her dress. Because the condensed rehearsals (albeit more substantial than on most films) occurred during the weeks right before shooting, he could not be as involved in that experience nor use it in the way a theatrical designer does: by that time, he and his staff were too busy with the actual shopping and construction.

Even with the advance work, shooting days were still an adventure: extras would arrive needing attention without prior fittings, camera angles were composed as they went. This meant having to make specific alterations to fit new information (which servingman's gloves would be visible, for instance). Here the specialist's craft sometimes put the designer in a very different (and more anxious) location than others: while they were simply pleased to have a hired horse-and-carriage appear to cart in the players, he had to consider the driver's clothes on the spot – although in the final cut they are not visible. Much of the difficulty involved not being able to test and evaluate in real time, not knowing what would "read" and indeed what would be included in the final cut. Whereas in theater improvements are ongoing, in film the designer can do little once the choices and sequence have been established; thus, after day five of shooting, it was more frustrating than helpful to be on set when continuity demands meant little could be altered.

On the other hand, Krass probably had a greater role in establishing the overall "look" and historical period for the film than do most designers. Having extensive experience with staged Shakespeare (including a Regency *Hamlet* at Barbara Gaines' Chicago Shakespeare Theater), he was eager to work on specifying the chronological context, whereas the directors were more focused on the actors' stories and the immediacy of the script's performance. The directors knew they wanted an American *Hamlet*, set sometime before World War I, in order to keep the fencing scene intact and plausible (although the Almereyda version suggests another way to arrange this without historical distancing). Pre-Civil War seemed too removed, which left a fifty-year window. Here again the different perspectives of design and direction arose: while co-director Simonson wanted an "abstract time," the story was being filmed in a realist mode and the design had to accord with that look. Although on a self-enclosed stage one can easily mix realist and non-realist elements – and one *can* abstract from a particular year's silhouette even on film – in a medium where detail is so much more visible, consistency also becomes much more important. If one is looking at "real leaves" outdoors and real rooms with real furniture inside, Krass noted, it would look messy and incongruous to mix in or abstract from clothes of different decades. To create a coherent vision, the designer needed to have a specific historical moment he was working off in creating this fictional American/Danish court – even if his collaborators and audience did not recognize it as such. He pushed, therefore, for the elegant silhouettes of 1907–9, using the paintings of Thomas Eakins to illustrate his concept. Given local choices, the directors would push towards the simpler and more modern alternative (no tie, not "poofy"); his job as designer was to interpret their preferences and translate them into plausible period style. As ever, compromise and collaboration were essential, sometimes adding layers to the fiction: for example, Scott's desire to signify Hamlet's adolescent-like resistance by wearing a black headband at the banquet both allowed some actors' business with Jamey Sheridan's Claudius and intruded inappropriately into the "look" of the court, in a way befitting a prince who feels the time is out of joint.

While the demands of film were often constraining and the process laborious, the project was also a labor of love: others agreed to participate out of loyalty to and belief in Scott, just as much as (if not more than) any desire to be in a Shakespeare movie *per se*. Certainly Blair Brown joined the project because she believed in the integrity of Scott's acting and vision. Playing Gertrude is not a particularly gratifying challenge for a veteran actress: compared to other roles she has performed onstage (including, soon after the film, "Prospera" in *The Tempest*), Gertrude was, in Brown's apt phrasing, "a haiku of a woman." With only one very brief "private" speech, itself cut from the film (the aside at 4.5.17–20 in the Pelican edition she used to rehearse her lines), the role provides little in the way of articulated thought or conscious reflection; as is often true in Shakespeare, Brown said, the woman's part is focused upon feeling and reacting rather than thinking. Indeed, in *Hamlet* the two women's parts are more easily understood as the two iconic love relationships in a young man's life than as independent beings. It helps to care about one's Hamlet.

The out-of-sequence shooting schedule, determined by the availability of locations, meant that Brown's film performance began on day one with the climactic closet scene. Serendipitously or through an act of will, starting at this "midpoint of her arc" helped Brown create her characterization: experiencing that scene of conflict with even more startling intensity as it came out of nowhere, she decided that "if it was going to get this bad with Hamlet, I really wanted to enjoy the beginning," her moment of pleasure. Accordingly she made the banquet scene a time of true celebration for Gertrude. She imagined herself as having been the younger wife (probably in an arranged state marriage) to a warrior king; this was a world in which "a handful of men run everything." While her husband battled Norway, his younger brother was *around*: Claudius, with his smooth political manner and enjoyment of Rhenish wine, seems to have been a creature not of the battlefield but of the same world as Gertrude. Meanwhile, her husband had aged to the point that, as Brown put it with scathing emphasis, "he took *naps* in the afternoon." At that point, it all became "incredibly simple": she did not regard the queen cynically as implicated in murder or even as stupid, but instead inferred that, given her social position, she just wouldn't know what was going on. With her older husband's passing, she became the consort of a man in his element – and hers – at a court banquet. This allowed her to begin with a sense of personal happiness (sexually and socially, in maintaining her position as queen) as well as civic responsibility (in helping to facilitate a smooth royal transition for Denmark). If only her son would behave, all would be joyful.

Instead, it went downhill fast – to the closet scene, and then her increasing isolation from Claudius in Hamlet's absence. For Brown, the maternal sensibility was very real – getting tetchy and protective as her son seemed increasingly difficult and out of control. The struggle to maintain her family became "like a war," which at least had the advantage of allowing Brown to make Gertrude "active," as she wished. (Like many other actresses recently, Lisa Gay Hamilton expressed a similar wish for Ophelia, a notoriously difficult part to make work this way on its own psychological terms; on Julia Stiles' version, see HODGDON.) In line with Brown's emphasis on natural affections, her Gertrude also wished her son to be happy in love; citing John Caird, Brown recalled a theory that *Hamlet* is a tragedy because Ophelia didn't have a child. With Ophelia's madness, the lid is off, and for Gertrude likewise everything is coming apart. The film signaled her emotional decline visually as well: when the mad Ophelia intrudes, Gertrude is drinking alone, her hair and manner unkempt. Truly mournful at Ophelia's graveside, she gets one last hurrah alongside Hamlet during the fencing scene, their relationship restoring her spirit and dignity. The wheel has come full circle: in a celebratory reassertion of maternal pride and love, she drinks her final glass of wine.

Creating a coherent throughline did not in itself make the role of "designated feeler" particularly demanding, or provide a huge amount of latitude for actorly interpretation. Having little to work with in terms of a scripted internal character nevertheless had its silver lining: Brown could step back and consider her place in the play as a whole, in a manner more akin to a director's or dramaturg's. (Although ideally part of any actor's work according to Stanislavski, this process is harder to achieve when one is attempting a larger, more multi-faceted role.) In accordance with her sense of screen acting, she saw her job as one of providing multiple choices, a wide range of specific interpretations, and then left it to the directors to decide in post-production which versions fit their overarching vision.

That vision, with which she was sympathetic, included capturing the more intimate, even claustrophobic dimensions of *Hamlet*. She recalled the power of Kozintsev's establishing shots of the Danish castle's isolation, and liked her directors' ideas for further scaling down this story of a state distilled into two families. The filmmakers felt Branagh's rendition was by contrast overblown and bombastic. They also wanted to clarify the play, or at least one understanding of it, rather than riffing off it like Almereyda or Luhrmann's *Romeo + Juliet*. The task, Brown notes, was trickier precisely because it was tamer, creating a film "like a pane of glass." In one sense, acting on film allows the actor to be quieter, to think, rather than to project or amplify: one is acting in "real space." But the language Shakespeare composed precisely for a non-realist stage setting sometimes conspires against small-scale representation. It calls for a liveliness of thought and scope in gesture that may seem like emotional indulgence within a visually enlarged but more nuanced screen world. If one scales back too much, however, one mutes the play's dynamic range, making the film excessively "quiet." Recalling the broadcast version of Nicol Williamson's Hamlet (see SHAUGHNESSY), Brown suggested that television was not usually "big enough" for Shakespeare. In attempting a comparatively modest, refined film of *Hamlet*, Scott and his collaborators were engaged in a balancing act: they strove to combine intimacy with a verbal and emotional scope perhaps more easily conveyed to an audience in the shared space of live theater.

Another aspect that appealed to Brown was Scott's desire to make an American *Hamlet*, with American actors but without feeling a need to announce that transposition in a showy way. Rather, the point would be that it is as "natural" for a modern American cast as for a British to perform Shakespeare on screen. Granted, certain performance conditions as well as prejudices may still make this harder. Having acted Shakespeare in repertory and with extensive experience in Canadian, British, and US productions, Brown emphasized the difficulty of developing classic roles without a community of training and tradition. Although American actors have the talent, seldom do they have the opportunity to cultivate it over time in the way promoted by British institutions; commenting on the value of a volume like *Clamorous Voices* in capturing a dialogue among Royal Shakespeare Company actresses who had played the same parts, she lamented the absence of such contexts to learn through comparison and conversation. In this regard, then, there was an added, specific challenge to making an American Shakespeare movie that maintains verbal facility and layered characterization.

All Brown's comments reinforced the importance of the artistic process as her focus of attention – indeed, her exclusive focus. While it may be true that, as scholar Mark Robson claims, we have so many *Hamlet* films because the makers want a "permanent record," seldom do the people involved talk that way. Only reluctantly did Brown attend the premiere, and then only to help Scott promote the film: as a rule, she does not watch herself on screen after performing, be it in film or television. (An exception proving the rule was Lars Von Trier's *Dogville*, in which her part was small enough that her desire to see that iconoclastic director's full conception outweighed her aversion to watching herself.) What might seem an affectation to an outsider makes more sense when one compares film process to theater performance: the experience in the moment, what one learns by embodied doing, sustains an actor's energy and interest. Familiar with the camera, Brown says she knows how to scale her performance to fit the medium, and considers the acting process her work and its own reward.

Perhaps this was why she did not even raise the issue of her largest speech as Gertrude not appearing in the film's final cut; she had in fact performed the description of Ophelia's drowning, although it was excised in post-production. Only in discussion with Campbell Scott did its disappearance arise as an illustration of both the losses and discoveries compelled by production constraints. He made in essence a four-hour film, and then had to cut it down to three. The first 45 minutes of cuts were not a problem, and indeed helped streamline some scenes and transitions; the process prompted some inventive montage sequences, such as those interweaving the reception of Hamlet's two letters (from 4.6, 4.7, a point at which performances often seem to drag). Excising the final 15 minutes, however, was hellish. The hardest was Gertrude's speech – both because of what it does to the actress's role and because they would have shot her entrance differently (emphasizing her face) had they known its meaning would come entirely through visuals. One can make the case that the absence of this weirdly located, lyrical set-piece actually allows greater surprise and empathy with Hamlet at Ophelia's graveside; some viewers, like our hero, may be startled at the direct realization of her death then, rather than having already digested it as material for aesthetic and intellectual contemplation. If so, it is another instance of unanticipated consequences and limited resources, rather than *auteurist* self-assertion, creating something fresh.

Some ideas that were indeed the filmmakers' creation also remained on the cutting-room floor or in Scott's imagination – among them, an extended series of establishing shots to be intercut with the titles sequence. In the final product, only the scenes between Gertrude and Claudius (demonstrating their sexual attraction, as well as introducing the first of many mirror/window/portrait viewing shots) and of Polonius (burning a letter, testimony to his policy and potentially sinister secrets) survived. Alas, there was no compensatory value in losing Horatio's late-night arrival, eating in the kitchen (reminding us of his marginal, comparatively powerless status); Laertes decadently indulging in olive-eating and deep kissing with a bevy of beauties (establishing his father's canny suspicions); or Ophelia looking up from outside Hamlet's window at the scholar reading, disappointed when his light is extinguished, then startled by his sudden presence next to her in the courtyard at twilight, awkwardly approaching an unconsummated embrace (confirming their special affinity and tragic importance to one another). Recalling these lost sequences, Scott concluded, "there is nothing controllable about film."

A sense of powerlessness not only factored into the artistic process but also appeared as a major theme in Campbell Scott's interpretation of Hamlet as a character. In a social context of empty carousing and false levity, of constraint and personal betrayal, the dislocated prince searches for someone to talk to, someone he can trust again. This is a Hamlet desperate for friendship: witness his pleasure in recognizing Marcellus as well as Horatio, before the presence of a third unfamiliar guard alerts him that their visit cannot be a simply personal reunion. As a result, the recognition of Rosencrantz and Guildenstern's employment becomes a major turning point, with Hamlet's eagerness to see childhood friends quickly turning to disappointment and then disgust. He realizes they too are not allies in this tricky, insincere world run by manipulators such as Claudius and his experienced minister Polonius. Moreover, those whom he does think about with the most affection – Horatio, Ophelia, the Players – are socially powerless, subordinated within the court hierarchy. And in any event, they could not help him assume the role unique to the prince as a son and heir coming of age.

For Scott, the emphasis lay in Hamlet's internal struggle with this sense of powerlessness, a psychological as well as social barrier. Unable to fit in Claudius' world, Hamlet becomes increasingly frustrated by the multiple expectations laid upon him, which he is "not yet ready" to assume. Even a Ghost demands that he perform in ways he cannot (yet). Saddled with burdens he cannot share, Scott's Hamlet is forced to talk to himself almost compulsively, his mind whirling with words at great speed, as he wrestles with this combination of social powerlessness and pressure to perform. Scott was quick to distinguish this from indecisiveness – "Don't tell me he's not decisive, he is *constantly* deciding things." Rather, it is *this* thing, this assumption of a specific role in the adult social order as others have constructed it, that he is not yet able to accept. The tragedy lies in his dying at precisely the moment when he becomes able to survive in that world as given, when he accepts "let be," and "the readiness is all." Scott argues that Hamlet's speech to Laertes prior to the fencing match – often drastically cut – crucially indicates this change, as for the first time "Hamlet talks like Claudius," without becoming passionate or intellectualizing excessively (his two characteristic "defense" modes for not being what he is supposed "to be").

If this sounds like an existential *Hamlet*, a story about creating meaning and becoming an adult, it is no coincidence. This is an actor who responds to questions about his target audience by noting the impossibility of knowing the effects of our actions, and invoking Camus' use of the actor as an exemplar of "The Absurd Man" (in *The Myth of Sisyphus*, that other classic text wrestling with the question of suicide). Scott's sense of the actor's labor as ephemeral yet profound – understood through "cellular knowledge" but not necessarily able to be articulated – emblematizes a dedicated humility about what one has the power to achieve. In describing the "let be" moment, he compared it to anyone reaching a crux in adulthood, when one becomes deeply anxious and can try to avoid "it" (through drink, denial, whatever) or else face and accept the situation, moving forward; this conclusion was not precisely fatalism nor suicidal on Hamlet's part, but rather a dimension of "being a grown-up." Hence, only during the final scenes (with Horatio and Osric, and then the fencing match) would Scott allow Krass to costume him as an elegant, collected princely figure.

This conception informed Scott's unconventional treatment of the Ghost as well, in particular that specter's reappearance as Hamlet dies. For Scott, the point was not to "Blame the Ghost" but to see him as part of the given context, clarifying why Hamlet's task was so hard and so important. Hamlet Senior contributes to the acknowledgment that Hamlet has done what is demanded of him, becoming the true prince. The Ghost likewise has an interpolated appearance at the crucial moment when Hamlet decides not to kill the praying Claudius. An immense amount of editing went into that sequence, primarily focused on determining exactly how much to show. Scott's initial inclusion of a full-body shot of father and son grappling was eventually scaled back to a mere suggestion – at which point they realized it was not even clear who was there (perhaps an uncanny resemblance to Peter Brook's "qui est là?"). They ended up showing just an arm – its appearance and the soundtrack establishing it as the Ghost – that with a sweeping motion lowers Hamlet's arm, discouraging his enraged attack. The intent was to help motivate Hamlet's speech in which he second-guesses his intuitive action, by reminding him (and the audience) of the true initiator of this plot; its goal was not just to kill the king but to fulfill the paternal requirement of appropriate revenge. Similarly, in the closet scene the Ghost doesn't simply "appear" to Hamlet: after Gertrude and Hamlet are startled by the bloody standing presence of the dying Polonius, the minister finally falls dead again to reveal (only to Hamlet) the dead king behind him. This shocking double "resurrection" vividly attests to the origin and cost of Hamlet's "almost blunted purpose."

Here as throughout, Scott employs the camera to create the Ghost effect, drawing on horror conventions as well as religious ones. (He told Krass that he wanted a real king embodied, leaving the work of making him otherworldly to the cameras and post-production.) A fan of US television's "Creature Features" as a boy, Scott's horror humor appears in the witty rendering of Act 1 scene 5 on a beach, where the "old mole" burrows around beneath the sands before a sword-bearing arm lunges up, like an Arthurian parody, to demand that Hamlet's companions "Swear"; its swift retraction slashes the swearers' hands, creating an eerie blood brotherhood. Arguably even the film's first approaching shots, moving in towards the guards at night, "belong" to the Ghost: we seem to be seeing the world from his perspective, reinforcing his role as the plot's prime mover. But characteristically, the association is suggested rather than overt; there will be no flamboyant exit through a Pepsi One machine, à la Almereyda. This *Hamlet* holds rewards for an attentive, thinking viewer, but is more interested in conveying Shakespeare's story than its own style. Tellingly, when discussing its impact Scott was most interested in whether the film had been clear and enjoyable for my non-specialist students.

For those students, perhaps his most surprising recognition was that it simply didn't matter much for the story or the character whether Hamlet's condition was "madness" or not – an admittedly odd perspective, but how it felt in performance. Such definitions became less and less significant over time. Although Scott himself found this surprising, it serves as a nice emblem of the gap between how we experience a drama (or a story, or life) and the categories of analysis we use to lend structure and lucidity to that experience. Academic disciplines try to construct clear and distinct ideas about their objects of inquiry through psychological models of "deviancy" or artistic labels such as "tragic flaw"; helpful as markers, in that they delineate sites of debate or social conflict, they become problematic when deemed adequate substitutes for the "object," when they replace or paraphrase a subject, process, or artifact. At that point, labels simplify to such an extent that they either block access to the experience or become (as in this case) irrelevant to it. For critics as well as students, it is useful to be reminded of such gaps and to consider how they affect our scholarly descriptions.

What's There?

What an audience member perceives need not be constrained, of course, by the filmmakers' intentions: even if Scott's ghostly additions seemed to him a local way to make sense of certain particulars, they may still seem to me an especially bold set of filmic choices. This difference becomes problematic, however, if one attributes or projects perceptions back onto the filmmakers themselves. For example, when Robson claims that a meditative belatedness "haunts" filmmakers and thereby accounts for the repetition of *Hamlet* on screen, one may counter that this sounds more like the anxiety of academia than of these artists: as scholars we struggle to find a new angle, whereas they often struggle just to get a shot completed. There's little mystery as to why an actor would want to play *Hamlet*, after all, and there were few signs that this group worried much about what had gone before or about their place in performance history. Occasionally a remark did imply a value placed on not merely echoing another version: early in rehearsals, Scott considered having the Ghost be an internal "voice," as if he were "possessed" – but then someone pointed out Jonathan Pryce had done precisely that onstage, and the idea seemed less fresh. Yet Scott's realization that filmically he could do things which he couldn't do so well onstage (like those flashes of a ghostly arm) seemed just as important a factor in the final conception as was the relationship to other productions. Certainly the positive idea of a big challenge, rather than worries about self-location, impelled this *Hamlet.*

Indeed, Scott's most frequently invoked metaphor was a mountain, a "place of great natural beauty"; rather than needing to justify the desire to go there, one simply appreciates the experience. It takes effort to get others to sign on for the climb, and requires responsibility en route, yet the aim is not to change it in order to "make it mine, different" but rather to partake of that recognizably beautiful and challenging space. The place becomes more special when you go with the friends you grew up with, those you know well: the communal experience becomes crucial to the event. And whereas scholars who have spent years reading and re-viewing *Hamlet* tend to get excited by the experimental, the odd, or the unexpected twist, Scott's goals included just "getting out of its way," letting the rich, multi-layered story speak for itself.

This attitude, when contrasted with Kenneth Branagh's more monumental *Hamlet,* may correspond to a national difference of acting emphasis as well. In making an American *Hamlet,* Scott said he was not at all "anti-Brit": he just wanted to perform, and allow other North American actors to perform, from their own perspective and without affectation, in effect adding another climbing route to those discovered in Britain, Russia, and elsewhere. Nevertheless, Scott sometimes appears stylistically the "anti-Branagh," focusing on the domestic, the intimate, and the understated instead of the political, the flamboyant, and the grand. (When Scott's Hamlet gets carried away, he is usually made to look foolish – a full-length oil painting of his father falling on top of the "rogue and peasant slave"; the professional actors glancing askance at his intrusive advice delivered in clownish make-up.) His film is much more humble in selling *Hamlet,* although it shares Branagh's populist goal of reaching a non-specialist audience.

Scott's particular emphasis included making the Polonius family African-American, illustrating again a difference from Branagh's casting practice and leading to some strange inferences by reviewers. In

91

the *New York Times*, Stephen Holden presumed this choice placed the story in the South and "suggest[ed] remnants of a plantation culture" with a decaying aristocracy "sipping juleps and toasting the memory of Robert E. Lee" – a description consistent with the tendency of Northerners to locate racism far from their own history, but with little basis in the film. In fact, *Hamlet*'s exterior shots were filmed at a house on Long Island, while several interior scenes were performed in a church crypt in Harlem. No signs, accents, or additions substantiated the claim of a Southern subtext. (Holden's favorable review also misreported that the film was a recording of the Huntington Theater production – perhaps a consequence of our culture's conventional focus on the director/star to the exclusion of other participants.) Whether directly attributable to this review or not, several other commentators have since perpetuated the Southern connection.

The *Times* review was at least right in noticing the film's consciousness of race as an inevitable part of our socially constructed reality. The personal choice of desiring to "climb the mountain with friends," notably with Lisa Gay Hamilton, also accorded with Scott's sense that making an American *Hamlet* demanded incorporating the nation's diversity in a responsible, illuminating way. Using racial difference as a social signifier, Scott was able to suggest unspoken barriers to Hamlet and Ophelia's love affair; as a marker of both (theoretical) illusion and (experiential) difference, race provided a more potent analogy for a modern audience than the similarly invested royal-versus-common "blood" distinction of Shakespeare's day. It added another dimension to Polonius and Laertes' protectiveness towards Ophelia (beyond gender condescension) and also suggested ways to conceive of Polonius as a more skillful yet constrained, wary politician: no matter how good he is at his job, he can never be "the King."

This latter point was crucial both in Scott's conception and in getting Roscoe Lee Browne to play the part. Called upon when health and other casting problems had left Scott with no Polonius near shooting day, the veteran actor had no interest in caricaturing a pompous fool; only when Scott stressed the potential for a more cunning, nuanced representation (and drew on their decades-old friendship) was he fortunate enough to get Browne to sign on. His presence becomes all the more important within Ophelia's story as well, especially when the film includes shots making her a silent witness to her father's scheming with Claudius and later to Hamlet's callous jesting about his corpse. For Hamilton, these shot sequences compounded her silenced frustration, her consciousness of Ophelia being objectified and used rather than able to shape her own story. As Scott noted, in another universe she would be going to France like her brother, or studying in Wittenberg like Hamlet, but in this socially confining world, she can't.

Awareness of race as well as gender thus compounds the text's tragic potential in a way utterly at odds with so-called "color-blind casting" (attempted famously by Joseph Papp at the New York Shakespeare Festival and adopted by Branagh alongside "nation-blindness" or "accent-blindness"; on this last, see HODGDON). For Scott, "color-blind" casting works from the dubious premise that we can bracket the perception of physical appearances and relationships conventionally assumed outside the theater; it distracts from verisimilitude to have, say, an Ophelia and Laertes who are visibly of different ethnicities, and thereby avoids rather than addresses the social realities in which we live. By contrast, non-traditional casting gestures at, without overtly alluding to, contemporary knowledge about the complexity of race in America. As Scott noted, we live in a time when we accept a Colin Powell as Secretary of State – but will we see a black President in our lifetime? Adapting the differences of class and status most definitely there in the text allows his *Hamlet* to address something that just as certainly matters now, in the construction of national identity and authority figures.

Even as I have tried to (de)construct and relocate "authority" and causality by analyzing the artistic process, I have been reminded vividly of my own scholarly investment in finding meaning through interpretation when watching Shakespeare on screen. A case in point: my reaction to the scene where Rosencrantz and Guildenstern come to capture Hamlet after Polonius' murder. In Scott's rendition, the cornered Hamlet reappears atop a stone statuary pedestal in the center of the room lined with confessional stalls (from which Claudius and Polonius earlier spied on him – the same spaces keep reappearing, budget limits as well as artistic craft reinforcing the intimacy and claustrophobia of this *Hamlet*'s courtly world). Then, in a wild burst, Hamlet leaps down onto his pursuers. I was delighted: my viewing was informed by earlier films and Peter Donaldson's thick description of Olivier's climactic (and dangerous) leap from atop a stone staircase to attack Claudius. I asked Campbell Scott about what I had seen as an allusion. Then the interpretive thud: he was not conscious of the connection, having chosen the reaction in the moment of performance. So much for my deft unearthing of film traditions and intertextuality. Granted, Scott's conscious memory is not the ultimate authority any more than is my own brain; it is only one check on what we call "misreadings" or "overreadings." Perhaps somewhere deep in his subconscious lurks an earlier viewing, a deep identification with Laurence Olivier that led him to this moment. But even if not, I can pursue the connection created on film where it leads me: I would only publish those pursuits, however, if I felt that my conclusions were premised neither on artistic intentions nor on my own desires alone. They would have to reveal something that an observer with no intrinsic reason to trust my authority would be able to follow and contest, using the evidence of the film, contextual knowledge, or rational argumentation. Those are not an artist's parameters, but a scholar's, in pursuit of valid truth (or plausibility) claims.

What may get lost in this pursuit is the nature of the gift itself, the film that initiated my interpretive discovery. For me, it would be a gift even if the giver did not so perceive it. But the gift is also a better analogy, based on my conversations, for what artists *think* they are providing than is the model of the argument, the document, or the "intervention." When we write about Shakespeare on screen, too often the artifact becomes the occasion solely for critique and argument – whether aesthetic or cultural – while the labor, energies, and actual conditions shaping it disappear from view. This leaves us with Shakespeare on screen as commodity fetish, rather than the product of complex, contingent relationships and transactions. Putting the artistic process back into our conceptual frame, by contrast, allows us not only to describe the artifact more fully but also to recall the other kinds of enjoyment that come through sensation, community, and chance. We need not lose the delights and insights that arise through rigorous interpretation and recontextualization in doing so. Indeed, I would argue that the interpretations become both more accurate and more provocative by taking into account the intricacies of process. And they may also encourage what seems a more authentic form of celebration of Shakespeare on screen as a thing in itself: as an act and sign of collective human creation striving, missing, and ultimately – in thought, gesture, or emotion – giving.

References and Further Reading

Camus, Albert (1955). *The Myth of Sisyphus and Other Essays.* New York: Vintage.

Holden, Stephen (2001). "And Who Knew That Shakespeare Was a Southern Author?" Movies, Performing Arts. *New York Times*, August 17, Section E: 8.

Robson, Mark (2001). "'Trying to Pick a Lock with a Wet Herring': *Hamlet*, Film, and Specters of Psychoanalysis." *EnterText* 1.2: 247–63.

Rutter, Carol (1989). *Clamorous Voices: Shakespeare's Women Today.* Ed. Faith Evans. New York: Routledge.

Shakespeare, William (1970). *The Pelican Shakespeare: Hamlet.* Ed. Willard Farnham. New York: Penguin.

Chapter 5

CINEMATIC PERFORMANCE

Spectacular Bodies: Acting + Cinema + Shakespeare

Barbara Hodgdon

Richard Burton slouches onto a (nearly bare) stage, sits, and throws away "To be or not to be" like a used laundry list, as though eager to rid himself of Hamlet's most familiar utterance. But as he says "when we have shuffled off this mortal coil," he sweeps both hands across his face, marking his hurried vocal delivery with a gesture of self-erasure. Glossing this film clip from Gielgud's 1964 stage production for colleagues at a recent symposium, I spoke of how this moment of performance condensed and fixed meaning, wrote Hamlet's words onto the actor's body, making what initially had seemed ordinary spectacularly visible. Yet as it turned out, what I had seen as riveting went unseen by everyone else; tied primarily if not exclusively to Shakespeare's language, they had *heard* Burton but had not noticed his gesture – or his body.

What is at stake in this scene of looking – or, rather, of *not* looking – can be focused more precisely with a moment from Laurence Olivier's *Henry V* (1944). Olivier frames his film with a recreation of a May 1, 1600 performance at the Globe: the audience gathers, hears Chorus speak the opening prologue, and responds to the play's initial scene, staged on the gallery above the platform stage. The camera then moves backstage to observe a flurry of activity, culminating as several heralds pass from background to foreground and move off right to make their entrance. For an instant, the frame is relatively empty; then, from left, Olivier, costumed as King Henry, comes into view in mid-shot. Pausing, he puts one hand to his mouth, clears his throat, and the camera pans to follow him as, now in a long shot of his back, he walks onto the stage. Doubly, even triply charged, the pause captures a liminal instant when the body acting (simultaneously Laurence Olivier and the Elizabethan actor he represents) becomes the body acted (King Henry) and – the moment might be called "An Actor Prepares" – focuses specifically on preparing the Shakespearean voice.

First of all, both scenes highlight an issue which, although central to understanding any performance, whether on or off screen, is especially pertinent to how spectators perceive Shakespearean acting in and for the cinema: the relationship between the emotive speaking voice and the still or moving body. While it is usual to consider the cinematic image as all-powerful, that is less the case with a Shakespeare film, which is not solely dependent upon the dynamics of looking, since vocal performance is not merely supplemental to but one of the central facts of the film experience: arguably, it is sound that makes the "Shakespearean body" whole (see Smith 1999). Second, since Burton's performance derives from a film which documents a stage production and Olivier's from one that is book-ended by an imaginary theatrical performance, both call attention to how stage acting and film acting share a frame of reference and exist in dialogue with one another: as Herbert Blau writes, "It is *theater* that haunts all performance whether or not it occurs in the theater" (1987: 164–5). Yet whereas the stage actor has considerable control over what Edgar Morin calls the "signifying direction and grain" of his performance, the film actor's presence is subject to sign systems that are not strictly speaking "of" live performance; indeed, in some sense, the film "performance" as such does not exist, for what viewers perceive is constructed by technological interventions (1960: 144). Writes Richard Dyer, "What you read into the performer, you read in by virtue of signs other than performance signs" (1979: 162). Yet adopting a semiotic vocabulary, which reduces acting to a grammar of signs or codes, loses the specificity, volume, and intensity of the individual's contribution to that polysemous performance.[1]

To think of the screen actor as creating a montage of behavioral and psychological fragments which are then composed into a "whole" invites rephrasing Stella Adler's famous advice to stage actors – that the talent lies in the choices – for on film, that talent also resides in the choices controlled and modulated by *mise-en-scène*, framing, camera movement, editing, and (other kinds of) sound, those aspects of film language which support and enhance the actor's performance. Such a strategy, which explores the full range of spectacular resources through which an actor articulates a role and views these in combination with the workings of filmic discourse – what might be called "distilled portraiture" – also recognizes that the body's visibility, the voice as the audible expression of the body, and the dynamic way in which body and voice occupy film space occur within sociohistorical contexts that can conceive both body and voice differently (Pavis 2003: 63–4). In short, the Shakespearean body on screen is, to inflect Paul Smith's apt phrase through Polonius, a socio-aesthetic-historical entity, a cultural production (1993: 219–20).

Since Shakespeare's language constitutes a central element of filmed performance, it offers a starting point for raising questions and sketching out several trajectories for analysis. Not only is voice the most difficult element of performance to detach from theater, but mainstream as well as academic critics prefer to hear Shakespeare sound "English" – spoken in the pre-signified rhythms of Received Standard Pronunciation (RSP). Thus naturalizing national identity to performance, the voice becomes both author-itative and authentic, promising (cinematic) access to early modern origins. Perhaps the most extreme instance of Shakespearean authority diffused through an actor's voice is Peter Greenaway's *Prospero's Books* (1991), which memorializes John Gielgud's performance as Prospero by having him speak (almost) all the lines. Yet far from attempting to pacify the voice to cinema, Greenaway's film makes it a sensual, even kinesthetic component, in part by constructing a lush visual regime – a compendium of Renaissance art, drawings, texts, and architectural spaces brought to moving life – that echoes and supports Gielgud's exquisitely modulated vocal performance, so that at all levels of its discourse, the film plays out the "size" of Shakespeare's writing.[2]

Because Shakespeare's language consistently reaches beyond the naturalist conventions of screen dialogue, sound becomes an unusually "thick" mode of production, most especially obvious in translating early modern conventions such as the set speech or soliloquy to the screen. In such moments of high audition, language is the primary register of acting: phrasing, pause, and emphasis construct the stilled body, bringing thought close to its surface, making it readable. As Gielgud delivers Henry IV's great speech on sleep in Orson Welles' *Chimes at Midnight* (1965), for instance, Welles simply puts the camera on Gielgud's austere figure and listens: as he speaks, the weighty cares and fatigue he bears leak into his vocal rhythms, becoming readable in his gaze and his effort to hold his torso erect. Sound becomes even more noticeable when it occurs as voiceover – what

Kaja Silverman calls a "voice on high" – often the most powerful speaking position on film and one which works to invert the usual image/sound hierarchy. In perhaps the most famous shot from Olivier's *Hamlet* (1948), the camera makes an astonishing move towards Hamlet's head as if, writes Antony Lane, "preparing to bore into his skull and continue its quest within the matching labyrinth of his brain. 'To be or not to be,' he asks gently, overlooking a boiling sea: a tempting drop, and an echo . . . of Hitchcock's *Rebecca*, in which Olivier had starred eight years before" (1996: 69). Similarly, when Kenneth Branagh (1989) begins Henry V's "Upon the king," for a moment his speech hovers over the image track in an invisible spatial register, transcending the body to assume a position of superior knowledge; imposed on the image, it turns the body "inside out," as though to display what is "inaccessible to the image, what exceeds the visible" (Silverman 1988: 48–9). Here, as in Hamlet's soliloquy, the voice sounds "close," stressing the link between voice and body, magnifying the illusion of interiority.

Each of these examples closely approaches an unspoken ideal: a deliberately historicized match (achieved in part through costume and *mise-en-scène*) between early modern language and modern bodies. Much more consistently, and especially (though not exclusively) in films of the late 1980s and 1990s, viewers experience some disjuncture between the two, whether in individual performances such as Michael Keaton's densely incomprehensible and physically quirky Dogberry in Kenneth Branagh's *Much Ado About Nothing* (1993), or throughout such films as Franco Zeffirelli's *Hamlet* (1990) or Oliver Parker's *Othello* (1995), where an international cast as well as a variety of accents and verse-speaking styles call heightened attention to the difference sound makes.

Arguably, Baz Luhrmann's *William Shakespeare's Romeo + Juliet* (1996) solves, or at least resolves, this disjuncture between voice and body, for the film's overtly postmodern milieu – a parallel universe comprised of late twentieth-century icons and inventive raids on the cinematic canon (from *Rebel Without a Cause* to Busby Berkeley, Fellini, Sergio Leone spaghetti westerns, and John Woo Hong Kong action films) – enables spectators to accept yet another fissure within an already fractured surround (see Hodgdon 1999). Indeed, in Luhrmann's film, scenography appropriates acting, taking on its role; in a sense the film stages its *mise-en-scène* as much as or more than its actors' performances. Here, however, at the opposite pole from Greenaway's homage to Gielgud's "voice beautiful" stands Leonardo DiCaprio's vocal performance. Writes Peter Travers, "As Romeo, he doesn't round his vowels ('tonight' becomes 'tanight') or enunciate in dulcet tones, but when he speaks you believe him. . . . DiCaprio lets the Bard's words flow with an ardor that you can't buy in acting class" (1996: 123–4). Moving from one to the other condenses a cultural paradigm shift in perceptions of Shakespearean performance, distinguishes between Gielgud's "pure" vocality, "filling the aisles with noises" (Lane 1996: 66), and DiCaprio's seemingly natural-born acting, his voice expressing not a kind of Shakespearean narcissistic autobiography but the body's emotive "truth." To write a cultural history of Shakespearean speaking on screen would be marked by changing protocols of verse-speaking inflected by generation, class, and by the rapid dismantling of the boundaries between high and low Shakespeares and between the art-house film and the mass market commodity.

Just as the Shakespearean voice sounds and resounds differently in different eras, mythologies of culture also precisely determine or precode the body's physical presence and gesture (see Gallagher and Laqueur 1987). But how does a particular actor's body become the bearer of texts, of sociocultural as well as cinematic histories? How does the filmed body become susceptible to meanings? And how does "character" get re-sited in relation to specific actors' bodies, inviting spectators to engage in a negotiation between actor and character and "to take part in the dance?" (Hodgdon 1998: 207; Pavis 2003: 67). To examine these issues further, consider how, in Olivier's and Branagh's films of *Henry V*, body (as well as voice) occupy and mark film space to activate meaning for a viewer (see McAuley 1999: 90).

Olivier's entrance as Henry V invites me to fantasize that I am indeed a time-traveler, present at the turn of a long-ago century, watching (a much slimmer) Richard Burbage walk forward onto the Globe's stage: as one among many actors who have played the role of the historical Henry, Olivier is just his most recent "walking shadow" (Macbeth's term for an actor). Working against theater historicity even as the setting declares it, what takes place here aligns productively with Joseph Roach's notion of surrogation – "an uncanny act of replacement acting, a deeply ambivalent replacement of previous performers and performances by a current behavior" (1996: 2–3, 9). Moreover, in that moment, the relationship between the body acting and the body acted changes; as the two are soldered together (again, in part by costume and make-up), the actor's body becomes canceled, hidden beneath that of the "character," who first appears "as a bodily effect in the image" (Comolli 1978: 41–3). Given Olivier's slim, elegant body and aristocratic features, he seems every inch a king; commanding the space physically as well as vocally, his is an authoritative, even charismatic presence – one crafted from Elizabethan-theatrical as well as mid-twentieth-century cultural fantasies of kingship.

Nearly fifty years after Olivier's performance, Branagh reauthored Henry's role: describing his initial appearance and linking it to film discourse, Stuart Klawans captures the "fit" between performing body and role which re-sites character:

> With his thatch of sandy hair, blunt nose and rounded jawline (suggestive of his boyishness and his native Ulster) Kenneth Branagh has the face of a commoner . . . [he] looks like the son of a usurper. He introduces himself in a set piece of old-fashioned movie spectacle: doors to the throne room swing open without human agency, while the camera, at floor level, looks up at a back-lit silhouette, which strides forward like every monarch who ever commanded the screen, rolled up with every gunfighter and Darth Vader, too. Then, as a fanfare continues on the soundtrack, a tracking camera presents Henry's point of view, with courtiers lined up on either side bowing to him, one by one. . . . Only after all this choreography do you see Henry's face – which turns out to be rather plain and emits a soft, controlled voice. The voice grows stronger throughout the film – though not right away – while the face and body, which hardly seem imposing at first, eventually take on the grandeur promised by the silhouette. (1989: 725–6)

Spectators encounter this Henry first as an empty mask, then as a character – one not only shaped by the specific class and ethnic markings of the actor's body but also given added weight by generic conventions quilted together from American film history. Moreover, like Olivier's before him, Branagh's body is impregnated by the surrounding culture, which is implicated in the processes of signification for both role and acting (see Pavis 2003: 66–7). This youthful king grips the throne-chair's arm with one hand, not yet secure, reigning himself in – a gesture that situates character within a whole cultural-historical frame of reference. Whereas, with England at war, Olivier's Henry flung his challenge to the enemy ("France being ours we'll bend it to our [will], / Or break it all to pieces") in ringing tones, Branagh's post-Vietnam, post-Falklands monarch addresses his courtiers and then, in a cut to close-up, whispers, "Or break it all to pieces," his level gaze anticipating, as though in a mirror, war's real effects. Branagh's performance, and his film, can be situated in terms of its relation to Vietnam films of the 1980s, to a renewed interest in history, and to popularizing Shakespeare. Not only did he seem to express tensions about masculinity alive in the culture just prior to the Persian Gulf War (see Aebischer), but his facility with making Shakespearean language sound like everyday idiom and with adapting himself to the limits and pressures exerted upon acting in the mainstream cinema also gave him near-instant stardom. For many, Branagh has become (as was Gielgud or Olivier for a previous generation) the conduit through which present-day viewers hold the mirror up to nature, the very model of a (post)modern performer – reinventing Shakespearean roles less by depending upon inherited traditions than by forging an emotional and psychological identification between actor and character that is understood by spectators within the familiar realm of contemporary behaviors (see Worthen 1997: 87).

Whereas Branagh's *Henry V* – and his performance as Henry – took cinematic shape from the generic conventions of contemporary war films but retained the aura of "Shakespeare-culture" in its *mise-en-scène*, Richard Loncraine's *Richard III* (1995), developed from a script co-authored with Ian McKellen (who plays Richard), reformulates Yorkist–Lancastrian dynastic culture and Richard's historically and theatrically sedimented identity to retail *Richard III* as a political thriller. Drawing on Edward VIII's sympathies for Nazism and on Hitler's strategic manipulation of power, the film nets in memories of totalitarian regimes, imagines what might have happened if a figure like Sir Oswald Mosley, leader of the black-shirted British Union of Fascists, had come to power in 1930s Britain. Situated stylistically within a web of signs quilted together from the British heritage film, American gangster movies, and TV/Media footage that work to relocate its fascination with fascism within mass culture, it intersects with Roach's idea of surrogation as simultaneously "an act of memory and an act of creation . . . that recalls and transforms the past in the form of the present" (1996: 29; see Walker).

No small part of that transformation entails reshaping the acting body for Richard III's role, one over which spectacular theatrical and cinematic performances, notably Olivier's highly theatricalized monster, cast long shadows. Except in close-ups of his exaggeratedly "old" face and bad teeth, McKellen's Richard does not appear physically grotesque – that is, putting it bluntly, he does not play the hump. Rather, he takes Richard's reference to himself as being "half made-up" to differentiate a "good" right side from a "bad" left side: one half of his face hangs somewhat, as though congenitally struck; he limps on the left leg, keeping his useless arm and distorted hand hidden within specially designed pockets (McKellen and Loncraine 1996: 29–30). And as he plots in private, the camera observes him through a haze of cigarette smoke, likening him to every 1930s or 1940s screen villain. David Denby captures his presence and aura: "Slender and starched, seemingly as bland as a mid-level Whitehall diplomat – a not quite handsome man, very tightly wrapped, very decisive but impersonal. Yet when he walks, you notice Richard's hump under the uniform and the walk itself, tilted and unsteady, like a yacht with its sails askew, turns into an adventure of pure will" (1996: 49). A coldly compulsive professional soldier, he first appears at war, and in war's body: dressed in camouflage fatigues, gas mask, and combat boots and armed with an automatic rifle, he leaps from a tank, his heavy breathing filling the screen: a postmodern action-film terrorist, part Terminator, part Darth Vader, he assassinates the king's son and the king; then, ripping off his gas mask, he shoots "Richard III" in huge blood-red letters onto the screen. Jam-packed with quotations from *Rambo*, *Die Hard*, Action Man comics, *Star Wars*, and video games, this introductory composite of ready-made allusions puts Richard where he has always wanted to be: a star player in a mass market commodity.

The celebrated two-hander between Richard and Lady Anne, its rhetoric of medieval debate condensed to semi-naturalistic screen dialogue, affords an especially stunning instance of how two actors marry line to gesture and how the shot frame patterns their ritualized interaction within a restricted space. Set in a military hospital morgue, the scene, which, ironically enough and in a potent alteration from the play,[3] takes its life from the dead body of Anne's husband laid out on a mortuary slab, becomes a test for actors' bodies. As she enters the morgue, Anne (Kristin Scott-Thomas) registers alarm at seeing her husband's corpse before crossing to him; throughout the scene's early section, camera position aligns the spectator with her: a high-angle shot of her husband's head and torso reveals his wounds; bending over him in half-embrace, she speaks her curses in his ear. Suddenly, magically ("What black magician conjures up this fiend"), Richard moves into view from behind her; his entrance, equally magical for spectators, begins a double seduction, for not only is he seducing Anne, he also is seducing the camera – and keeping his "good" right side towards both.

Edging closer, he removes his hat to honor the dead, looks at the corpse as though to assess the accuracy of his killing wounds; in a slowed-down variant of Cary Grant and Rosalind Russell's wooing dance around the newsroom desk in *His Girl Friday* (1939), he moves around the slab from head to foot as Anne deftly keeps herself between him and her husband's body, avoiding his sight. Shot set-ups consistently give Anne the more powerful right-screen position, forcing Richard not just to play to her but to "win" the space.[4] When he lifts the blanket to cover the corpse's foot, Anne lunges across the slab, protecting her husband's body from his touch, and he moves forward to left foreground for his most startling remark, "Your bed-chamber," spoken in close-up as a soft aside to the camera.[5] Not only is Anne more brightly lit than he but less distance separates the two when the camera aims at Richard past her shoulder, as though by this time complicit with him. His back is towards the camera when Anne spits at him, full in the face, her veiled contempt made physical: ironically, it is she who initiates a sexual economy grounded in body fluids, objects – and gestures – that Richard will turn back on her body.

Richard removes the glove from his good hand with his teeth, and a handkerchief (magically) appears, with which he dries his face and delicately wipes away his own tears, prompted by remembering his father's death. At Anne's "Out of my sight!" he obediently turns his back; as she adds, "You do infect my eyes" and he speaks of his "manly eyes," spectators see neither hers nor his. Throughout, Anne's face has been studiedly impassive, but at Richard's "Teach not your lip such scorn, for it was made / For kissing, lady," her eyebrows lift slightly, her eyes half close, and her head tilts down. Reading these signs of sexual tension prompts him to pick up a scalpel, force it into her hand, and kneel before her; when she drops it, he again offers it; then (it's no risk) puts the knife against his jugular. On "But shall I live in hope?" he elongates the open vowel, the circular "o" anticipating his next gesture. For just an instant, as Richard removes his signet ring with his tongue (exactly the right body part, the silvered tongue speaking killing words), he holds both knife and ring, and then the one is exchanged for the other as, sliding the ring, wet with his saliva, down her finger, its blood-red nail the only color, he performs a crudely perverse marriage rite, answering what had come from her mouth with his own (McKellen and Loncraine 1996: 84).

Rising, Richard smartly salutes the corpse; lowering her eyes, Anne acknowledges the gesture, her submission nearly complete. The camera pulls back to show Richard leaving, but he stops and turns (a final test): "Bid me farewell" – half question, half command – to which she acquiesces; but once he is out of sight, her body sags in long shot, relieved but defeated. As for Richard, his risky verbal and psychological dexterity transforms into physical dexterity: completely free within the space, and having gotten the girl of his dreams, he dances up a flight of stairs like Fred Astaire to a reprise of the cheeky jazz tune sung earlier at the Yorkist ball to Marlowe's lyric, "Come live with me and be my love." Glossing his performance, McKellen writes: "This celebratory soliloquy of triumph . . . breaks through the convention of naturalism as effortlessly as a song in a musical. . . . On the take used in the film, I spontaneously paused at the top, for another full-stop to the scene, a clenched fist flung in the air before leaving round the corner" (McKellen and Loncraine 1996: 88).

Present-day Shakespeare films, especially those such as Loncraine–McKellen's *Richard III* or Branagh's *Henry V*, work to marry Shakespeare to a psycho-physiological mode of acting which draws on Stanislavskian or Method protocols, currently the dominant paradigm (see Zarilli 2002: 85–98). Indeed, Shakespeare + Stanislavski offers a loose descriptor for the invisible work lying behind McKellen's and Scott-Thomas' performances – work which travels towards but may not become visible *as* performance (Donnellan 2002: 12–13; see also HENDERSON). But what happens when a film *sees* the actor's invisible work, exposes the acting-ness of acting itself? Al Pacino's *Looking for Richard* (1996) does just that, demonstrating a process in which "character" becomes a kind of passing narrative transmitted by a body trained in Method protocols. In Richard's extraordinary soliloquy of conscience, the image track shifts from mid-shots of Pacino-as-Richard to high-angle shots of Pacino-as-actor and cross-cuts between the two: as character and actor address each other across the cut ("Is there a murderer here?" "No," answers Pacino, to which Richard responds, "Yes"), which is the dancer, which the dance? Cuts between the two simultaneously refuse the possibility of synthesis and encourage it, so that spectators seem to watch "rehearsal" set beside "performance." Fragmenting the actor's person in brief, disjunctive takes, the editing interrupts both modes of acting but never controls its significance: rather, the camera contains and then elides over performance, allowing Pacino to restate his presence – and performance to rediscover itself – across ruptures of cinematic style (see Testa 1990: 121, 129). On the one hand, creating a gap between fictional character and performer invites severing the two; on the other, it simultaneously constructs a more complex dynamic, one especially attuned to conveying Richard's doubt and displaced sense of interiority. Not incidentally, rather than relying on conventions familiar from

classical Hollywood cinema, a mode that supports the actor's authority and privileges star presence, Pacino's neo-Brechtian performance
works to deconstruct conventional star acting.

Many spectators, of course, also may see Pacino's Richard as a
character with a cinematic past. For in the savage blankness of his
face, the slightly hooded eyes, the slight twitch of the mouth, evanes-
cent as smoke, before he turns on his prey, his performance as *The
Godfather's* Michael Corleone (1972) comes into view, generating a
productive collision between roles. That phenomenon, where one
role seems to shadow another, and where at times the performer's
presence or persona inhabits both simultaneously or even effaces the
performer–character relation, has become increasingly familiar in
recent Shakespeare films, especially those which move ever closer to
systems of representations and verisimilitudes in the culture and which
feature actors whose bodies and voices, faces and behaviors are associated more with mainstream Hollywood offerings than with Shakespeare. Indeed, at times the link between spectator and performer
does an end run around dramatic character, or bears only an oblique
relation to it, so that a distance opens up between character and
actor, role and person.

It is, for instance, difficult to forget that it is Elizabeth Taylor and
Richard Burton playing Katherina and Petruchio in Franco Zeffirelli's
Taming of the Shrew (1967), even though the celebrity star couple's
presences give their roles an aura of immediacy and authenticity.
Furthermore, an actor's star image may be perceived as stable in non-
Shakespeare films but unstable in Shakespeare films, as with Mel
Gibson's crossover from high-action thrillers such as *Mad Max* and
Lethal Weapon to *Hamlet* (dir. Zeffirelli, 1990). In psychoanalytic terms,
however, celebrity presence provides spectators with a ground, based
on the apparently absolute status of the star, which is fed by whatever topicality burrs onto the actor as representative of the prevailing
culture and of those character traits most admired and/or feared by a
peer community (see McAuley 1999: 95; Quinn 1990: 155–6, 158).
That phenomenon also ties into an erotics of celebrity, especially
apparent in Internet chat rooms associated with recent Shakespeare
films, such as Luhrmann's *Romeo + Juliet*, whose stars, DiCaprio and
Clare Danes, not only brought a fresh immediacy to their roles but
also seemed to embody the dilemmas experienced by young adults
coming of age in a present-day culture of violence.

Although Luhrmann's film marks the onset of a "new wave generation" of Shakespeare films directed towards a youth audience, the

figure who has most energized that phenomenon is Julia Stiles, whose roles in two so-called spinoffs – Kat in *10 Things I Hate About You* (1999), Desi in Tim Blake Nelson's *O* (2001) – and as Ophelia in Almereyda's *Hamlet* (2000) have made her a star, giving her celebrity status. An authoritatively naturalistic actor, she brings an unusual aura of authenticity to Shakespearean acting: completely in her body, absorbed in the moment, her awareness of the camera works to amplify her performances. As Ophelia, she offers a portrait of a young woman who is doubly subjected to the visions of others – within the narrative, to her father, her brother, and Hamlet, as well as by cinematic techniques of *mise-en-scène*, framing, and editing. Given little to say (by Shakespeare and even less in Almereyda's script), hers is a silent performance: Hamlet's photographs, capturing her in close-up, plumb her stillness, conveying the sense that she has lost any subjectivity save as an image – ironically offset by her own penchant for taking, and later destroying, photographs. Not only is she the youngest actor in the film, but her performance rests primarily on how her relatively small body is seen in space. Surrounded from the outset by male figures who attempt to control and manage her, keeping her away from Hamlet, she appears unable to affect what happens to her: frequently, she gets pulled from the center of a shot into shadow or tries to move off screen, seemingly extraneous to the spectacle, a figure who inhabits its margins.

Seen alone for the first time by a waterfall fountain as she waits for Hamlet (who never comes), she walks along its rim, carefully balancing her body. Enhancing the sense that she is forced to live on the edge, this balancing recurs in several key spaces – the fountain, curving windowed walls that open onto emptiness, a swimming pool, the Guggenheim Museum's tiered spiral staircase-ramp. However spare, her performance crackles around those edges: although she seems to be doing less, she is actually doing more, calling up thoughts and emotions that fill her to the brim but which she cannot, dare not, express. It as though she imagines that what Michael Chekhov calls a gossamer veil descends, "veiling" those feelings, generating an economy of expression and sense of presence which a spectator experiences kinesthetically (1991: 165).

When Polonius (Bill Murray) warns her about Hamlet, father and daughter sit on a window seat, the cityscape visible behind them. Avoiding his eyes (her look may betray her), Ophelia gazes at her lap, where she holds a kind of Joseph Cornell box, a nightmare forest from Grimm's fairytales which links metonymically to the other spaces of loss she inhabits; attempting to enter its depths, her fingers explore its surface, but Polonius, wresting it away, further infantilizes her by raising her leg onto his lap and tying her shoelaces, his own ineffectual attempt to manage her body. Later, he pulls her with him to the edge of the indoor swimming pool, where she stands slightly behind him, embarrassed, her head down and body held rigid; the camera tends to ignore her while Polonius, his ramrod-straight back intensifying his ill ease at exposing private matters in public, explains to Claudius and Gertrude that Hamlet is mad, delivering a seemingly pre-rehearsed speech and showing them the poem that Hamlet has written to Ophelia, who ineffectually tries to take the paper from him. As she drifts forward along the poolside and off-screen, Polonius continues ("What do you think of me?"), and the camera "finds" her in a tight close-up which not only marks her pain but also is accentuated by her vision of the water's depths, echoing the earlier shot of the boxed nightmare wood. As her father gestures towards her ("My young mistress thus I did bespeak: / 'Lord Hamlet is a prince out of thy star'"), the camera frames her from behind in midshot, poised on the pool's edge, and then moves slowly in (non-diegetic electronic sound supports the shot). At Polonius' "This must not be," suddenly, seen from below the surface, her figure plunges into the pool, where she sinks, both hands covering her eyes, before a cut returns to the midshot of her from behind at poolside, her head registering ever so slightly a startled reaction, to close off the fantasy. Patching her into a silent soliloquy in space, the sequence gives her a stunning, if momentary, sense of interiority, made even more striking because Hamlet's "To be or not to be," spoken as voiceover, follows immediately from and is keyed by her "not to be" – the actor's, and Ophelia's, perennial answer.

Later she again is manipulated by her father as, while Gertrude and Claudius watch, he sets her up to entrap Hamlet: everything about the *mise-en-scène* – a young woman standing on a low table attended and dressed by others – evokes another, more familiar (or familial) scenario of wedding preparations. But instead of being fitted for a bridal gown Ophelia, her cheeks wet with tears, is being strapped up with a wire. And in the film's equivalent of the nunnery scene, set in Hamlet's apartment, it is her inability to dissemble and her desire for Hamlet that betrays the device. Taking letters from a box, she begins matter-of-factly but cannot bring herself to look at him; when he interrupts ("Are you honest?"), she seems caught unaware by Hamlet's "I loved you not," which strikes her like a blow. As though intensifying their fractured intimacy as well as allowing her to regain her composure, the film cuts away from their figures to follow a jet's vapor trail ascending through blue sky before returning to a midshot of Ophelia, whose shift into profile, masking her tears, keys her whispered "I was the more deceived." Moving closer, Hamlet embraces her, and the camera moves in as Ophelia reaches hungrily towards his kiss, cut off when he discovers the microphone pinned to her shirt. Rising, she utters small animal-like cries, rips off the wire, gathers the letters, and stuffs them back into the box with the wire thrown angrily on top of them: like the film's other surveillance devices, it has canceled out not just the letters but all that has passed between them. The gesture of jamming the lid on the box suggests her realization that her love for him has been thwarted and that ultimately it will destroy her. Characteristically, the scene ends by taking away Ophelia's words and showing her body – in a long shot that follows her pedaling her bicycle through city streets to her studio darkroom where, in midshot, and with Hamlet's words ("Take this plague for your dowry . . . we will have no more marriage") as a gloss, she burns his Polaroid image.

The last time she appears, a high-angle shot reveals her circling the Guggenheim stair, her black-clad figure diminished against the vertiginous space, and then there is a cut to her confrontation with Gertrude, where, standing at the edge of the abyss and about to topple over into it – a visual echo of the fairytale woodland and the pool's depths – the suppressed animal cries of the nunnery scene turn, in her madness, to a full-throated scream, answered (again, characteristically) by one of Claudius' henchmen manhandling her out of sight. Finally (it is a coda), she passes out her photographs of flowers to Laertes and the others, sliding her body, which moves like liquid within the space, along the boundary of a window-walled circular space. Aside from Gertrude's epitaph, the rest is silence.

These are, of course, Hamlet's last words, yet not only do they seem to suit Stiles' arresting performance, they also call attention to a paradigm shift initiated by Branagh's quasi-revolutionary *Henry V*. That shift was predicted and perhaps is best summed up by Salinger's Holden Caulfield: "I just don't see what's so marvelous about Sir Laurence Olivier, that's all. He has a terrific voice and he's a hell of a handsome guy and he's very nice to watch walking or dueling or something but . . . [he] was too much like a goddamn general instead of a sad screwed-up type guy."[6] Although Hamlet's famous speech to the players, "Suit the action to the word, the word to the action," has been read as authorial advice to actors, present-day Shakespearean screen acting might bespeak its own suitability to and within shifting contemporary performance practices with a difference – might, for instance, say, "Play down the voice, play up the body." If nothing else, that phrase gestures towards what might be called the "other performance" – the one lying beyond (Shakespeare's) words. And that, in turn, raises further questions about what methodologies – historic and aesthetic categories, semiological descriptors, body work and effects, star presences, and so on – most usefully can be brought to bear on analyzing such performance work.

Notes

1 On semiotics, see Pearson (1990) and Quinn (1990).
2 Here and throughout I am indebted to Richard Abel.
3 In Shakespeare's text, the body is that of Anne's father-in-law, King Henry VI. An early shooting script marked the refrigerator doors with the names of Shakespeare's rival playwrights, Christopher Marlowe, Thomas Kyd, and Ben Jonson among them. See McKellen and Loncraine (1996: 70).
4 McKellen writes, "Richard inspires himself by playing the fantasy role of romantic lover. . . . [H]e has razored a moustache of screen heroes like Clark Gable, Clifton Webb, David Niven, Douglas Fairbanks" (McKellen and Loncraine 1996: 80).
5 Scott-Thomas did not want to hear the phrase "as it would lessen the later shock of Richard's approach." See McKellen and Loncraine (1996: 76).
6 J. D. Salinger's *Catcher in the Rye*, cited in Ethan Hawke's introduction to Almereyda (2000: xiii).

References and Further Reading

Blau, H. (1987). *The Eye of Prey: Subversions of the Postmodern*. Bloomington: Indiana University Press.
Chekhov, M. (1991). *On the Techniques of Acting*. New York: HarperCollins.
Comolli, J.-L. (1978). "Historical Fiction: A Body Too Much." *Screen* 19.2: 41–53.
Denby, D. (1996). "Bard Again." *New Yorker*, January 15: 49–50.
Donnellan, D. (2002). *The Actor and His Target*. London: Nick Hern.
Dyer, R. (1979). *Stars*. London: BFI Publishing.
Gallagher, C., and T. Laqueur, eds. (1987). *The Making of the Modern Body: Sexuality and Society in the Nineteenth Century*. Berkeley: University of California Press.

Hodgdon, B. (1998). "Replicating Richard: Body Doubles, Body Politics." *Theatre Journal* 50.

—— (1999). "Everything's Nice in America? *William Shakespeare's Romeo + Juliet.*" *Shakespeare Survey* 52: 88–98.

Klawans, S. (1989). "Review of *Henry V.*" *Nation,* October 11: 725–6.

Lane, A. (1996). "Tights! Camera! Action!" *New Yorker,* November 25: 66–77.

McAuley, G. (1999). *Space in Performance: Making Meaning in the Theatre.* Ann Arbor: University of Michigan Press.

Morin, E. (1960). *The Stars.* New York: Grove Press.

Pavis, P. (2003). *Analyzing Performance: Theater, Dance, and Film.* Trans. David Williams. Ann Arbor: University of Michigan Press.

Pearson, R. E. (1990). "'O'er Step not the Modesty of Nature': A Semiotic Approach to Acting in the Griffith Biographs." In Carole Zucker (ed.), *Making Visible the Invisible: An Anthology of Original Essays on Film Acting.* Metuchen, NJ, and London: Scarecrow Press: 1–27.

Quinn, M. L. (1990). "Celebrity and the Semiotic of Acting." *New Theatre Quarterly* 22: 154–61.

Roach, J. (1996). *Cities of the Dead: Circum-Atlantic Performance.* New York: Columbia University Press.

Silverman, K. (1988). *The Acoustic Mirror: The Female Voice in Psychoanalysis and Cinema.* Bloomington: University of Indiana Press.

Smith, B. R. (1999). *The Acoustic World of Early Modern England: Attending to the O-Factor.* Chicago: University of Chicago Press.

Smith, P. (1993). *Clint Eastwood: A Cultural Production.* Minneapolis: University of Minnesota Press.

Testa, B. (1990). "Un Certain Regard: Characterization in the First Years of the French New Wave." In Carole Zucker (ed.), *Making Visible the Invisible: An Anthology of Original Essays on Film Acting.* Metuchen, NJ, and London: Scarecrow Press.

Travers, P. (1996). "Just Two Kids in Love." *Rolling Stone,* November 14: 123–4.

Zarilli, P. B. (2002). *Acting (Re)Considered.* 2nd edn. London and New York: Routledge.

Chapter 6

Shakespeare, Sex, and Violence: Negotiating Masculinities in Branagh's *Henry V* and Taymor's *Titus*

Pascale Aebischer

In recent years, Shakespearean performance studies have benefited from a lively dialogue with film theory and gender studies, resulting in fascinating analyses of the representation of the female body on stage and screen. The same theoretical frameworks can be employed for a consideration of the male body. Both playtexts under discussion here, *Henry V* and *Titus Andronicus*, are concerned with warfare and involve a crisis of masculinity which coincides with a crisis in bodily integrity. Representing the warrior-hero seems, for Shakespeare, to entail a testing of his masculinity to the point at which it risks being fractured, showing a vulnerability of the body culturally associated with femininity.[1] Kenneth Branagh's and Julie Taymor's transposition of the plays into film – a medium which frequently uses the "abnormal body" as a means of "defining . . . the normal body" (Davis 1995: 151) – works to amplify the playtexts' concern with the martial male body's precariousness. Through analysis of key scenes in which masculinity is challenged and/or reaffirmed, I want to establish how these contemporary directors, both of whom had experience staging or performing their respective plays in the theater,[2] make use of the opportunities offered by the film medium to explore these Shakespearean crises of masculinity. What is the impact of the directors' own backgrounds on their treatment of martial men? When the early modern playtexts present the directors with a nexus of sex and violence organized around the male body, how do they negotiate this in terms accessible and relevant for a turn-of-the-millennium audience?

Branagh's *Henry V*: "Saving Your Majesty's Manhood"

Branagh's 1989 *Henry V* not only represented the beginning of a new phase of productivity in the history of Shakespeare on screen, but it also heralded a distinctly turn-of-the-millennium re-vision of Shakespeare's portrayal of martial heroism. In the decade preceding Branagh's film, soldiers and warfare had become heavily mediated through Hollywood's investigation of the traumatic experiences and legacies of Vietnam (e.g., Cimino's 1978 *The Deer Hunter*, Coppola's 1979 *Apocalypse Now*, and Stone's 1986 *Platoon*). In these cinematic representations of modern warfare, the body was the site of intense cultural anxiety about violent masculinity. Soldiers were, on the one hand, glorified for their muscular potency and patriotism (in ways reminiscent of and indebted to the western), and, on the other hand, vilified paradoxically both for their excessive aggression (often sexualized in representations of Americans assaulting Vietnamese women) and their "weakness" in response to trauma (taking drugs, breaking down in tears, losing control of their minds and bodies). Political ambivalence about the justification for war was played out, in these films, on the bodies of the soldiers, for whom – as in Hal Ashby's 1978 *Coming Home* – politically acceptable "male" heroism could sometimes be possible only at the expense of physical disability.

Meanwhile in Britain the Falklands conflict of 1982 had left a similarly complex legacy. The initially patriotic response to the Argentinian invasion of the British islands off the coast of Argentina was increasingly mitigated by resentment of the task force's inadequacy and misgivings about the motivations behind the war. Emblematic was the public perception of Conservative Prime Minister Margaret Thatcher. In her combination of stylized femininity with icy sexlessness, "masculine" aggression, and rigorous policing of the dispossessed at home, Thatcher appeared to be a direct descendent of Shakespeare's own threateningly androgynous Virgin Queen.[3] Not surprisingly, in

113

view of these challenges to conventional masculinity, compounded by the increasing visibility of feminist activists and gay rights campaigners, the late 1980s saw the emergence of a new masculine ideal in the media and advertising. This was "the passive, beautiful, and seductive young man" of Calvin Klein-type advertisements, who was "displayed in ways previously reserved for desirable young women, and given poses and facial expressions previously reserved for the iconography of femininity" (Solomon-Godeau 1995: 70). In the 1980s, then, the stereotypically "masculine," heterosexual warrior-hero of popular culture existed in a dialectic relationship with his "flip-sides." Rambo, the able-bodied patriotic Vietnam veteran who transcends his trauma and reasserts his masculinity through violence, coexisted with disabled fellow-soldiers (shaggy-haired Tom Cruise attempting to lose his heartthrob image as paralyzed Vietnam veteran Ron Kovic in Oliver Stone's 1989 *Born on the Fourth of July*) and passive, beautiful, vulnerable, and sensitive "new" young men, muscular yet without aggression, and of ambivalent sexual orientation.[4]

Kenneth Branagh's body can be read as the site on which this tension between conflicting types of masculinity played out using Shakespeare's (pre)text. The form of heroism embodied by Laurence Olivier in the 1944 film of *Henry V* needed to be revised in 1989. As many critics have pointed out, Olivier's film, sponsored by the wartime British government and with its dedication to the "Commandos and airborne troops of Great Britain," can be seen as part of British World War II propaganda, the battle of Agincourt standing for the anticipated invasion of German-occupied France. Not only did Olivier cut many of the lines in which Shakespeare allows some ambivalence about Henry's project to balance the patriotic appeal of his successful campaign, but certain directorial choices were also clearly designed to enhance the protagonist's heroic status. Olivier's "medieval" battle of Agincourt with its colorful soldiers, elaborate choreography, and extravagant cinematography is beautiful to watch. Its violence is minimized to the extent that, in spite of the high number of casualties referred to in the playtext, "we see very little of the *pain* of combat, very little of its terror – and no blood at all" (Donaldson 1990: 15). The film's attitude towards male heroism is reflected in the body of the king. Literally a knight in shining armor, Olivier's Henry is never anything but clean and impenetrable, as if the metal on his body reflected an inner quality of valor, integrity, and strength. Even though, in stroking the head of the sleeping boy on the eve of Agincourt, Olivier's Henry appropriates the "feminine" quality of nurturing and has something of the effeminate beauty of the matinée idol, this androgyny is, as Donaldson suggests, put at the service of "resuscitati[ng], in an age of doubt and cynicism, . . . the mythology of the loving father-king" (1990: 19). The king's sexual orientation and his leadership are not challenged by his picture-book prettiness, and his integration of traditionally "feminine" features does not seem to come at the cost of self-division.

For Branagh, this unfractured representation of the warrior's body, mind, and mission was not an option. In the introduction to his screenplay, he took issue with Olivier's "seeming nationalistic and militaristic emphasis" and decided that his own interpretation would try to convey "the qualities of introspection, fear, doubt and anger which [he] believed the text indicated." *Henry V*, he thought, "could work as a political thriller, as a detailed analysis of leadership and a complex debate about war" (Branagh 1989b: 9–10). In order to "make it the truly popular film [he] had in mind," he was, in implicit contrast with Olivier's fairytale atmosphere, going to be "gritty" and "realistic" (1989a: 220).

As a result, his heavily edited screenplay contained a whole host of lines in which Shakespeare stresses the violence of warfare, the threat it poses not only to the civilian population but also to the physical integrity of the soldiers and their own perception of their virility. As Michael Williams poignantly muses on the eve of Agincourt, men who go to war risk dismemberment and death: "all those legs and arms and heads chopped off in a battle shall join together at the latter day and cry all 'We died at such a place'" (4.1.135–8). The king's body, too, though idealized in the Chorus' references to the "warlike Harry" who "assume[s] the port of Mars" (0.5–6), is ultimately but a "frail and worthless trunk" (3.6.153), a body whose bones he challenges his opponents to sell as his ransom (4.3.91), anticipating his own physical disintegration. In Branagh's film, with its siege of Harfleur deliberately nodding to the trenches of World War I in which so many soldiers lost their limbs and lives, and its sodden huddle of disenchanted soldiers who would not look amiss in a Vietnam film, mutilation and death are plausible outcomes of battle. Regardless of Henry's displays of physical strength as he throws the herald to the ground when speaking of his potential dismemberment into bones and trunk, his words ring true because he is at that moment also strikingly unarmored and exhausted in mind and body. At its most extreme, the martial ideal of masculinity may well mean leaving one's "valiant bones in France, / Dying like men" (4.3.98–9).

Branagh ventured beyond Olivier in retaining Henry's unexpect-edly gendered and sexualized threats in his speech to the Governor of Harfleur, cut entirely from Olivier's script. While Harfleur is feminized by Shakespeare's Henry – "I will not leave the half-achieved Harfleur / Till in her ashes she lie buried" (3.3.8–9), with "achieve" carrying the charge of "to have sex with" – "impious war . . . with his smirched complexion" (3.3.15–17) is gendered male. Henry, in fact, threatens to assault just about anyone who is not as manly as his "rough and hard of heart" "fleshed soldier[s]" (3.3.11): Harfleur's "fresh fair vir-gins" and "shrill-shrieking daughters" whose locks will be defiled, its silver-bearded fathers whose "most reverend heads" are to be "dashed to the walls," and its "flowering" "naked infants" who will be "spitted upon spikes" (3.3.14, 35–9). The more one listens to Shakespeare's soldiers talk, the more war sounds like rape and sexual conquest – even the Dauphin worries that Frenchwomen, disgusted with French-men whose "mettle is bred out," "will give / Their bodies to the lust of English youth" (3.5.29–30). In Shakespeare's playtext and Branagh's screenplay, the abstract concept of warfare is made concrete (and male) through the bodies of the king and his soldiers, political vio-lence is made personal, and territorial invasion is troped as sex through the repeated threat of rape.

Sexualized warfare is even given a face and body in Princess Katherine, who is significantly first introduced straight after Henry's conquest of Harfleur, with Henry's threat to the virgins still ringing in the audience's ears. Her attempts to learn English, which result in her inadvertent pronunciation of "foot" and "gown" as homonymous with French *foutre* ("fuck") and *con* ("cunt"), have been described by Claire McEachern as a "semantic invasion" of the Princess, in which the "pleasure of punning tempers the pressure of rape" (1994: 54). Katherine's body is not only the site of figurative rape but also of figurative dismemberment. The lesson she learns is, in fact, a Petrarchan blazon of her body, a listing of limbs in which the parts do not quite add up to a whole. Thrusting her hand through the curtains, Katherine, played in Branagh's film by Emma Thompson, merrily enacts the fragmentation of her body as the viewer's eye is repeatedly directed to participate in the inventory of her limbs. Visually and semantically fragmented, with her chaste gown punningly and coarsely revealing her genitals, Katherine is dispossessed of her body. She is a synecdo-che of her country, the virginity which she is forced to yield to Henry equivalent to the "maiden walls" of France's cities, her identity re-duced to being Henry's "fair flower-de-luce" (5.2.317–18, 207–8).

Henry's self-contradictory declaration "I love thee cruelly" (5.2.200) concisely expresses the "incongruity of configuring violence as romance" (McEachern 1994: 54).

It is the more significant, then, in view of Branagh's stated desire to analyze war and his decision to retain most of these lines in which martial masculinity is problematized, shown to be potentially out of control, sexualized, and leading to mutilation and death in the name of "manhood," that his film ultimately evades the issues of sexualized warfare and dismemberment. Henry's victory at Agincourt is turned into the reward for individual fortitude and achievement and his arrogation of Katherine's body transformed into a mutual falling in love, her happy acquiescence in her figurative fragmentation and literal appropriation erasing the associations of violence in their union. If anything, Olivier showed greater awareness of the linking of war and sexual conquest when he made the Dauphin express his anxiety about Frenchwomen's bodies in the presence of Renée Asherson's innocent Princess Katherine, who gasps in horror. Branagh, by contrast, keeps more of the problematic lines but frames them in such a way as to cancel out the aural information through the visuals he provides. His Henry's private relief, whenever he realizes that he need not carry out his threats of violence, is obvious and works to diminish the simultaneous awareness that the threats were genuine (he *does* hang Bardolph). As a result, it is now widely accepted that this film, in spite of its director's insistence on his critique of war, ends up glorifying warfare. Key to this effect is Branagh's representation of his body as an icon of vulnerable and sensitive, yet ultimately unassailable, heterosexual masculinity and the repression of this body's dangerous "others": the dismembered war veteran and the beautiful, passive, potentially homosexual young man of advertising.

Branagh's first appearance as King Henry in the film already heralds his insistent – and narcissistic – self-framing as a strong phallic male. Described by many as a "Darth Vader" figure (e.g., Pursell 1992: 270; Loehlin 1997: 134), Branagh's back-lit silhouette emerges upright and threatening in the open doorway leading to the council chamber. The cinematography for this entrance corresponds to what Paul Smith has identified as a "semiotics of the heroized male body" in Hollywood films, using a mixture of "under-the-chin shots," heavily back-lit shots, and facial close-ups (1995: 83). The approving looks of Henry's courtiers as he walks through their ranks establish him as an unchallenged figure of respect. The exchange of gazes also establishes the atmosphere of sporty camaraderie that characterizes much of the film's representation of warfare: Henry's courtiers clearly are at ease with each other physically, a close-knit group of men sizing up their young leader and keen to go get some action. The scene's assertion of phallic authority is complicated by the fact that when Henry finally sits down and we see his face, his youth and vulnerability are suddenly stressed: the throne dwarfs his normally stocky body while the visible eye make-up gives him a campness that jars with his rugged features. The film's opening thus sets the "ideal" of masculine authority against the disconcertingly "real" androgynous youth who, in the course of this scene and throughout the film, must grow to become the virile leader heralded by the "Darth Vader" entrance.

How much was at stake for Branagh in this first scene is evident from his autobiography, *Beginning*. In it he records that, his voice having gone up an octave in the first take, he reshot his opening speech to make it "considerably butcher" – an adjective he uses several times to denote the type of manhood he is striving for (1989a: 225). *Beginning* is marked by its author's repeated expressions of anxiety about his virility, which seems under constant threat from implications of homosexuality (1989a: 35, 43–4, 49, 50) and peer-group bullying (1989a: 26–7, 224). The anxiety increases with his choice of an acting career, since in his account the profession is strongly associated with campness and homosexuality – the very attributes that were also newly foregrounded in advertising and that Branagh is keen to distance himself from. The result is a rigorous self-scrutiny of Branagh the actor by Branagh the director, so that Branagh emerges as the ideal viewer of the film, both wielder and object of the camera's gaze, the prototype male spectator and critical consumer of his particular brand of "butch" (read: "straight") virility.

This "butchness" is first put under pressure and tested in the scene of the traitors' unmasking (2.2). Expunged by Olivier, this scene plays a key role in Branagh's attempt to bring out the "political thriller" in the play. The handsome young traitors' entrapment is charged with homoeroticism as Henry, surrounded by his courtiers-turned-soldiers, lures them into a false sense of security and physical closeness. The ground for this scene is prepared by Exeter: in his explanation of the particularly intimate relationship between Henry and the treacherous Lord Scroop, the words "bedfellow" and "foreign purse" enter into a peculiar anachronistic play with each other. For while to modern ears "bedfellow" is sexualized, for audiences attuned to Shakespearean bawdy, "purse" is charged with the meaning of "genitals," making it sound as though Henry's lover Scroop had sold him in exchange for

French sexual favors (2.2.8–10). This misinterpretation is given weight in Branagh's *mise-en-scène* by Henry's reassuring grasp of Scroop's hand which, for a moment, looks as though Henry were about to reach for Scroop's crotch. Henry's gentle stroking of the traitor's face is followed by an enraged attack in which he pushes Scroop down on a table and leans over him. Framed as an intimate two-shot, the assault resembles a violent reenactment and/or parody of homosexual union. Scroop's attractive face and lithe body, like the bodies of his fellow-traitors, would not look amiss in a Calvin Klein or Versace advertisement, so their violent rejection by the more stocky, rougher-faced Branagh can be read as a first expulsion of "inadequate" forms of masculinity from his entourage.

The repressed homosexuality of this scene resurfaces in the midst of the dirty scrum of Branagh's Agincourt which, like Olivier's version of the battle, is both heavily edited and vastly amplified with extra-textual material. Gone are not only Pistol's ransom scene, but also Henry's ruthless order for the execution of all French prisoners and Exeter's account of the deaths of York and Suffolk. Though Exeter's lines are cut, their homoerotic charge is translated visually by Branagh's presentation of the final moments of York, one of the last beautiful athletic young men of Branagh's court. The account Branagh cut is, in fact, striking for its figuration of death on the battlefield as a gory *Liebestod* in the tradition of *Romeo and Juliet*. It involves a recognition of the dead loved one by York, a last embrace and kiss, the promise that their souls will be reunited in heaven, and the pathetic union of the lovers in a tableau of death: "over Suffolk's neck / he threw his wounded arm and kissed his lips, / And so, espoused to death, with blood he sealed / A testament of noble-ending love" (4.6.24–7). Branagh's filmic narrative does not include a kiss and last embrace, but the conventions employed to capture York's death are borrowed from mainstream cinema's standard representation of sex scenes. In slow motion, underlined by Patrick Doyle's dramatic music on a soundtrack on which all battle sounds except the splashing of mud and clashes of weapons are momentarily erased, York is surrounded by six adversaries. Stabbed in the groin (the location of the wound invisible but inferable), his body arches backward, his face contorted in an expression of intense feeling that could denote either agony or orgasm (or both). Followed immediately by a shot of Pistol's grief-stricken face affectionately bending towards that of the dead Nym, the death of York is full of disavowed homoeroticism. Even the spurt of blood from his mouth has a disturbingly erotic quality in this intimate battle sequence which neatly fits Steve Neale's analysis of popular cinema's repression of homosexuality. Since the implied viewer of mainstream cinema in general (and Branagh's film in particular) is male, Neale argues, the eroticism of looking at the male body and/or any explicit presentation of homosexuality is routinely disavowed, repressed, or dealt with obliquely. This "repression of any explicit avowal of eroticism in the act of looking at the male," Neale suggests, "seems structurally linked to a narrative content marked by sado-masochistic phantasies and scenes" (1993: 16). The violence of York's battlefield death and Henry's unmasking of the traitors can, then, be read as allowing an erotic look at the attractive male body in which the object of the gaze is punished for his implied homosexuality and erased from the film through his death.

The ideal of masculinity which emerges through this elimination of alternative modes (including the expunction, one after the other, of the grotesque Falstaff, Bardolph, and Nym, followed by Pistol who slinks out of the film) is that incorporated by Branagh himself. Surrounded by images of steely men – the French knights slamming down the visors on their helmets and the massive figure of armor-clad Exeter – Branagh's body, in its textile and leather outfit, looks dangerously vulnerable and coded for its penetrability. Yet Branagh's awareness of "the horrors of a hand-to-hand medieval combat" notwithstanding (1989a: 141), mutilation is not represented on his battlefield – even York's emasculation is only gestured at. Dismemberment is replaced by the ubiquitous mud (which is disabling only in the mildest sense) and the repeated camera focus on "English" faces distorted in physical effort.[5] The literally disabling experience of battle is thus transformed into something which, though physically taxing, can be eventually washed and slept off. Branagh's heroic virility is forged through his combination of vulnerability and momentary weakness (he collapses twice from exhaustion after battle) with physical endurance and sheer willpower. The victory of Branagh's Henry, who is not so much a medieval knight in shining armor as a "complicated, doubting, dangerous young professional" (Branagh 1989a: 139), is one of driven determination translated into physical stamina.

This is one of the crucial ingredients that make the "Non nobis" sequence which concludes Agincourt such a powerful moment. The tracking shot that follows Henry's painful progress through the devastated battlefield and concludes by looking up at his erect and victorious figure on a cart is the type of shot conventionally associated with the cinematic representation of the triumphant male hero (Smith

1995: 83). Cinematically, the shot is thus linked with Henry's first "Darth Vader" appearance – but now there is no longer a discrepancy between the "ideal" and the "real." As for that first scene, Branagh seems to have taken extra care to monitor his performance, playing it back on video after each take to make sure that he got it right (Branagh 1989a: 236). The tracking shot is accompanied by a rousing chorus of male voices that builds irrepressibly towards an emotional climax which visually is firmly associated with the lone figure of Henry. We have just seen him at his physical lowest, barely able to stand up. Next thing we know, to the choral accompaniment that seems to be singing his, rather than God's, praises, he overcomes this weakness not to fight another battle, but to carry a dead boy. This is an altruistic show of strength, homosocial in its purpose and, through the roughly affectionate way in which Henry's gloved hand ruffles the boy's hair, unambiguously coded as sexually disinterested ("butch," in fact). With the same gesture, the now very world-weary and adult Henry differentiates himself clearly from the androgyny associated with his own earlier "boyhood" in the oversized throne.

The screenplay describes the final Agincourt close-up on Henry's "blood-stained and exhausted face" as revealing "the dreadful price they have all had to pay for this so-called victory" and suggests that Henry's lowered head is a sign of "shame" (1989b: 114). What I see is different: a male rite of passage in which the young initiate has overcome his physical weakness. Though vulnerable (no armor) and sensitive (his show of emotion at the deaths of others), he has proved himself to be a man and is now celebrated by a chorus of approving grown men as their leader. The bent head is a show of humility, yes, but the type of humility one associates with "stooping to accept the Olympic Gold medal in the traditional and familiar close-up of a successful challenger" (Pursell 1992: 272). With the English army virtually reduced to the rugged, righteous, sturdy, and middle-aged, Branagh emerges from the mud of battle like a newborn hero, ready to be scrubbed clean to get the ultimate manly prize: the French princess. In its expurgation of alternative bodies, the price that has to be paid for the acquisition of the "butchness" necessary to win Katherine/Emma Thompson and lead the disenchanted British soldiers/unruly Brian Blessed towards ultimate victory/financial success, Branagh's film exposes the crisis of masculinity at the end of the 1980s. In its peculiar blend of "new man" sensitivity and "butchness," the film offers, in the end, a consolidation of rather than a challenge to conventional martial masculinity. But the very self-consciousness that goes into the erasure of alternative bodies and the sadness that accompanies the deaths of Bardolph, York, and the boy betray Branagh's own discomfort with the "depressingly male piece" that was to be the basis of his international success (1989a: 237).

More Muddy Men: Taymor's *Titus*

Julie Taymor's 1999 *Titus* was the first full-blown Shakespeare feature film to be directed by a woman and also the first feature adaptation of Shakespeare's most brutal play. More than any other play, *Titus Andronicus* violates the integrity of the human body and reveals how easily metaphors of dismemberment can punningly slip into literal mutilation – "lend me thy hand and I will give thee mine," says Titus to Aaron in preparation for his hand-amputation (3.1.188). Here, the threat of physical disintegration and sexualized warfare contained in the words of *Henry V* is carried out on the bodies of the characters, who are raped, hacked to pieces, disemboweled, burnt, and ground to dust. The play does not allow either director or viewers to look away from Shakespeare's disturbing picture of the human body at its breaking point. Taymor seems to have been drawn to the play precisely because of the way it interrogates Western culture's fascination with violence as entertainment and its potential to illuminate the horrors of the twentieth century (Taymor 2000a: 174). Instead of Vietnam and the Falklands, the Holocaust is a central influence and Fascist Italy literally provides the backdrop for her film, with Mussolini's government buildings and 1930s fashion constituting key elements of Dante Ferretti's design.

Richard Burt's assessment that Taymor's "indirect references to the Holocaust via Italian and German Fascism . . . help save her film as a serious engagement with a serious tragedy" (2001: 80) is ungenerous and ignores the fact that her horizon stretched far beyond Fascism to the theater of violence of Roman antiquity; genocide and mutilations in the early 1990s; and contemporary high school shootings and drug crime in the United States. Particularly resonant throughout her film is the Balkans war. Its putative combatants and victims literally enter the film in the Coliseum scenes, which were shot in Croatia just before a renewed flaring-up of the conflict, using members of the Croatian police academy as Titus' victorious army. On the DVD, Harry Lennix (Aaron) comments wryly that the policemen "have a history of being much more than adorable." In interviews, moreover,

Taymor repeatedly linked the "honor-killing" of Lavinia to the widely reported Bosnian practice of killing women who, during the war, had been raped by Serbs in a systematic campaign of rape-as-ethnic-cleansing. By 1998–9, the paradigm of Vietnam had been superseded by images of "clinical" warfare in the Gulf, masterminded by experienced older professionals like General Schwarzkopf and Colin Powell (both of whom Taymor explicitly compares to Titus [2000a: 174]). More relevant than the "Vietnam syndrome" now was the deranged, primitive ethnic violence of massacres, rapes, and mutilations in Rwanda and the Balkans, and the seemingly unconnected, inexplicable aggression evident in American youth culture.

Complementing these historical points of reference in Taymor's film are cultural/artistic images of the human body, such as her deliberate layered invocations of Degas' ballerina, Marilyn Monroe, and Grace Kelly in her portrayal of Lavinia. This is possibly where her film differs most from Branagh's. True, Branagh's construction of masculinity was inflected by popular culture, but he scarcely ventured beyond simple allusion. Taymor shows far greater awareness of the fact that the body is comprehensible to us only through representation and that this representation is inflected by cultural preconceptions and archetypes which determine how bodies are "read." None of the bodies in her film simply "is"; instead, bodies are positioned in a cultural hall of mirrors, where each reflects a multitude of other bodies that have gone before. As a result, her bodies demand to be read on two levels at once, both as themselves (a *referential reading* that might include allusion to historical context) and as pointing to a larger construct beyond immediate referentiality (a *symbolic reading*). Christine Gledhill's analysis of popular fictions provides a useful framework: "On the one hand," she says,

> the human figure commands recognition by its reference to social, cultural and psychic attributes – gender, age, class, ethnicity, sexual orientation, and so on – on the other hand the human body functions metaphorically, symbolically, mythically. . . . [T]he archetype exceeds its socially specific sources, emerging as a distillation of stereotypical features and evolving through an accretion of uses across decades, forms and national cultures. (1995: 75, 81)

The playtext Taymor is working with is particularly appropriate for such a perception of the human body as both referential and symbolic, reflecting archetypes, since a vacillation between the literal and the metaphorical is a key element in Shakespeare's script. If read merely on a literal level, the mutilations, murders, and fancy recipes are simply absurd – there is no way that Lavinia would still be running around after the loss of blood she has been suffering, and from a cookery point of view, pastry made of ground bones does not sound like a good idea. The play only begins to make sense if the reader/ spectator learns to interpret a body like Lavinia's both as that of an individual sufferer, the mutilated rape victim, *and* as a representative of "headless Rome" (1.1.189), the seat of civilization that has come under attack from barbarism. What Taymor's film achieves is an extension of Shakespeare's dual representation of the body to encompass distinctly twentieth-century referential and symbolic meanings.

Taymor's opening sequence functions as a preface in which she introduces her viewer to the type of multi-level reading she favors. It takes the spectator from a bourgeois twentieth-century kitchen through a time-warp to the center of a Roman arena. The "modern" boy playing with action figures of Roman soldiers with which he stages his own little theater of kitchen-table violence is transported into an ancient Rome that nevertheless remains firmly contemporary, mediated through the boy's eyes. When the toy soldier the boy has dropped in the mud is reflected and multiplied in the "real" muddy soldiers who suddenly fill the arena, the effect is unsettling because referentiality itself is disturbed: is the toy a representation of the soldier or the soldier a representation of the toy? The blurring of boundaries between "real" and "representation" here suggests that the "real" itself is already a representation of a preexisting mental image.

The bodies of the soldiers, their "armour and visible skin . . . cracked and black as soot as if emerging from an inferno" (Taymor 2000a: 20), are layered with multiple significations. On a referential level, they are simultaneously the soldiers of Titus' army, the "real" Croatian policemen who may have been involved in the atrocities of the Balkans war, and Taymor's recreation of "the Chinese terracotta soldiers when they found them, that whole army" (Johnson-Haddad 2000: 35). Symbolically, they are living toys (suggesting a lack of autonomy and individuality) and figments of the boy's imagination conjured up by his violent play, revealing how easily the presumed innocence of boys' play can metamorphose into full-blown violence. The soldiers can thus be read as grown-up versions of the boy whose fleshly, "soft" vulnerability is transformed into the implicit "hard" brittleness of clay figures. Part men, part statuesque machines, they are Taymor's representation of archetypal warriors, dehumanized, with bodies that are at once steely – even their skins are caked in armor-like clay – and susceptible to mutilation. Their description in the screenplay is telling: Taymor writes that their right arms "appear *as* swords" (Taymor 2000a: 24, emphasis added), suggesting a prosthetic substitution of swords for chopped-off hands which is a sign both of their own susceptibility to dismemberment and their ability to become phallic weapons threatening other bodies.

The brittleness of martial masculinity is fully revealed in the next scene, which is set in communal baths. "As the clay streams off the bodies of the soldiers, revealing their skin," Taymor explains, "the actors transform from archaic sculptures to human beings. In essence, the film moves into a mode of 'reality'" (1999: 226). It is here that their vulnerability is most shockingly exposed and made to resonate with Western art's obsession with the fragmentation of the body and its aesthetization through painting and sculpture. For here, the beautiful, muscular nude bodies of the soldiers are clearly fetishized by the camera, held up as erotic objects of contemplation while the narrative momentarily stops in the way typical of mainstream cinema's presentation of the *female* body.[6] As our eyes read the image from the left of the frame to the right, enjoying those statuesque nudes, our gaze is violently arrested by the sight of the last soldier in the row, whose right leg is amputated below the knee. At the moment in which the dismembered body is seen, the spectator's pleasure is fractured. The missing limb functions as a sobering "reminder of the whole body about to come apart at the seams. It provides a vision of, a caution about, the body as a construct . . . always threatening to become its individual parts" (Davis 1995: 132). Taymor wrenches her viewers from the position of consumers of erotic *art* to a *real*ization of the violence that lies behind it, a realization that involves the viewers' recognition of their own physical vulnerability at the sight of dismemberment. As with the violence which underlies the scenes of repressed homoeroticism in Branagh's film, here, too, the male body seems to be available to the viewer's eroticizing gaze only at the cost of its wounding. When the clay is washed off, the soldiers and their statuesque bodies are imbued with life and reality, and the "perfection" (invoking the Latin sense of "completeness") of the nude is transformed into the "imperfection," the lack, the vulnerability of the naked body. Taymor here mobilizes the distinction made by art critic Kenneth Clark between the "nude" and the "naked" – between the body "clothed" in art, "balanced, prosperous, confident," versus the "huddled and defenceless" naked body "deprived" of protective clothing (1985: 1) – and reveals that the "nude" already contains the "naked" in it. The unassailable, beautiful body of the warrior, dressed in artistic photography and held up as an erotic object of contemplation, is also the unprotected, dismembered body of the war veteran.

The power of this moment – which is actually very brief but can be seen as emblematic of the whole film's treatment of the human body – lies in the layers of its revelations. For, having de-aestheticized and exposed the soldier in his nakedness, the film then prompts us to redress him in "art" once we realize that the missing leg evokes the fragmented statues of Roman and Greek antiquity. At the moment at which we recognize the allusion to ancient art, to our cultural heritage (a link which is reinforced through the film's deployment of fragmented statuary in sets, props, and "Penny Arcade Nightmare" collages), the momentarily horrifying body becomes beautiful again. The panic of fragmentation Taymor briefly provokes, seeking to "activate a masochistic gaze, capable of identifying with loss and suffering" (McCandless 2002: 488), is overlaid by the aesthetically distanced appreciation of the image and its clever allusion.

But there remains something to the allusion that is naggingly "wrong," namely the body's sex. Within Western culture, the aestheticized dismembered body – the existence of countless limbless statues of male figures (and of male real-life amputees) notwithstanding – is gendered female, its prototype the Venus de Milo.[7] In her "Director's Notes," Taymor explicitly evokes the Venus, yet the body she models on her is not that of a male warrior but Lavinia's, "stripped to her torn petticoats on the top of a truncated column . . . soon to be completed with truncated limbs and all" (2000a: 184). It is the body of Lavinia which bears the principal burden of metaphorical and physical disintegration in Shakespeare's playtext in her triple mutilation of hands and tongue, *her* body which is subjected to rape, *hers* which is associated with mud in Titus' description of her as "the spring whom [the rapists] have stain'd with mud" (5.2.170). Even the dismembered body politic of Rome is gendered female in this playtext which, while it includes male mutilation, chooses to focus its anxieties about dismemberment on the female. Titus' hand-amputation may well take place onstage, but throughout the play he remains the able body to Lavinia's disabled one, comparing her inability to beat her chest with her hand and express herself with his ability not only to beat his chest, but also to "interpret all her martyred signs" and speak for her (3.2.36). His own amputation is associated with hers to the point that it is she who ends up carrying his hand in her mouth in an iconic image of grotesque physical dislocation.

What happens in Taymor's film, then, is an intriguing reversal of Shakespeare's gendering of dismemberment. In the playtext, Lavinia's body is re-membered verbally by the men who love her. When they do so, as in Marcus' lamenting evocation of her absent "pretty fingers," "lily hands," and "sweet tongue" (2.3.42, 44, 49), the blazon's enumeration of limbs (like the blazon of Katherine's English lesson in *Henry V*) only works to exacerbate her fragmentation. But in the film, Lavinia's hands are quickly restored through her nephew's thoughtful provision of wooden prosthetics. As though the sight of female dismemberment was too much to bear, too literally Medusa-like in its power to make grown men like Lucius fall to the ground in figurative emasculation (3.1.65–6),[8] the film literally reassembles her body into an optical whole. Not only that: after the initial horrible image of her helpless figure on a tree-stump in the midst of a swamp ravaged by fire – an image which hauntingly incorporates the playtext's association of Lavinia with lopped branches and a muddy spring – Taymor "cleans up" her Lavinia. In the course of a few scenes, Lavinia's broken-up, grotesquely leaking body is restored to its original beauty and seeming physical perfection through the use of camouflaging costume, prosthetics, hairstyle, and camera-work. Disturbingly, as David McCandless notes, "The iconic hands re-dress Lavinia's loss. . . . Combined with the focus on her unflawed face, they enable her to inhabit the phantom cultural body and even, as a fragile, still-beautiful woman, to attract a desiring look. . . . [T]hat look implicitly disavows her lack" (2002: 508). Femininity, in Taymor's film, is coded less through its susceptibility to penetration and fragmentation than through its impermeability, emblematized in Tamora's golden body-armor and metal dresses. Tellingly, these costumes were designed specifically to suggest Tamora's "masculine and feminine powers" (Taymor 2000a: 181), giving her a third gender (androgyny) that places her beyond the predicaments associated with either sex.

Contrasting with patched-up Lavinia and unassailable Tamora are the wounded *male* bodies which the film insistently parades before us. Physical pain and dismemberment, in Taymor's vision, are gendered male. Her screenplay tellingly distinguishes between the mental "trauma" and "shame" felt by mangled Lavinia and the physical "incredible pain" suffered by the freshly amputated Titus (2000a: 93, 105). Unlike the elaborate prosthetic twigs and woodcarvings used for Lavinia's stumps, Titus' stump is insistently kept "unrepaired," merely

127

wrapped in towels or capped in black plastic. Its wound is reopened, his body's vulnerability insisted on in the scene where Taymor sits his hunched naked body in the bathtub, making him write mad messages with blood drawn from his stump with a syringe-pen. Blood is also drawn from bare-chested Alarbus prior to his offscreen mutilation and disembowelment, his gleaming entrails brought back for onscreen ritual burning. Later, in one of the "Penny Arcade Nightmare" sequences, Alarbus' wounded, panting torso reappears surrounded by chopped-off arms and legs that swirl towards the viewer. Another collage combines the head of Mutius with the body of a sacrificial lamb. The enormous, definitively broken-up, and eroding sculpted hand and foot that lie in the streets of Rome look male, as opposed to the female limbs in the woodcarver's shop which are used for the re-membering of Lavinia. Male prisoners, like Titus' sons and Aaron, are presented to us tied up and bare-chested in images that, once more, seem to punish the male body for its exposure to a potentially eroticizing gaze. Aaron's body, in particular, is first constructed (through a combination of costume, body art, and camera-work) as an erotic/exotic object of orientalist desire, whose ritual scarring works simultaneously as a performance of racial difference and as an intimation of the wounding that attends the male body in this film.[9] When he is subsequently subjected to Lucius' physical violence and finally turned into a sacrificial Christ-figure, outstretched arms tied to a pole and wearing a loin cloth, we are aligned with the wordless audience in the Coliseum's bleachers, our passive spectatorship making us complicit in his punishment.

A side effect of this regendering of vulnerability and pain as male is that Shakespeare's representation of sexualized warfare through the rape of Lavinia is deprived of its sting, as is a large part of Taymor's invocation of the Balkans conflict as a context in which to read Lavinia's fate.[10] For while she uses Bosnian "honor-killings" as a means of justifying Titus' killing of his daughter, normalizing an act which even Saturninus describes as "unnatural and unkind" (5.3.47), when it comes to using the same historical context of waging war on an ethnic group through the impregnation of its women, Taymor shies away from the paradigm of Bosnia and seeks refuge in the idea of the corruptibility of innocent youth. Far from being portrayed as the rapist-soldiers of ethnic warfare, or as the playtext's perverters of Petrarchan love conventions and Rome's barbarous assailants, Chiron and Demetrius share the campness of Alan Cummings' Saturninus and are visually associated with disenchanted Western youth culture.

Their lithe young bodies, dressed in extravagant clingy outfits or tight leather trousers, are akin to *fin-de-siècle* camp, the conventions of heavy metal, and the gay iconography of Mapplethorpe and Calvin Klein. They are clearly distinguished in terms of body type, gestures, and accessories from the self-sufficient masculinity embodied by Lennix's Aaron and the more traditionally virile ("butch"?) bodies of Titus' kinsmen who would not look amiss in Branagh's army. Surrounded by the paraphernalia of disaffected turn-of-the-millennium youth – video games, rock music, beer, drugs, cigarettes – their aggression is explained away as the effect of social circumstances and indoctrination by evil Aaron, just as Saturninus' wickedness is associated with Tamora's control over him. Aaron and Tamora thus function in the film, as in the playtext, as two alien, exotic, powerfully sexualized creatures onto whom evil can be comfortably displaced. In an interview, Taymor herself explained that, in her eyes, these "boys aren't killers or rapists; they didn't come up with the idea on their own. But it's amazing how innocence can be twisted" (Johnson-Haddad 2000: 36).

Chiron's androgyny is particularly disturbing in this context: the more mindlessly aggressive of the two brothers and eventually the embodiment of Rape, he is also the more "effeminate" in traditional terms. When the brothers' sparring takes on the shape of parodic love-making, Demetrius, a phallus-shaped cushion squeezed between his legs, jumps on top the spread-eagled passive and "feminized" Chiron. Chiron sometimes wears his long hair in pigtails, he slouches in the manner of a teenager ill at ease in his body, and when acting out the concept of Rape, he appears in drag. Even though Taymor insists that Chiron's appearance in stockings, knickers, and a little girl's training bra was meant to suggest the destruction of innocence, the male body in female underwear is more likely to evoke transvestism. Rape, then, is not the effect of sexualized warfare and male aggression pushed to its destructive worst. Instead, it is represented as the result of the fumbling for sexual and gender identity of a confused, drugged-out, disenchanted, turn-of-the-millennium teenager who could easily have let out his frustrations by shooting his classmates and teachers instead. His aggression is neither primarily sexual, nor truly political, but an expression of restless frustration and confusion.

Taymor's distinction between the Andronici's "straight" and virile bodies (even if fractured) as opposed to the "queer," decadent bodies of their opponents reinforces the traditional valorization of the former and the demonization of the latter. It also allows for a conventional recuperation of "queerness": since Chiron's confused aggression is linked to his youth, the film suggests that, had he survived being baked into a pie, he might well have turned into a decent citizen later in life (after all, though he has killed a man, raped a woman, and then hacked her into pieces, Taymor says he is no rapist or killer . . .). Seen in this context, Young Lucius' exit from the film with Aaron's baby in his arms can be read as the victory of decency over decadence. The sensitive and compassionate boy survivor walks into the hope-filled dawn of the new millennium, where he will use his knowledge about the vulnerability of the male body to good effect and save lives rather than destroy them. Over the sacrificial body of Aaron, the black man who becomes both Christ and, through the evocation of lynching rituals, the embodiment of white American culture's collective racial guilt, the white boy can pick up and nurture the black baby in a brighter land of the future. Though the film ends, as it more or less begins, in the Croatian version of the Roman Coliseum, invoking once more the contexts of Italian Fascism and warfare of the Balkans, these contexts are finally superseded by the American frames of reference. As the remnants of the old world with their sexual murkiness, fractured bodies, and ethnic and religious warfare between white communities are covered up by plastic sheets, the dawn the boys exit towards seems to be a utopian America of racial integration and physical integrity. The abandonment of the European frame of reference, the literal cover-up of the butchery at Titus' dinner table, and the distinct artificiality of the dawn Young Lucius is moving towards reveal the strain that accompanies this upbeat ending. In both these films that interrogate masculinity in Shakespeare's playtexts and late twentieth-century culture, a heavy price is paid for the final integrity of the male body.

Notes

1 See de Lauretis on the cultural gendering of subjectivity, violence, and action as male and the association of femininity with the positions of passive obstacle and victim (1987: 43–4). Thanks to Philip Shaw and Mark Rawlinson for their thoughts on the male body and to Rob Hardy and Emma Depledge for their feedback.
2 Branagh played Henry for Adrian Noble's 1984 RSC production; Taymor staged *Titus Andronicus* for "Theater for a New Audience" in New York in 1994.

3 See Shaughnessy (1994) and Loehlin (1997) on Branagh's stage and screen Henrys in the contexts of the Falklands and Thatcherism.
4 See Bordo's chapter "Beauty (Re)Discovers the Male Body" for the bisexual appeal (and gay origins) of the passive young men in advertising (Bordo 1999). The casting of lithely muscular Tom Cruise as the disabled veteran epitomizes the association of these seemingly opposed figurations of the male body in that decade's cultural imagination.
5 The fullest analysis of Branagh's mud use is Hedrick's (1997).
6 Mulvey (1975) provides the standard discussion of the implicitly male camera's fetishization of the female body in mainstream cinema.
7 Both Nead (1992) and Davis (1995) discuss the aesthetic tradition of truncated Venuses at length.
8 See Davis' analysis of the disabled body's Medusa-like qualities (1995: 131–40).
9 For a more extensive analysis of racial difference in *Titus*, see Aebischer (2004: 118–21).
10 On the politics of Taymor's treatment of rape, see Aebischer (2002).

References and Further Reading

Aebischer, Pascale (2002). "Women Filming Rape in Shakespeare's *Titus Andronicus*: Jane Howell and Julie Taymor." *Études Anglaises* 55: 136–47.
—— (2004). *Shakespeare's Violated Bodies: Stage and Screen Performance*. Cambridge: Cambridge University Press.
Berger, Maurice et al., eds. (1995). *Constructing Masculinity*. London: Routledge.
Bordo, Susan (1999). *The Male Body*. New York: Farrar, Straus, and Giroux.
Burt, Richard (2001). "Shakespeare and the Holocaust: Julie Taymor's Titus is Beautiful, or Shakesploi Meets (the) Camp." *Colby Quarterly* 37.1: 78–106. Repr. in Burt (2002b).
Clark, Kenneth (1985 [1956]). *The Nude: A Study of Ideal Art*. Harmondsworth: Penguin.
Davis, Lennard J. (1995). *Enforcing Normalcy: Disability, Deafness, and the Body*. London: Verso.
de Lauretis, Teresa (1987). *Technologies of Gender: Essays on Theory, Film, and Fiction*. Bloomington: Indiana University Press.
Gledhill, Christine (1995). "Women Reading Men." In Pat Kirkham and Janet Thumim (eds.), *Me Jane: Masculinity, Movies and Women*. London: Lawrence and Wishart.
Hedrick, Donald K. (1997). "War is Mud: Branagh's *Dirty Harry V* and the Types of Political Ambiguity." In Boose and Burt, eds.: 45–66.
Johnson-Haddad, Miranda (2000). "A Time for *Titus*: An Interview with Julie Taymor." *Shakespeare Bulletin* 18: 34–6.

McCandless, David (2002). "A Tale of Two *Titus*es: Julie Taymor's Vision on Stage and Screen." *Shakespeare Quarterly* 53: 487–511.

McEachern, Claire (1994). "*Henry V* and the Paradox of the Body Politic." *Shakespeare Quarterly* 45: 33–56.

Mulvey, Laura (1975). "Visual Pleasure and Narrative Cinema." *Screen* 16.3: 6–18.

Nead, Lynda (1992). *The Female Nude: Art, Obscenity and Sexuality*. London: Routledge.

Neale, Steve (1993). "Masculinity as Spectacle: Reflections on Men and Mainstream Cinema." In Steven Cohan and Ina Rae Hark (eds.), *Screening the Male: Exploring Masculinities in Hollywood Cinema*. London: Routledge: 9–20. Repr. from *Screen* 24.6 (1983).

Pursell, Michael (1992). "Playing the Game: Branagh's *Henry V*." *Literature/ Film Quarterly* 20: 268–75.

Shakespeare, William (1995). *Henry V*. Ed. T. W. Craik. London: Routledge.

Shakespeare, William (1995). *Titus Andronicus*. Ed. Jonathan Bate. London: Routledge.

Shaughnessy, Robert (1994). *Representing Shakespeare*. Hemel Hempstead: Harvester Wheatsheaf.

Smith, Paul (1995). "Eastwood Bound." In Maurice Berger et al. (eds.), *Constructing Masculinity*. London: Routledge: 77–97.

Solomon-Godeau, Abigail (1995). "Male Trouble." In Maurice Berger et al. (eds.), *Constructing Masculinity*. London: Routledge: 68–76.

Taymor, Julie (1999). "*Titus*." In Eileen Blumenthal and Julie Taymor, *Julie Taymor: Playing with Fire: Theater, Opera, Film*. New York: Harry N. Abrams.

Chapter 7

Figuring the Global/ Historical in Filmic Shakespearean Tragedy

Mark Thornton Burnett

I

Over the past decade, attention in the humanities and social sciences has been turning with a new urgency to the phenomenon of globalization. Dramatic changes in the organization of production and social relations, a compression of the time-space continuum, and interpenetrations at the level of politics and culture – all have been singled out as among globalization's constituent components. Other manifestations include deterritorialization and the diffusion of identical consumer goods, as a result of which border crossings have become commonplace and cultural homogeneity normative. One of the most salient incarnations of the global, however, is to be found in film, with Hollywood representing a forceful cinema industry that has put its competitors into the shade. As recent studies such as *Global Hollywood* (Miller et al. 2001) and *Hollyworld: Space, Power, and Fantasy in the American Economy* (Hozic 2001) indicate, the tendency has been to foster dominant screen images, practices, and expectations that have dictated filmmaking in a variety of styles and environments. This essay argues that, in deploying modes of popular entertainment, editorial restlessness, action-oriented narratives, intertextual borrowings, and postmodern registers, a discrete group of Shakespeare films – Jeremy Freeston's *Macbeth* (1997), Kenneth Branagh's *Hamlet* (1996),

Michael Bogdanov's *Macbeth* (1998), Michael Almereyda's *Hamlet* (2000), Gregory Doran's *Macbeth* (2001), Billy Morrissette's *Scotland, PA* (2001), and Stephen Cavanagh's *Hamlet* (2005) – displays an acute responsiveness to the conventions and exigencies of the global Hollywood machine.

But this is not to suggest that these screen versions of two of Shakespeare's most celebrated tragedies are marked by a deindividualized sameness. On the contrary, this essay contends that, because "the 'global' is itself constructed through local practices" (O'Byrne 1997: 73), these films betray a complex relationship to mondial models, wed local and global concerns, and reveal an ultimately "glocal" appearance.[1] In the case of film versions of *Macbeth*, the local, perhaps not surprisingly, suggests itself as Scotland and as all things "Scottish." Where film versions of *Hamlet* are concerned, the local, less obviously, is enshrined in evocations of, and references to, Ireland. Writing recently on Shakespeare in the theater, Sarah Werner observes that, "One of the persistent myths of scholarship, despite the body of theory that tries to counter it, is that we can objectively scrutinize our subjects." She concludes: "the role of the personal is a crucial element in working with performed Shakespeare, a factor that is impossible to separate out from the seemingly discrete status of 'the text' and 'the production'" (Werner 2001: 70). Taking on board Werner's salutary counsel, this essay makes no rash claims for objectivity. Instead, it takes as its point of departure the mixed cultural location of its author. I am an Englishman with Scottish ancestry living and working in Northern Ireland and, as such, am regularly confronted with the productive, if uneasy, implications of teaching, and thinking about, an icon of the British establishment in a problematically postcolonial context. My own experience leads me to figurations prompted by a particular critical environment and to connections which may not be as striking to another onlooker. Discernment and interpretation are themselves part of a "glocal" process, which means, in this case, that even if Scotland and Ireland do not appear immediately relevant, they will feature as important for the appropriately located commentator. Films take on different complexions according to the different perspectives from which they are judged.

With these provisos in mind, this essay argues that, via Scotland and Ireland, which are associated both with the national particular and with constructions of past traditions, screen versions of *Hamlet* and *Macbeth* enter into a critical dialogue with the historical process. Here, of course, one faces the thorny question of precisely how "history" can be defined and constituted. Commentators such as Michel Foucault argue that history must be understood as an expression "of rupture, of discontinuity" (Foucault 1986: 4) rather than as a continuous, upward development; moreover, because there is no "inviolable identity of . . . origin" (Foucault 1977: 142), the past is impossible authentically to recover. As Jacques Derrida writes, "the past . . . can never be lived in the originary or modified form of presence" (Derrida 1991: 42). Other commentators build upon these formulations. Hayden White contends that history is essentially fictional due to its "irreducible ideological component" (White 1973: 21), while Fredric Jameson claims that "'real' history" has been superseded by "aesthetic styles" (Jameson 1991: 20) and effects.

Such a skeptical and dismantling treatment of history is itself, perhaps, one consequence of globalization; as Alan Munslow writes, "the growth of exploitative capitalism, with its commodification of labour . . . and the worsening dispossession of . . . the underdeveloped globe" (1997: 15) has made it increasingly difficult to believe in metanarratives of progress, in the reliability of representation, and in the possibility of objective judgment. As a result, history has generally been reconceived both as the necessarily flawed endeavor to reconstruct the mediated traces of experience and as a practice that, obeying certain rules and conventions, governs the production of knowledge. In this context, the films under discussion are once again pertinent. Aware of their own methods and techniques, they demonstrate the ways in which the past is recoverable only via signs and stereotypes even as they yearn for, and find inspiration in, an ideal of unblemished historical resurrection. Thus, the unwilling conclusion of the screen *Macbeth*s is that Scotland, rather than a "compelling metaphor for the transnational playground," as Courtney Lehmann has recently argued (2003: 231), can survive as no more than a memory or supplement. By the same token, the impression granted by recent filmic *Hamlet*s is that Ireland exists not so much as a workable "reality" but as a ghostly subtext that contests, and on occasions is forced to submit to, more powerful paradigms. Despite gestures towards the local and efforts to carve out individualized histories, then, filmic productions of *Macbeth* and *Hamlet* operate inconsistently, their unpredictability a function of their reliance upon the characteristics and requirements of the global scene.

A subsidiary argument of this essay is that films of *Hamlet* and *Macbeth* "figure," or symbolically represent, the "global/historical." To conjure with the figural makes sense in view of Derrida's view that, because we cannot attend "to the [historical] source itself," we need to concentrate rather upon the "figures [and] metaphors . . . into which the source has deviated" (Derrida 1998: 201). Ideally, writes Derrida, the "metaphor is the relation between signifier and signified"; in practice, however, a "play of signifiers" (Derrida 1976: 275) takes over and the clarity of metaphor begins to falter. This "figure," he states, changes "places," displacing the subject even when the speaker "believes he is designating it, saying it, orienting it, driving it, governing it like a pilot in his ship" (Derrida 1998: 102). History, too, is figurative, and because articulated through language, can move in unforeseen directions: the figure, like the films themselves, rarely establishes single meanings but, instead, proliferates multiple and contradictory interpretations. In this sense, the figural is akin to the global. Derrida's geographically infused description of the uneven workings of metaphor takes us back to globalization and, in particular, to Arjun Appadurai's argument that the global is marked by asymmetric flows and "growing disjunctures" (Appadurai 1996: 37). The global and the metaphorical, and the metaphorical and the filmic, form an uneasy alliance that exercises a significant influence upon Shakespearean cinema and the irregular contours of its representational operations.

II

In Freeston's and Bogdanov's screen versions of *Macbeth*, global influences, as they feed through American representational practice, are particularly apparent. The close of Freeston's feature film discovers tartan-clad warriors falling to their deaths upon rows of sharpened stakes; here, it self-consciously borrows from both Kenneth Branagh's *Henry V* (1989) and Mel Gibson's *Braveheart* (1995), successful productions backed by the US corporations of the Samuel Goldwyn Company and Paramount. These films were marked, above all, by their respective endeavors to make Shakespeare palatable to non-European audiences and to indulge mythologized delineations of Scotland for American consumption. In Bogdanov's *Macbeth*, too, the pressures of Hollywood are keenly felt, although, in this television production, it is the postmodern tendencies of that cinematic counterpart that are replicated. Not least in the prominence accorded Macbeth's (Sean Pertwee) Landrover and Lady Macbeth's (Greta Scacchi) pill-popping, Bogdanov's *Macbeth* rivals other Shakespeare films of the 1990s in which identical properties and habits are highlighted: one thinks of Ian McKellen as Richard III daring the world from his Landrover in Loncraine's 1995 film, or Diane Venora as Lady Capulet swallowing tablets in Baz Luhrmann's 1996 release, *William Shakespeare's Romeo + Juliet*. Both of these, of course, are films consecrated to the virtues of postmodernity, as their use of staccato editing and stylistic fragmentation, among other elements, indicates. More unsettlingly, perhaps, the opening of this *Macbeth* plunges us into an abandoned quarry masquerading as the "blasted heath" (1.3.75) in which dummies, burned-out cars, and televisions litter the scene. Because a television set is foregrounded in this landscape recovering from a "global catastrophe," we are forced to acknowledge a further dimension of the postmodern – the extent to which war, in Slavoj Žižek's words, has been "deprived of its substance" and replaced by "the spectre of an 'immaterial' war where the attack is invisible" (Žižek 2002: 17, 37). The production's opening, filmed in black and white, would seem to establish an appearance of mondial homogeneity, and, indeed, there is little to choose between this supposedly "Scottish" environment and other nuclear wastelands characteristic of recent Hollywood cinematic outings.

In many ways, Doran's television production of *Macbeth* is cast in a comparable mold. Its predilection for lurching tracking-shots and low-resolution green lighting is evocative for viewers sensitized to recent political events (the Gulf Wars) and popular television series (*The X-Files*). Via these contemporary registers, we come to inhabit a world with no firm dividing lines or sharpened edges: one modality of being fades into, and is synonymous with, the next. If camera-work inculcates an impression of sameness, so, too, do the production's visuals. Filmed in the stark, brick-lined interior of the Old Round-house Theatre in London (see SHAUGHNESSY), Doran's *Macbeth* gives no clue as to its imagined geographical anchorage and favors only the bare narrative essentials. No attempt is made to suggest either factions or individual affiliations: each major player is, literally, cut from the same dun cloth. The effect of this prevailing visual grayness is that the mindset of the individual becomes the psychology of the collective. Antony Sher writes that the production aimed for a sense of a "modern world but one you can't easily identify . . . and you can't say which war this is either." He concludes: "we remind ourselves of images we've seen on TV recently: earthquakes in Turkey, the war in Kosovo – again and again images of modern societies made primitive"

(Sher 2001: 340–1). Global homogeneity, in short, is the production's interpretive template or rationale, and it is applied in such a way as to collapse temporal specificity and flatten national borders.

It might be concluded from the discussion thus far that these film versions of *Macbeth* center upon the exclusion of all "Scottish" signifiers. But, in fact, the very opposite is the case. Hence, Freeston's film of *Macbeth*, according to the video jacket, "is authentically set in eleventh-century Scotland [and] . . . conjures a grim world of battlefields, desolate moors, forbidding castles and haunted caverns." Certainly, such markers of Scottishness are continually underscored: shots of snow-clad mountains, deer, and castles join company with the indigenous accents of the cast. Visuals embrace the heraldic "lion rampant" (used on later medieval Scottish flags), which, initially featuring on Macbeth's shield, later appears on Malcolm's military accouterments in an evocation of the resurgence of genuine royalty. In Bogdanov's production, Scotland is similarly a suggestive presence. The emphases, however, are less obvious, taking the form of seemingly understated visual messages. Thus, while the characters mainly appear as street fighters dressed in combat gear, tartan detailing in epaulets implies local affiliations and, in view of tartan's historical applications, military points of contact. Because Malcolm (Jack Davenport) is figured as a soldier who wears a full tartan cap and scarf, complemented by a tartan insignia on his collar, an impression of his unadulterated Scottish identity is afforded. When tartan detailing consorts with pale-colored garments, white takes over as the dominant indicator of Scottishness, an impression which is reinforced in the scene in which Lady Macduff (Ruth Gemmell), in a creamy white interior, feeds her children porridge. Here, as elsewhere, traditional modalities (the consumption of porridge) are deployed as signs of virtuous Scottishness, and this extends, as well, to constructions of technological preference (Banquo [Michael Maloney], despite being a twentieth-century military commander, still elects to ride a horse). Scottishness, according to Bogdanov, is not pervasive; rather, it is periodic and occasional, subject to the ebb and flow of political vicissitude.

What Bogdanov's *Macbeth* seizes upon as its ultimate theme is the extent to which signifiers of Scottishness can be deployed self-consciously for ideological purposes. The accretions of interpretation, and layerings of invention, that have typified the history of Scottish identity become the central issue. For example, at the start, the fact that Macbeth is represented as wearing only a small scrap of tartan points to his distance from established, and Scottish, sources of authority. Before the murder of Duncan, moreover, Macbeth and Lady Macbeth are dressed in a black tie and a black silky dress respectively, the implication being that, for them, power inheres in English aristocratic practices. Indeed, as the production gathers pace, it is increasingly Englishness, rather than Scottishness, that is cultivated by the central protagonists as a superior set of values. Admittedly, this interpretive decision does not entirely accord with the play's geographical citations or peregrinations; it does, however, have the advantage of underscoring the class elements of transgression and the extent to which Macbeth's ambition is destructive of ideals of national purity and unity.

The logic of a selective usage of Scotland reaches its endpoint of evacuation in Doran's *Macbeth*. Variously homogenizing and suppressing, this television film excises many Scottish references; taking note of Etienne Bonnot de Condillac's remark that "memory . . . consists . . . in the power of reminding ourselves of the signs of our ideas, or the circumstances which accompanied them" (Derrida 1991: 88), however, allows for an alternative perspective. For Scotland, or a version of it, does project itself into this *Macbeth*, yet only at the level of recollections, of a "memory" that needs "signs in order to recall the nonpresent" (Derrida 1991: 133). Once again, we here find a further bridge to the global, since, as Andreas Huyssen argues, "local and national memory practices contest the myths of cyber-capitalism and globalization and their denial of time, space and place" (2000: 37). In Doran's construction of the signs of memory, first the visual and then the aural are invoked. At the entrance of Duncan (Joseph O'Conor), for instance, a back-lit drawbridge descends to reveal the king flanked by churchmen and dressed in white and gold; the sounds of a Latin chant complete the effect. Later, the eerie wail of Celtic pipes is enlisted as Duncan prepares for sleep. For Doran, then, what is Scottish is also what is older, Catholic, and institutional, the implication being that Duncan incarnates an anterior "golden age."

As the production develops, Scotland comes to signify, through the application of memory, a sense of historical continuity. Here, the aural is particularly important, with Celtic pipes being played when Macbeth cries "Banquo!" (3.1.142) and harks back to his bloody resolve to dispatch his closest associate: because of the meanings already enshrined in the music, the production gestures towards connecting various members of the "true" Scottish nobility. More complicatedly, the returning refrain of Celtic pipes during Malcolm's "testing scene" allows the lineal theme to incorporate a quasi-divine dimension; taking place in a church, the disquisition on Scotland implies that England, the bastion of the spiritual, is a harbor from Scotland, a "nation miserable" (4.3.104) now plagued by a profane monarch and a monstrous secularity. But these suggestions are further ambiguated by the production's conclusion in which the witches, lamenting Macbeth's fall, intone over his body a final Latin requiem. By extension, Scotland, seemingly repressed, is reinstated as the unearthly and the mystical. In fact, what Doran's *Macbeth* demonstrates at this point is the phenomenon of Scotland as a ghostly recurrence. As Derrida states, commenting upon questions of "repetition," "a spectre is always a *revenant*. One cannot control its comings and goings because it *begins by coming back.*" "Think . . . of Macbeth" (Derrida 1994: 11), Derrida concludes. Through a process of accretion and transformation, Doran's *Macbeth* comes to be haunted by that which it endeavors to remember.

In view of its multiple applications and uses, it is clear that Scotland – a realization of the local in conversation with the global – is, in these films, by no means straightforward or transparent. On the one hand, the suggestion is that Scotland is incapable of retaining individuation in the face of English hegemony. (The coronation scene of Bogdanov's *Macbeth* is resonant here: the new king enters attired in black leathers and shades, while his consort, reclining on a red throne, presents herself in a red and black tartan outfit, complete with black choker: the choker arguably signifies the strangulation of the local and the distinctive.) On the other hand, Scotland is figured as existing at no more than the level of the stereotype. Žižek writes that "what we experience as reality is not the 'thing itself,' [for] it is always-already symbolized, constituted [and] structured by symbolic mechanisms" (1999: 73). When Freeston's *Macbeth* focuses upon thundery skies, homespun tartans, and witches appearing amidst ruined buildings, therefore, this is not Scottishness; rather, it constitutes a second-hand, "always-already symbolized" construction of Scottishness that is hardly "authentic." In fact, what Freeston purveys is a construction of Scotland mediated through English Romanticism. As Jeffrey Richards states, this invented Scotland was "characterized by wild landscape, music and song, and by the supernatural" (1997: 178). Since all of these are staple ingredients in Freeston's film, the local in his reading of *Macbeth* assumes a fraught and problematic status, which is riven with reminders of an older tradition.

Romanticism is also a feature of Doran's *Macbeth*, or, at least, of the documentary *The Real Macbeth* that aired on Britain's Channel Four the same night that the production received its premiere. Although the documentary strives to uncover the "secrets behind the real king" and to reveal "what the old Scotland was like," it executes its intentions via rehearsals of fog-encrusted landscapes, lakes, and ruined abbeys: once again, we are appealed to via "always-already symbolized" Scottish images. *The Real Macbeth* fills in those Scottish spaces that Doran's *Macbeth* neglects or is incapable fully of accommodating; it provides an extra-textual opportunity for a longing for the local to be articulated; and it celebrates the residue of the postmodern impetus to strip *Macbeth* down to a neutral core. However, because *The Real Macbeth* was broadcast as a sister-piece and as an addition to Doran's *Macbeth*, it might be more apt to see the documentary as a prosthesis. As a supplement, it chimes with David Wills' view that the "artificial addition" is "about" nothing less than "placement, displacement, replacement . . . substituting . . . supplementing" (1995: 9, 226). *The Real Macbeth* is the historical crutch upon which is supported a *Macbeth* that, in the same moment as it disperses and generalizes history, finds itself gravitating towards the fragments of an anterior narrative. Or, to put it another way, the documentary form offers further corroboration of the ways in which the local, even as it is put to historical work, is dictated to by larger national, and ultimately global, ideologies.

III

Just as screen versions of *Macbeth* work in complex, if contradictory, ways to reveal key aspects of the present global moment, so, too, do cinematic realizations of *Hamlet*. Michael Almereyda's film is no exception to the rule. Consistent with the opening figuration of Elsinore as a global empire in turn-of-the-century New York, his *Hamlet* invests throughout in images of corporate anonymity, material excess, and technological reification, with commodities and advertisements answering to a reading of dominant commercial imperatives. More subtly, but no less powerfully, Branagh's *Hamlet* likewise constitutes a film centered upon developments in mondial organization. Via an epic emphasis upon a new fluidity of human movement (carriages give way to locomotives), the steady advance of instruments of communication (ambassadors' reports are replaced by newspaper editorials) and the dissolution of national borders, the film might be said to linger over the emergence and facilitation of a more expansive global landscape. More importantly, matching the sweep of the film's 70mm format is an arresting conceptualization of an outside world that traverses and transforms Denmark's dominions. Incarnated in Fortinbras (Rufus Sewell), this new order casts aside Elsinore's nostalgic immersion in the iconic symbols of both pre- and post-revolutionary Russia, suggesting a force which will not only supersede both phases of this polyglot Euro-country's fortunes but will also replace them with the uniform markers of a broader world identity. Pertinent here is the film's conclusion in which the homogeneous grey of Fortinbras' military anonymity blots out an Elsinore that has been colorfully individualized.

Conjuring the dystopian vision of national development and destiny enables Branagh to lodge his *Hamlet* within a resonant historical register. A sense of history is immediately made available via editorial choices, with Branagh mobilizing the *Hamlet* narrative to chart his own place in the history of Shakespearean representation. Consistently foregrounding the decision to realize the play in its entirety by using the 1623 First Folio (plus – see WALKER), the film aspires to establish Branagh as the leading Shakespearean interpreter. To this end, it avails itself of seasoned veterans of Shakespearean performances. There is a lively intertextuality involved in casting Derek Jacobi as Claudius, for instance, in that the actor played Hamlet in 1979 at the Old Vic and directed Branagh in the role for the 1988 Renaissance Theatre Company production (Branagh 1996: vi–vii, 175). If Jacobi is Branagh's filmic stepfather, then Branagh is Jacobi's theatrical son, the descendent of a metaphorical parent who both throws into relief and authenticates the younger actor's colonization of hallowed terrain. A justifying imperative would also appear to lie behind the casting of John Gielgud (Priam) and Judi Dench (Hecuba) in nonspeaking appearances; once again, Dench directed Branagh in the past and, since *Hamlet*, has added to her imprimatur of gravitas and Shakespearean authority by playing Queen Victoria, "M," and Elizabeth I herself. At the same time, Branagh displays a predilection for utilizing Hollywood box-office stars, which simultaneously precipitates subtextual conflicts and shifts the sources of Shakespearean ownership and interpretation. Charlton Heston, in his cameo role as the Player King, executes his performance in a familiar venerable vein, but Jack Lemmon (Marcellus) and Robin Williams (Osric), who are associated with essentially comic conventions, arguably deflect attention away from an evocation of tradition and legitimacy. On the one hand, by drawing upon the pooled resources of Stratford-upon-

Avon dignitaries and Hollywood legends, Branagh sets himself up as another epic filmmaker, as a bardic reanimator with impeccable credentials. On the other, his casting choices reinforce for audiences Branagh's paradoxical position within a "glocal" niche (see HENDERSON).

History inheres, too, in the reverberations inaugurated by the exterior setting of Blenheim Palace, which substitutes for Elsinore. Following the defeat of the French at Blenheim in 1704, the palace was constructed for the Duke of Marlborough as thanks for a landmark victory. Sir Winston Churchill was born at Blenheim in 1874, and members of the family still live there. With these contexts in mind, Branagh's *Hamlet* emerges as a synecdoche for historical conflicts between England and France, between England and Germany, and between the English royal family and democratically elected political organizations. The setting, in fact, could work finally to suggest that one global conflict may be indistinguishable from the next. While Gielgud and Heston commemorate theatrical values and cinematic glories, they simultaneously point to unsettling parallels between the fates of empires. As a despairing Priam, Gielgud presides in the film over the fall of ancient Troy; as a liberating Moses reincarnated, Heston brings to mind the fate of the biblical Israel. Moreover, because the *mise-en-scène* highlights compositions of characters encircled by flames and conflagration – Priam is glimpsed in this manner, as is the implacable Fortinbras – the implication is that the vulnerability of the "civilized world" is a universal condition and that decline and destruction take on transhistorical characteristics. Whichever moment in history is favored, it seems as if the world is at the mercy of identical changes and comparable transformations.

For Branagh, then, and to a lesser extent Almereyda, worldly change, variously articulated, is very much to the fore. Indeed, this agenda is subtextually signposted, for the two *Hamlet*s deploy a globe as a highly charged personal and public leitmotif. In the case of Branagh's *Hamlet*, the globe is located in the private space of the protagonist's study, its presence communicating the fragility of local constructions and recalling the dangerous materiality of the world beyond, not least in the scene where Hamlet strikes his head against it ("I . . . can say nothing" [Branagh 1996: 72]) in a passion of frustration. In Almereyda's Hamlet, the first frame of Hamlet's (Ethan Hawke) film-within-a-film (*The Mousetrap*), which is significantly a silent film, similarly privileges a turning globe as a self-conscious conceit. Here, the arrangement of shots illuminates the threat posed to ideals of family, community, and original kin by the forces of globalization.

Simultaneously, of course, this globe draws attention to its own arti-ficiality – in addition to signifying Shakespeare's theater, a globe is the logo of Universal Pictures and thus a pertinent indicator of the repressive influence exercised by a globally financed movie industry.

Crucially, in the same moment as these films spotlight the dom-inance of the global, so do they make available alternatives. Given the contingencies upon which globalization depends, it is perhaps not surprising that the *Hamlet* films also extend to embrace locally inflected considerations. At once these cluster around the figure of Branagh himself. Simultaneously locally rooted (his continuing com-mitment to his Northern Irish birthplace is well documented) and overtly pledged to a mass market (global) Shakespeare, he signifies *par excellence* the perennial artist who finds himself only when he has vacated his homeland. And implicitly posited against the rush of glo-bal forces in both films is the specter of an Ireland both illusive and elusive. Echoing the political neutrality of the Republic of Ireland is Elsinore's political isolation, one of the most arresting aspects of the visual vocabulary of Branagh's *Hamlet*. Blinds are invariably shot as drawn; the gates of the castle always feature as closed; and the mir-rors that decorate the state hall stand as testimony to a court that looks inwards rather than outwards, backwards rather than forwards. The most important of those backward glances, of course, is directed towards Old Hamlet (Brian Blessed), who appears both as a species of the local and as a particular construction of Ireland. Not least because of his colossal proportions and his association with bogs and quag-mires, Old Hamlet evokes the Irish giants of antiquity: among these, Brian Boru, a mythical giant Irish king, was perhaps the most cele-brated. Yet, at the same time, in his sallow, pale manner and hollow, preternaturally blue-eyed appearance, Old Hamlet could form a con-nection with historical Irish giants such as Corney Macgrath, who was exhibited in the eighteenth century and whose ossified remains are still on display in the Anatomy School of Trinity College, Dublin. Like Macgrath, Old Hamlet, in his posthumous manifestation, experiences exhibition, only in the form of a statue rather than a skeleton. The following case might be made: Branagh's delineation exposes a Victor-ian and quasi-romanticized perspective and hints that, for him, the value of Ireland as counterpoint resides in its earlier incarnations.

Less obviously, but just as forcefully, Almereyda's *Hamlet* presents Ireland as one among a range of possibilities conjured to eschew global pressures. Critically to apprehend the ways in which Ireland figures and, in particular, the extent to which it functions as a contestatory metaphor, it is important to recognize that Hamlet is constructed throughout as disoriented – in thrall to floating simulations. The protagonist stands as a cipher for Jameson's concept of the "human body" struggling "to organize its immediate surroundings perceptually, and cognitively to map its position in a mappable external world" (1991: 44). As the film understands it, Hamlet is dislocated in direct relation to the faux-historical nature of his urban contexts. Imitative Chippendale markers on skyscrapers, the pseudo-real South Street Seaport, and ersatz architectural symbols in New York have resulted in a fragmentary landscape in which the inhabitant can only be angst-ridden, melancholic, and isolated. The horrendous material realities of 9/11, which Almereyda's film pre-dates, have brought into tragic focus the sense of psychological affliction with which the city was already colored.

Countercultures and filmmaking/videomaking offer possible escape routes out of Hamlet's impasse. In contradistinction to multinational chrome and universal blank modernity, for instance, Hamlet's room appears as a refuge, its furniture implying an antique and eclectic dispensation, and its alternative appearance running against the vertical grain of the surrounding urban terrain. Filmmaking/videomaking, too, provide an enclave, a means of cognitively "mapping" a personal script. Thus, Almereyda's camera dwells repeatedly on Hamlet's *auteurial* eyes, as if alerting us to the ways in which he visualizes a history that is otherwise lacking (see Donaldson). In addition to screening moments from his past, Hamlet mobilizes seemingly unconnected filmic fragments, which involve an appetitive cartoon dragon, a skeleton of a dinosaur, and a series of heads from Renaissance frescoes. Within its own logic, the sequence posits a Hamlet who, caught in a "time" that is "out of joint" (Almereyda 2000: 35), will look to the evolution or origin of things as a means of contesting late capitalist modalities of consumption. The dragon functions to indicate that, from Hamlet's perspective, the Elsinore corporation has become an infantilized caricature of an earlier incarnation. Now, the film suggests, Hamlet aspires to be in command of his own history – of a different narrative to that promulgated by the state – and thus it is singularly appropriate that he should simultaneously be discovered as playing with an egg-timer. Borrowing from high and low in his confrontation with mortality, Hamlet appears as the archetypal postmodern filmmaker, his cannibalizing practice an accusatory reflection upon a regime that also preys upon its own in order to guarantee its continued existence.

Ultimately, however, it is Ireland rather than filmmaking/ videomaking which is formulated as suggesting an alternative *modus vivendi*. Most obviously, Ireland is aurally and visually evoked. For example, because Horatio (Karl Geary) boasts a Dublin accent, Wittenberg can be linked to Dublin and a history of national conflict, one which is reified by the map of Ireland on Hamlet's wall and reinforced by a simultaneous shot of a TV monitor broadcasting burning images redolent of the internecine strife of Northern Ireland's inner-city "troubles." The notion of Ireland as the spiritual home of the Shakespearean hero sits comfortably with Hamlet's more general predilection for revolutionary iconography. But the glance towards Ireland is more intimately rooted. An accompanying two-shot establishes a parallel between the political persecution of the Irish nation and Hamlet's own domestic experiences. For the upright, bullying Hamlet *père* (Sam Shepard), bypassing a US construction that associates the actor with the "wild west," replicates the geographical site occupied by England on the map, while a crouching, subordinate Hamlet *fils* imitates the shape and location of a subordinate Ireland. This cartographical configuration notwithstanding, the ultimate location of Ireland is more slippery than that allowed by the film's elaboration of a liberationist ideology. The imagery of Ireland used, and the meanings generated, deny the material complexities of sectarian conflict, reducing them to a simple colonial paradigm. Similarly, the messy history of partition is elided in the relationship between Horatio and Marcella (Paula Malcomson). An alliance of north and south (Marcella's northern intonation is the counterpart to Horatio's Dublin vowels) suggests Ireland as a seamless ideological unity. (Interestingly, Marcella is the name of the controversial protagonist in Pat O'Connor's ground-breaking *Cal* [1984]; set in the Belfast of the 1970s, the film is more stridently preoccupied with the perils and possibilities of Protestant/Catholic rapprochement.) In fact, what is finally made visible through such a romanticization of Ireland is the nation's commodification in a global economy. Thus, while Hamlet gestures towards Irish models, so, too, does Claudius (Kyle MacLachlan): ensconced in his limousine, the CEO reaches out to touch a television image of Bill Clinton, a highlight of whose presidency was the brokering of the Northern Irish peace agreement. As a site for social values remote from corporate capitalism, Almereyda's Ireland emerges both as a dissident ideology and an imagined idyll spectrally present in spite of current political realities.

"At bottom," writes Derrida, "the spectre is the future" (1994: 39), and, if this is the case, then the ghost of Ireland in Almereyda's *Hamlet* also gestures to what is to come. This is confirmed in the film's penultimate shot of Augustus Saint-Gaudens' sculpture of General William Sherman, which stands in New York's Grand Army Plaza (just off Fifth Avenue). Accompanying the figure of Sherman is the ethereal angel of Nike, who leads his horse forward with triumphant purpose. It is perfectly possible, of course, to read into the statue an allusion to Fortinbras and to detect in Sherman's repression of the "south" in order to save the "north" a codified comment upon the bipolar structure of Ireland's political organization. Yet Fortinbras seems less forcefully evoked here than Hamlet who, via the statue of Sherman, is situated in a historical idiom: the protagonist eventually resolves his vexed relation with time and with the metropolis. Moreover, because Saint-Gaudens was born in Dublin and, shortly before his death in 1907, was working on a huge figure of Charles Stewart Parnell, the revolutionary Irish leader and spokesperson for agrarian agitation and land reform, the suggestion is that Hamlet, akin to the sculptor, is being claimed by his national forefathers and guided towards a culturally emancipated species of spiritual destiny. A passing shot of an airplane's jet trail confirms the impression and works as an analogy for a soul-in-progress. Even this reading, however, is compromised by the presence of Nike, and not least because this classical goddess has been hijacked as a logo by the Nike Corporation, one of the most infamous of world sports industries.[2] The question of Hamlet's ultimate destination is balanced in the final montage between both local and global scenarios, and any sense of resolution hinges upon this uneasy equipoise.

Uneasily haunting these filmic versions, then, is an Irish specter, one that assumes different shapes but that consistently connotes possibility and registers desire. As a synecdoche for the local, Ireland becomes what is not global in the same moment as it constitutes itself as a necessary component of the mondial make-up. Out of these reworkings of *Hamlet* emerges an Ireland that is a metaphorical landscape both local and global ("glocal") in orientation. A material enactment of such cinematic "glocalism" can be found in the 1997 European premiere of Branagh's *Hamlet*. Taking place in Belfast, and supporting local charities, the event explicitly figured Branagh as a homegrown talent who was introduced to, and welcomed by, the audience as "your boy." However, audience expectation was dashed when the local hero appeared in ghostly form available only via a videotaped message, albeit one put together especially for the occasion. Notwithstanding the local sentiments espoused in Branagh's communication, the lure of the mondial stage had proved "metal more attractive" (Branagh 1996: 87). (Branagh had commenced filming his role as an American detective for Robert Altman's *The Gingerbread Man* [1997].) Intriguingly, one of the main charities to benefit from the premiere was "First Run Belfast," an organization founded in order to enable local thespians to study drama and stage theatrical ventures outside Northern Ireland. Both encouraging a movement away from the local, and simultaneously embracing its worth and particularity, the occasion exemplifies the dilemma of a creative practitioner who aspires to local participation in the same moment as he is molded by the global enterprise of the Hollywood phenomenon.

IV

At first sight, Morrissette's *Scotland, PA* and Cavanagh's *Hamlet* would appear to have little in common. *Scotland, PA* is an American satirical comedy set in the 1970s that takes *Macbeth* as its narrative model. By contrast, Cavanagh's *Hamlet*, made and financed in Londonderry, Northern Ireland, adheres to the Shakespearean tragic imprint. Closer investigation, however, reveals a number of unexpected correspondences and a comparable final conjunction of global, local, and historical considerations. On immediate impressions, *Scotland, PA* represents a felicitous contemporary translation of its source, sounding variations on Macbeth's name and evoking the play's fascination with maternity, as in the lament of the female stallholder at the football game: "that young man's just crying out for a new mamma." Echoes of *Macbeth* are heard, too, in the diegetic use of music (like Shakespeare's protagonist, the songs of the group Bad Company are preoccupied with masculinity and "destiny") and in the parodic reinvention of its celebrated speeches (the "Tomorrow, and tomorrow, and tomorrow" [5.5.18] soliloquy, an apocalyptic insight into meaninglessness and futility, is realized as the Buddhist chant, "Tomorrow is tomorrow is not today," whose ideal end is knowledge and enlightenment). Other modalities of translation invert cultural icons and utterances from the 1970s to make discrete thematic points. The opening frames of the TV detective, Sam McCloud (Dennis Weaver), chasing a criminal in a helicopter remind us of the premise of the series: a rustic country sheriff routinely succeeds in exposing the corruption of Manhattan business magnates. In *Scotland, PA*, the formula is reversed, with Lieutenant Ernie McDuff (Christopher Walken) leaving the city for the country in order to execute justice. Similarly, visual allusions during the shooting trip to Michael Cimino's *The Deer Hunter* (1978) serve to recall that, in this Pennsylvania-set film, Nick (again Christopher Walken) was precipitated into the "heart of darkness"; in *Scotland, PA*, however, the actor's role is comically directed towards ridding the local community of precisely such a descent into nihilism.

Such references discover *Scotland, PA* as flirtatiously concerned with time and causality as they express themselves at particular historical junctures. The film first broaches early modern history in the ramifications attached to "Scotland": the Pennsylvania town was founded by seventeenth-century émigrés fleeing religious persecution and thus reflects back upon some of the ideological complexities animating the "original" playtext. Secondly, the film elaborates a construction of the 1970s in order proleptically to conjure global developments during the 1990s and beyond. It is not to be wondered at, then, that the dialogue of *Scotland, PA* consistently gestures forwards. Typical here are Norm Duncan's (James Rebhorn) promise that "Tonight, you two are going to witness history" and Joe McBeth's (James LeGros) comment that "Intercom" is "the way of the future." Although not explicitly invoked, that "history" and "future" embrace the disappearance of the small-scale food outlet and its replacement by large-scale multinational franchises. What is suggested through "McBeth's," in fact, is the emergence of McDonald's, an incorporated global industry: the acronym "PA" in the film's title may well be deliberate. More specifically, the "identical" status of McDonald's and "Americanization" (Giddens 2002: xxi) is suggested in *Scotland, PA*'s engagement with the signs of US hegemony, with McBeth sporting a stars-and-stripes outfit.

But *Scotland, PA* does not only thematize McDonald's rise; it simultaneously hints at its decline. In 2002, soon after the film's release, the McDonald's corporation reported its first major loss; share prices slumped to half the chain's peak; key eateries closed; and health-oriented rivals successfully competed for customers. The prominence accorded to McDuff's vegetarian restaurant and his "garden burger" at the film's close encodes a meditation upon this more recent trajectory, upon the ways in which the global is invariably forced to adapt and co-opt, and upon the increasingly uncertain purchase of US cultural domination. In this respect, it is striking that *Scotland, PA* does not endeavor to represent *Macbeth* as quintessentially either "Scottish" or "Shakespearean": the play and its national context are only comprehensible inside an American register. The isolation of the Pennsylvania town, I would argue, ultimately points to a sense of inwardness and to a historically particular illusion of invulnerability that, before 9/11, was actively entertained and may now be attempting to re-establish itself. Hence, the sequestered nature of the film's setting is purposeful, linked, as it is, to fictions of self-sufficiency, to the inevitable interpenetration of external influences, and to the dialogic condition of the global (contrast LANIER).

A comparable path for the Shakespearean filmmaker presents itself intriguingly in Cavanagh's *Hamlet*. To understand his *Hamlet* is to acknowledge the history of Derry and to recognize its origins as a contested English plantation founded by the Corporation of London in 1613; its status, following the famous siege of 1689–90, as the savior of Protestantism; its narratives of internecine Catholic/Protestant conflict; and its association with the civil rights movement, the culmination of which was the "Bloody Sunday" march of January 30, 1972 during which thirteen unarmed participants were killed at the hands of the British parachute regiment. Because of this setting, those Irish specters lurking within the *Hamlet*s of Branagh and Almereyda are, in Cavanagh's film, granted a more complete embodiment. The use of English in a Northern Irish intonation, for example, allows the dissident accent of Marcella in Almereyda's *Hamlet* to be formulated as a type of universal. Almereyda's linguistic sub-plot here becomes a major consideration, pointing to the telescoping of that director's local gaze. Similarly, the quasi-revolutionary subtext of Almereyda is pushed to an extreme by Cavanagh and, in this respect, Derry is once again richly evocative. During the 1970s, part of the city was declared "Free Derry," a Utopian Catholic enclave inside the "occupied six counties"; the location signifies a material enactment of the idealized political space Hamlet (Stephen Cavanagh) is represented as striving towards.

Lending Ireland the central role while still managing to accommodate the Shakespearean original, Cavanagh's film opens up new avenues for exploring the relationship between the Shakespearean local and the Shakespearean global. Global gestures are easily discerned: the narrative pace of the film is quick and compressed, and guns and cameras, the insignias of Luhrmannesque Shakespeare (there is cross-fertilization between filmic borders), are given pride of place. Yet, at the same time, by translating *Hamlet* to Derry, the director explicitly draws upon, and makes full use of, the associations embedded in a locally charged environment. Although overt "political statements" (Cavanagh 2003: n.p.) are avoided, political images, in particular, are privileged, with Derry's famous seventeenth-century walls featuring prominently, as do torchlit soldiers in combat gear and the Guildhall, seat of a fractured administration. Such visual paraphernalia have a twofold effect. On the one hand, they lend the film an acute historical suggestiveness, positing the siege of the city (in which the Protestant "apprentice boys" of Derry famously held the city against the Catholic James II) as an event whose mythological overtones are still being replayed. And current political pressures, which have a highly charged importance in Northern Ireland, are felt throughout, as in the alarmed disclosure that Old Hamlet has been seen and Hamlet's own anxiety that his colleagues will "reveal" (1.5.123) his precious secret. There is, as Cavanagh admits in interview, a "high security culture under Claudius" (Cavanagh 2003: n.p.) and the all too familiar presence of governmental surveillance. On the other hand, the film's appeal to the eye brings the Shakespearean "original" back to mind, making of Hamlet a type of resistant apprentice and forging a bridge between Derry and Wittenberg, home of Protestant radicalism. Unlike the *Hamlet*s of Branagh and Almereyda, which concentrate respectively on nineteenth- and twentieth-century manifestations, Cavanagh's filmic reading addresses Shakespeare through a longer and more uneven timeframe of Ireland's political fortunes, thereby establishing the inescapable interrelation of the past and the present. Thus, while globalization dictates the film's typology and style, Cavanagh's subjects remain locked in a richly determined local distinctiveness. As such, his *Hamlet* offers us a denser reading of the Irish "heritage" and suggests that the local is at its most communicative only when it has absorbed its historical particularity.

Local distinctiveness can also blur interestingly into a confrontational exclusiveness. Whereas Almereyda and Branagh deploy the local to reduce the global, Cavanagh deploys the local to confront Shakespeare and, in particular, his global status as transnational voice. Offering a verbal counterpoint to Branagh's notion of a cross-cultural Shakespearean tongue and granting the most famous speech its most local purchase, "To be or not to be" is delivered in Irish. Such an innovative directorial undertaking is explained by Cavanagh as follows: "Hamlet has the idea that Claudius is listening and he doesn't want to be understood. He doesn't want his intentions to be transparent from what he says" (Cavanagh 2003: n.p.). The use of hand-held camera-work in this scene, as elsewhere, allows for a "visceral" impression and makes a virtue of the linguistic decision, forcing us to be "complicit in [Hamlet's] emotional life" (Cavanagh 2003: n.p.). More arrestingly, the notion of an Irish-speaking protagonist brings to mind the ways in which Irish has been used in Derry in opposition to British dominance and helps to formulate Hamlet's bifurcated identity in terms of the unresolved resonances of a disappearing national language.

As it is screened more widely, more will be learned about the relationship between Cavanagh's *Hamlet* and its wider environments. No doubt the activities of a multinational film industry will have an influence upon the film's reception and reputation, dictating the degree of prominence that the local can be afforded. Appadurai reminds us, "mass consumption" is all too often the precondition for the articulation of "resistance, irony, selectivity, and, in general, agency" (1996: 7). Yet with these byproducts of the global in mind, perhaps a *Hamlet* that sets out, as does Cavanagh's, to "terrorize" (Cavanagh 2003: n.p.) its audience will be granted a privileged place in Shakespearean cinematic history.

V

Using an appropriately late capitalist metaphor, Derrida notes of the reading experience that "you are immediately plunged into the consumption of another text that had already, out of its double bottom, set this text in motion" (Derrida 1998: 133). Such intricately functioning connections are abundantly evident in filmic Shakespearean tragedies, and demonstrate that cinema never operates in an isolated, or local, context. The coexistence of homogeneity and difference, and the fluidity and variegation of history, are among the considerations these recent films explore, the diversity of preoccupation reflecting the range of significations that the "figural" is capable of embracing and precipitating. In short, the films discussed in this chapter operate in similar capacities to Derrida's construction of the "metaphor" that "retires, withdraws from the world scene, withdrawing from it at the moment of its most invasive extension" (1998: 104). They reach outwards to the global in the same moment as they retreat to the local, revealing a "glocal" complexion that enables them to negotiate the ultimate locations of authority and hegemony. As Foucault remarks, "It is possible that the . . . local [and] regional . . . are indissociable from . . . our discovery of the manner in which power is exercised" (1977:

215). And, in exposing these operations, the Shakespearean filmic impulse sensitizes us anew to history as unmediated and intertextual, to the continuing effects of cross-cultural conversation, and to the place of the individual critic in the broader intellectual consensus.

Notes

1 The term "glocal" has been pioneered by, among others, Robertson (1995).
2 I owe this felicitous suggestion to the generosity of Courtney Lehmann.

References and Further Reading

Appadurai, Arjun (1996). *Modernity at Large: Cultural Dimensions of Globalization*. Minneapolis: University of Minnesota Press.

Cavanagh, Stephen (2003). Interview with Mark Thornton Burnett. Londonderry, April 4.

Derrida, Jacques (1976). *Of Grammatology*. Trans. Gayatri Chakravorty Spivak. Baltimore and London: Johns Hopkins University Press.

—— (1991). *A Derrida Reader: Between the Blinds*. Ed. Peggy Kamuf. New York and London: Harvester Wheatsheaf.

—— (1994). *Spectres of Marx: The State of the Debt, the Work of Mourning, and the New International*. Trans. Peggy Kamuf. London and New York: Routledge.

—— (1998). *The Derrida Reader: Writing Performances*. Ed. Julian Wolfreys. Edinburgh: Edinburgh University Press.

Foucault, Michel (1977). *Language, Counter-Memory, Practice: Selected Interviews and Essays*. Ed. Donald F. Bouchard. Oxford: Blackwell.

—— (1986). *The Archaeology of Knowledge*. Trans. A. M. Sheridan Smith. London and New York: Tavistock.

Giddens, Anthony (2002). *Runaway World: How Globalization is Reshaping our Lives*. London: Profile.

Hozic, Aida (2001). *Hollyworld: Space, Power, and Fantasy in the American Economy*. Ithaca and London: Cornell University Press.

Huyssen, Andreas (2000). "Present Pasts: Media, Politics, Amnesia." *Public Culture* 12.1: 21–38.

Jameson, Fredric (1991). *Postmodernism, or, The Cultural Logic of Late Capitalism*. London and New York: Verso.

Lehmann, Courtney (2003). "Out Damned Scot: Dislocating *Macbeth* in Transnational Film and Media Culture." In Boose and Burt, eds.: 231–51.

Miller, Toby, Nitin Govil, John McMurria, and Richard Maxwell, eds. (2001). *Global Hollywood*. London: BFI Publishing.

Munslow, Alan (1997). *Deconstructing History*. London and New York: Routledge.

O'Byrne, Darren (1997). "Working-Class Culture: Local Community and Global Conditions." In John Eade (ed.), *Living the Global City: Globalization as Local Process*. London and New York: Routledge: 73–89.

Richards, Jeffrey (1997). *Films and British National Identity: From Dickens to "Dad's Army."* Manchester: Manchester University Press.

Robertson, Roland (1995). "Glocalization: Time-Space and Homogeneity-Heterogeneity." In Mike Featherstone, Scott Lash, and Roland Robertson (eds.), *Global Modernities*. London: Sage: 23–44.

Shakespeare, William (1997). *The Norton Shakespeare*. Ed. Stephen Greenblatt, Walter Cohen, Jean E. Howard, and Katharine Eisaman Maus. New York: Norton.

Sher, Antony (2001). *Beside Myself*. London: Hutchinson.

Werner, Sarah (2001). *Shakespeare and Feminist Performance: Ideology on Stage*. London and New York: Routledge.

White, Hayden (1973). *Metahistory: The Historical Imagination in Nineteenth-Century Europe*. Baltimore and London: Johns Hopkins University Press.

Wills, David (1995). *Prosthesis*. Stanford, CA: Stanford University Press.

Žižek, Slavoj (1999). *The Žižek Reader*. Ed. Elizabeth Wright and Edmond Wright. Oxford: Blackwell.

—— (2002). *Welcome to the Desert of the Real*. London: Verso.

Chapter 8

CROSS-CULTURAL INTERPRETATION

Reading Kurosawa
Reading Shakespeare

Anthony Dawson

In the *New Yorker* in 2003, Alex Ross addressed the way cultural studies has infiltrated the world of pop music, transforming it from simply music that is popular to an "emanation of an entity called popular culture," where the focus is on commodification rather than on the music itself. Describing a conference that brought academics and journalists together, allowing the latter to "drop arcane allusions" and the former "to loosen up a little," he writes amusingly about academic obscurantism:

> Some of the presentations ... lapsed into the familiar contortions of modern pedagogy. Likewise, in the many pop-music books now in circulation, post-structuralist, post-Marxist, post-colonialist, and post-grammatical buzzwords crop up on page after page. There is a whole lot of problematizing, interrogating, and appropriating goin' on. . . . I made it a rule to move to a different room the minute I heard someone use the word "interrogate" . . . or cite any of the theorists of the Frankfurt school. Thus, I ducked . . . when I heard a sentence that began . . . "Invoking Walter Benjamin." And I bailed on a lecture entitled "Bruce's Butt" – Bruce Springsteen's butt as seen on the cover of *Born in the USA* – when the speaker began to interrogate the image of the butt, which, under sharp questioning, wouldn't give anything away. (2003: 88)

Now Ross can himself be tempted by rhetorical excess, but his critique nevertheless hits home. Reading it in an elegantly written journal like the *New Yorker*, I wince. One part of me wants to protest, to defend the tribe, to insist on the value of specialized vocabulary and controlled abstraction: "hold on, there is such a thing as *good* academic writing!" But another part of me knows perfectly well that scholarly writing in the humanities often invites, even requires, Ross' brand of irony. Probably the most painful phrase in the quoted passage is "the familiar contortions of modern pedagogy." What's implied is that educated people everywhere recognize the display, and for the most part discount it. It's just academics doing their tricks – the only problem being that the audience is limited to other academics; they are simply mimes performing for other mimes, contortionists for fellow human pretzels.

The wedge between the educated public and academic discourse is not a new subject, and my raising it is no doubt "familiar." But since the problem hasn't gone away, since we've fallen into the habit of accepting, perhaps with a groan but nevertheless accepting, obscurantist rhetoric, then it might not hurt to remind ourselves of the problem. The particular occasion for my jeremiad is my emergence from a period of reading about Shakespearean film. Like pop music, film, I am told again and again, is an "emanation of popular culture," a marketplace commodity, a forum for the reproduction of social imbalances (racial, sexual, economic), a mark of what Hamlet calls an inward "imposthume" on the smooth face of capitalism. Shakespeare too is popular, so the argument goes, not because his language is incomparable, or because the stories he tells and characters he illuminates are themselves intrinsically satisfying, but because our culture has found a way to exploit his works to perpetuate its evident injustices. The efflorescence of Shakespeare films in the 1990s is thus addressed as a revelatory feature of late capitalism rather than as something that emerges from the aesthetics of film itself, a new understanding of the value of Shakespeare's plays, or a need for something good amidst the prevailing schlock.

While it's hard to deny that some of this work is apt and true, I often feel that it misses the point. Of course film is part of commodity culture, it is distributed within a global marketplace, and there are injustices associated with this kind of practice. Shakespeare wrote his plays within a developing entertainment market, he was a member of a company (in the commercial as well as the artistic sense), and he bought himself a big house with the proceeds. There were plenty of injustices around then too. But this hardly confines the stretch of his plays to the reproduction of oppression; nor does it mean that the best way of approaching them is in relation to how they negotiate the interplay between subversion and containment. It's a mistake to imagine that just because the plays or films emerge out of a particular social configuration their meanings are limited to that milieu.

Approaching Shakespeare in an international context, as I have been asked to do, we often confront similar position-taking – Shakespeare as tool of colonial or postcolonial hegemony, as the good cop of Western capitalism, softening up unsuspecting Others for the carefully staged entrance of the bad cops of industrialization and globalization. I've said elsewhere that I don't think that's very fruitful, since, when other cultures and languages import and translate Shakespeare, they tend to make him serve their own purposes. This has been going on at least since Shakespeare began to be translated, and no doubt before, and always involves two-way traffic – "Shakespeare" has never been only one thing.

This is not to deny the value and importance of some of the insights that have arisen from the cultural studies model. It has, for one thing, helped us see the objects of our attention in a global context, made us alert to the intersections of local and global, and encouraged us to situate ourselves as observers. Indeed, if Shakespeare has become global, we can now see that he has done so through adaptation to a thousand different locals, starting with one called, prophetically, the Globe Theatre in Bankside. But what does it mean to say that Shakespeare is "global"? First of all perhaps that his plays are astonishingly plastic and adaptable; this clearly is a crucial element in his genius, this ability to appeal to so many different temperaments and cultures. It is the ground of his universality; too often, I think, especially in circles that distrust the very idea of the universal, this element is misinterpreted as a bland and homogenizing sameness, when what it really means is variety, scope, and difference. So if Shakespeare is global, it is because his work is able to inhabit so many different locals.

This mixed habitation has, in an awkward neologism, been named "glocal," a term that carries with it a two-pronged political agenda: (1) that "universal" values are suspect, mainly a screen for cultural or political domination, and that practitioners who appeal to such values are either deluded or complicit; and (2) that the "local" is a potential antidote, resistant to hegemony though perhaps powerless against it. The odd thing is, however, that it is often the "universal" values themselves that are the ground of resistance; in eastern Europe, for example, liberal ideas such as individual freedom in the face of state oppression have often marked productions of *Hamlet*. In such locations, the "local" is the space of oppression, the "global" of liberation. Hence recent celebrations of the "glocal" might seem a bit straitened, overly eager to find in the local the possibility of escape from an oppressiveness which is too easily identified as "Western" or "European," as if those terms were themselves single and uncomplicated. The local can be as much of a straitjacket as the universal.

But not always, of course – take, for example, a film from Singapore, *Chicken Rice War* (dir. Cheah Chee Kong, 2000), an adaptation of *Romeo and Juliet* that plays humorously on the familiarity of both Shakespeare's play and Baz Luhrmann's 1996 film, while at the same time staking its own claim. One of the ways it does this is through the liberal use of "Singlish," a patois that mixes English with the forms and vocabulary of local languages. As Yong Li Lan argues in a splendid essay to which I am indebted, Shakespeare's international cachet enables a partnership between local and global, freeing the demotic language as a kind of resistance to cultural standards, even as the comic use of Singlish pokes fun at (to adapt Theseus' phrase) local names and habitations. At the same time, of course, Shakespeare and the cross-cultural values associated with him provide the occasion by which such moves are enabled and justified. Even more to the point, perhaps we should be looking for ways to ask different questions, ones that move away from political negotiations. What alternatives to the cultural studies path might be worth following?

Akira Kurosawa's Shakespeare films, which were designed partly as meeting grounds for Western and Japanese classical modes, offer a possible route (or several: I shall here address only *Ran* and *Throne of Blood*; his *Hamlet* adaptation *The Bad Sleep Well*, set in 1960 corporate Japan, raises different questions). Unabashedly Japanese, they are also profoundly Shakespearean. Local and global meet on an even terrain, and there are additional mediations – between, for example, the literary and the cinematic, text and image, a version of the kind of interplay that has been conducted throughout the history of Shakespearean performance. Although to say so goes against the critical grain, it seems to me that Kurosawa is deeply interested in the literary elements of Shakespeare;[1] to some degree he negotiates the distance between reading and seeing, literature and performance. How, we might fruitfully ask, does Kurosawa read Shakespeare? In seeking ways to address that question, I want to try out a rounded, aesthetically oriented approach to Shakespeare film, one that is alert to cultural difference, and hence indebted to much recent work, but not concerned with commodification or oppression. What sorts of pleasures, gains, and losses does the cinema, in the hands of a "foreign" master, offer when it confronts Shakespeare's texts? We have learned from materialist theory that art and interpretation are always *situated*, never free of myriad cultural constraints. Kurosawa, while an independent artist with his own vision, is also a Japanese man of a certain generation; he is embedded in his and his country's history, deeply affected by its traditions, and involved in one of the most collaborative of art forms. My own history, tradition, and cultural/intellectual milieu similarly affect my approach to interpretation. All this informs my readings; indeed, such considerations underpin the encounter that I seek to construct, bringing to bear both my knowledge as a "Western" Shakespearean and my ignorance of, but curiosity about, things Japanese. What happens when these two collide or coalesce? In asking this question I define my approach – wanting to speak across cultural boundaries without implying the superiority of either and hoping that, by recording the passage as carefully as possible, something about film, about Shakespeare, about Kurosawa, might emerge into the light.

I confess at the outset a certain resistance to some of Kurosawa's cinematic strategies. His image-making sometimes irritates me with its obviousness. In *Throne of Blood* (or, more accurately translated, *The Castle of the Spider's Web*, 1957), for example, repeated shots of clouds, the overly insistent fog, the web-like forest through which hapless riders charge back and forth for far too long, filmed always through a tangle of branches – such images smack of significance writ large, and for me feel intrusive (though I seem to be in the critical minority). At one key moment, for example, just as Washizu/Macbeth (Toshiro Mifune) takes the fatal spear with which he is to kill his lord, there is a shot of the crescent moon, symbol of the feudal lordship, with a screeching crow crossing in front of it; this seems an attempt, like the shrieks of night birds that punctuate the soundtrack, to find a visual equivalent to Lady Macbeth's "The raven himself is hoarse / That croaks the fatal entrance of Duncan / Under my battlements" (1.5.38– 40). But for me it falls flat – it's too literal. Even the subtle framing of scenes, often praised by film critics, can seem overly contrived – such as when, near the beginning, Washizu and Miki sit to rest before their triumphant return, with the distant Castle of the Spider's Web caught between them. They sit one on each side of, almost outside, the frame, while the castle, the object of their competition in the narrative to come, occupies the center of the shot. It is a strong visual marker and one gets the point. But it is produced in a labored way

159

that severely strains credibility, even in an insistently symbolic version like this one, since up to this point they have been in a desperate rush to reach the castle. Because I'm interested less in the didactic point and more in the ways that the films resist their overt morals, I'd rather approach them through what might be seen as literary categories – elements that critics have often thought to be downplayed in his films – such as character, motivation, dialogue. I want to trace how literary/performative values complicate what at first seems all too obvious a message, conveyed directly and not always subtly via certain purely "cinematic" visual strategies. In saying this I am claiming that Kurosawa looks to Shakespeare not only for story or imagery, material ripe for imagistic transposition, but also for deeper thematic possibilities, richer portrayals of character, elements that stretch the cinematic reach, bringing it into dialogue with the literary. His films are not just adaptations of *King Lear* and *Macbeth*, but readings of them.

The first thing one notices when coming to *Ran* (1985), Kurosawa's version of *King Lear*, is splashes of primary color in an expansively green landscape; the sense of fragile human imposition on a vast and beautiful territory is strongly marked in the opening sequence, which features horsemen engaged in a boar hunt. As the credits roll, the horses stand etched on the brow of a hill against the sky, their riders poised, expectant, and unmoving. The boar snuffles through the grass and the chase is on. Close-ups of an old man loosing an arrow are followed by a cut to a static circle of brightly dressed figures inside a fluttering yellow and black marquee. We soon learn that Hidetora, the old man and Lear figure, has been the one to kill the boar (naturally, since he's the one with the power and his sons and underlings defer to him). But the hunted boar is also an ironic figure for Hidetora, himself a destined prey; indeed, he makes this explicit in the dialogue by linking the old and tough-skinned boar with himself. So the successful imposition of human power over nature (the boar), is recast as futile or even illusory, a perception enhanced by the rest of the long opening movement of the film.

Inside the roofless enclosure, the men sit isolated in the mountain landscape, their effulgent clothing and the heraldic backdrop the only marks of human presence. A bit later, outside the space defined by the black and yellow silk fence, the old warlord announces his intention to divide his lands; within the film's feudal Japanese setting, what this means is that he will make Taro, his eldest son (not daughter), the lord of the first castle and head of the clan, while the other two sons must content themselves with submission to Taro and with secondary and tertiary castles. The outspoken Saburo, the Cordelia figure, protests and is banished, along with a faithful retainer (Tango) who, like Shakespeare's Kent, supports Saburo. The latter's marriage negotiations with attendant noblemen are abruptly cut off, only to be picked up again a few minutes later when one of the lords, in the spirit of Shakespeare's King of France, rides after the banished Saburo and Tango to offer shelter and his daughter's hand.

As a Shakespearean, one notes the parallels of plot and character (including a derisive Fool); but beyond such similarities, the film at first seems deeply foreign to Shakespeare's text.[2] Gradually though, Kurosawa's interpretation of Shakespeare makes itself felt. Take one tiny detail in the opening segment: Hidetora, before announcing his retirement, falls asleep while sitting cross-legged in the grass. The others in the circle look embarrassed or uncertain and move away; the Fool leaps about; Saburo pulls out his sword, and, ignoring the cowering Fool, crosses to a small sapling. He cuts off a few branches and places them so as to provide flecks of shade for his sleeping father. The countryside, while lush and grassy, is practically devoid of trees ("for miles around there's scarce a bush," as Gloucester says of the heath to which Lear is exiled); the one shrub inside the enclosure stands as a potential sign of love in the all-hating world. Kurosawa condenses features of the play's symbolic landscape into this moment: Cordelia's aggressive love, the emptiness of the heath, an isolated moment of tenderness (as when Cornwall's servants prepare a balm for the blinded Gloucester), the frailness not only of age, but also of human life generally. Indeed, this whole opening sequence, while recounting Hidetora's personal, military, and political rise to power, keeps reminding us of the fragility of such achievement by setting it in a space that both invokes and contrasts with the interior, courtly setting of Shakespeare's first scene, while simultaneously resonating with the emptiness evoked later in the play.

After his nap, Hidetora bursts out of the enclosure, his face wild with his dream of "being alone in the wide world." The actual abdication then takes place out in the open, at the edge of the vast ridge. While *King Lear* moves painfully from indoors to outdoors, from protection to exposure, *Ran* begins outside and exploits the sense of nature's distance from, and indifference to, humankind – an awareness that emerges only gradually in Shakespeare's text. Though the lush green landscape is not at all like the bleak wintry ones of Peter

Brook's or Grigori Kozintsev's films of *Lear* (1971 and 1969, respectively), the sense of distance is almost as pronounced; the primary colors of the sons' clothes, the fluttering marquee with its symbolic sun and moon, the pallid white of Hidetora's clothing and make-up, all contrast with the insistent green, and the chilling whine of the cicadas. As Hidetora tells his story of conquest in such a setting we get the distinct sense, despite his boasts and the sycophantic bowing of most of his retainers, of a diminished human world, a brightly colored speck, but a speck nevertheless.

Such feelings are rife in the film. The vision of isolation persists to the end, when we see Tsurumaru, who had been blinded by Hidetora and whose ruined castle is the backdrop for much of the second half of the film, silhouetted on a ruined parapet, as a black bird flits across the screen. The sequence begins from a great distance, with Tsurumaru barely visible; jump cuts bring us close enough to see him in profile, feeling his way to the edge of the parapet, bereft of his beloved flute. He drops the image of Buddha his murdered sister had given him and it lies unheeded on the rocks; then the jump cuts are repeated in reverse, back to the distant shot, where the whole devastated landscape lies in the fading orange light, and there is nothing left but the fierce call of the flute.

"Only the birds and beasts live in solitude," says Hidetora when banished from his second son's fortress, but he quickly learns that, with Buddha "gone from the world," there is no escaping the pain of isolation. Solitude is more than loneliness; it means being cut off from communal life. Thus the ruined castle becomes the ultimate symbolic space in the film, akin to the hovel in which Poor Tom seeks in vain to shelter his nakedness. Western critics (e.g., Mack, Strier) have long stressed the prevalence of community and service in *King Lear*, its appeal to values of hospitality, and its insistence on the calamity of breaking social bonds. *Ran* represents, I think, a strong reading of the play from this perspective. In fact, the turning point of the whole story (a departure from Shakespeare's plot but in keeping with his thematic interests) is the betrayal of the old lord by one of his trusted followers, Ikoma, who lures him into an ambush at the third castle (which we have just seen taken over by Taro's men). The untrustworthiness of Ikoma is signaled by the Fool, who mimes smelling a fish, but Hidetora pays no attention; nevertheless, we get the distinct impression that had Hidetora followed his feelings and taken refuge with Saburo instead of heeding his double-crossing advisor, all would have been made right. Such moments not only keep the issue of loyal service in the forefront, but also shift sympathy to the old man, in spite of repeated reminders of his past cruelties. Indeed, as in *King Lear*, sympathy prevails over moral condemnation.

Social relations predominate within fixed and limited spaces, typically the castles and courtyards where much of the action occurs. In the opening sequence, the distinction between inside and outside, and more distantly, between ordered and deteriorating social relations, is prophetically blurred through the use of the roofless enclosure and the movement from inside to outside for the division of the realm. As the civil war heats up, castles are burned, and fratricide and what Hamlet would regard as incest[3] infiltrate the social world. The ruined castle, which used to belong to the blind Tsurumaru and his gentle sister, Sué,[4] is thus the ideal backdrop to suggest this twisted set of relations. Hidetora ends up there with Kyoami, the Fool, who sees it as an earthly hell. It becomes a kind of harbor for all the refugees, including Tsurumaru and Sué, Tango, and even, briefly, Saburo. It is a liminal space, halfway between inside and outside, "topsy turvy" as the Fool insists, earth and sky transposed in its strangely labyrinthine vistas.

Because of the importance of home and homelessness in *King Lear*, Kurosawa's focus on buildings and their destruction resonates with the original. In Shakespeare the motif is recurrent: "I can tell why a snail has a house . . . Why, to put his head in" (1.5.27–30); "He that has a house to put 's head in has a good head-piece" (3.2.25–6); "You houseless poverty . . . How shall your houseless heads and unfed sides, / Your looped and windowed raggedness, defend yourselves / From seasons such as these?" (3.4.26–32). When the castle doors are shut against Lear, houses, such as the hovel in the storm or the small farmhouse attached to Gloucester's estate, provide a possible refuge. Though Lear descends on Gloucester's castle in Act 2 he never in fact enters it, delivering his great speech about need and superfluity ("Reason not the need") in the courtyard, and then being "thrust out" of the gates – as Gloucester is too after his blinding. This means that after Act 1 Lear spends most of the play outdoors, just as Gloucester does once he is mockingly told to smell his way to Dover. Other meanings cluster around the word "house" – the household, for example, and the people in it; the royal line itself, with the pomp and authority that should attend it; or the symbolic place of implacable refusal: "this hard house / (More harder than the stones whereof 'tis raised . . .)" (3.2.63–4) which refuses entry to Gloucester and the injured Lear. Thus houses are associated not only with refuge but also

163

with lineage and authority, and their rampant abuse. The houses in the play mirror the elaborate system of deference that permeates it (in which even great lords such as Kent and Gloucester are represented as servants). Being out of the house generally signals a distance from this system, and therefore a loss of self in relation to the only order that can sustain personal identity. Being moved outside, as Edgar, Gloucester, and Lear are, is then a terrible risk, a self-exile, because selfhood is constituted in terms of one's place in a house.

Kurosawa responds to this feature of the play by building his film around a number of households. Primary among these is First Castle, which Taro inherits but which is dominated by his wife Kaede, whose family, displaced by Hidetora, once held it. Her identification with and power over that space, along with the revenge plot she engineers in an attempt to maintain mastery, threaten the male dominance associated with the samurai code (Howlett 2000: 123–5). Even more important is Third Castle, the one associated originally with Saburo (the Cordelia figure), the destruction of which forms the centerpiece of the film. Hidetora, lured there through a plot, sits impassively, almost meditatively, in its upper reaches during the siege mounted by the older sons, his stillness broken by occasional darting moves as he looks for a sword. But he is unable to commit hara-kiri for lack of a weapon, his troops are overwhelmed by gunfire, and the whole place is torched. He emerges almost magically untouched from the flames, walking slowly down the stairs as the opposing troops part in what looks like awe. He passes out of the gates to his final "house," the ruined castle of Tsurumaru, where he, like his Shakespearean counterpart, must live outside and separated from the order of deference and status symbolized by the various castles. The whole interplay of outside and inside in the film reframes *King Lear*'s intense focus on houses and houselessness, but transposed from the implied use of stage space in Shakespeare's open-air theater, itself ambiguously both interior and exterior, to the illusionistic three-dimensional space made available through the technologies of film (the various weird and unsettling camera angles in the scenes at the ruined castle bear this out).

The sense of an unraveling self, cut off from hierarchical relations and caught in the mazes of a threatened and ultimately destroyed castle, also haunts the earlier *Throne of Blood*, often considered the greatest of all cinematic adaptations of Shakespeare. There too we confront a powerful sense of isolation, counterpointed with the memory of belonging. One of its most affecting scenes registers its hero's distance from his past and his painful awareness that there is no way back. In a significant departure from *Macbeth*, which the film follows much more closely than *Ran* does *King Lear*, we witness Washizu trying desperately to communicate with his mad wife, the seemingly indomitable Asaji. Even cooler and more determined through most of the action than her counterpart, Lady Macbeth, she now kneels, scouring imaginary blood off her hands over the same bowl she casually used in the scene directly following the murder. But there is no watching physician or lady to frame the scene; rather, Washizu himself has rushed to her room. The sequence is introduced by cries of "My lady" and Washizu dashing along the matted hallways in his characteristic half-run, legs pumping and upper body immobile; a point of view shot catches Asaji's lady-in-waiting cowering in a doorway, which is blocked by a large frame with a kimono spread scarecrow-like across it. Washizu is brought up short. The kimono hangs finely and formally, except for the left arm and shoulder, which have slipped off the frame like a broken wing. He pauses, then tears the garment off, revealing the kneeling, oblivious Asaji, scrubbing her hands. He kneels, tries to distract her, crying out her name in desperation, but her focus never bends from the "smell of blood." More shouts, and then comes the news of the forest moving towards the castle, barely giving Washizu time to mourn; thus does the fulfillment of the equivocal prophecy mark the imminent end of Washizu's increasingly demented reign.

Both the sequencing and the scene itself stress how utterly alone Washizu has become. Slightly earlier, upon learning that the promised heir has been born dead (because of the baby in Asaji's womb, lord and lady have plotted the murder of Miki/Banquo and his son), Washizu is seen in a bare room shouting "fool, fool." His grief is palpable, and ironically inflected by the emptiness of the room, furnished only with a small chest on which sits the symbolic helmet of power.[5] Fixed mockingly to the helmet is the emblem of feudal hegemony, a huge crescent moon, which we first saw adorning the head of the murdered Lord Tsuzuki (Duncan). Later, watching as Asaji scrapes at her hands, Washizu is just as thoroughly alone as he was in that sparse room: screaming to get through to her, he is helpless to do so. Thus Kurosawa subtly shifts the Shakespearean emphasis. While *Macbeth* also traces its hero's growing isolation, it follows a somewhat different course. After the killing of Duncan, a gulf begins to widen between husband and wife; Macbeth alone plans the murder of Banquo and his son, telling his lady to be "innocent of the knowledge . . . Till thou applaud the deed" (3.2.45–6). In *Throne of Blood* the plan comes from Asaji, with only grudging acceptance from her husband. This not only adds to the monstrosity of the female (of which more later) but also maintains the idea of team-work, which, while still present in *Macbeth* (as at the banquet), is less prominent. Washizu's need for his wife grows rather than diminishes as the action continues – or at least is more graphically presented. Once again Kurosawa develops hints already there in Shakespeare's text ("She should have died hereafter" [5.5.17]). Having Washizu witness directly his wife's descent into madness gives a special tonality to his isolation, stressing once again the crucial importance of community and its loss, an idea with transhistorical as well as local implications.

The film begins and ends with the image of an isolated mountain-scape shrouded in fog, a piercing flute, and jabs of percussion accompanying the chant on the soundtrack. A lonely wooden monument, marked with fading characters, is all that's left of Washizu – a decaying post, a text that speaks hauntingly from the past like *Macbeth* itself. The spectral voices emphasize the "murderous ambition" and the moral of Washizu's fall is made all too clear. The action, however, doesn't really fit the moral. Washizu may be ambitious, but he's very reluctantly so. Just as readings of *Macbeth* in terms of ambition tend to flatten the play, so Kurosawa's own script belies the complexity of his representations. Washizu is as loyal as he is ambitious, and though we are told several times that every samurai harbors in his heart of hearts a desire to be lord of a castle, what we actually see in the film's early parts is relative contentment with the position one holds. When, as a reward for his loyalty in defeating the rebels, Washizu is made lord of the North Castle, the initial images are of a life of pastoral contentment, peasants working the fields in bright sunlight, horses being exercised, a chorus of young retainers talking about paradise – the bliss of communal life.

Behind the sliding panels, however, a darker conception takes shape. "Have you made up your mind?" asks Asaji, the serpent in the garden. So talk has been going on, instigated by the curious prophecies voiced by the forest spirit (i.e., that Washizu will soon be master of Cobweb castle and Miki's son will inherit it). Washizu is restless and displeased, wanting none of this talk: "Enough!" Asaji, however, is not easily deflected from her purpose; her mask-like face hardly changes expression, but she has the power of her own certainty, always a strong weapon against the kind of indecision that plagues Washizu. She knows hearts, she says – her husband's and those of his rivals; she "knows" Miki is ambitious and will use what he learned from the forest prophecy to bring down Washizu: "Children kill their parents for less." Again, the scene mirrors and departs subtly from *Macbeth*. Washizu is even less ambitious than his counterpart, more troubled and uncertain, while Asaji is much darker and more implacable than Lady Macbeth. She is the driving force throughout and, like Lady Kaede in *Ran*, is unalloyed in her evil, lacking even Kaede's motivation of familial revenge.

Even more than Shakespeare's, Kurosawa's women seem to function symbolically. In *Throne of Blood* there are really only two women, and they are mirrors of each other – Asaji and the strange, ambiguously gendered spirit in the forest, who spins her wheel and knows, perhaps even controls, the fates of vain and mortal men who "end in fear." It is a man's world, but it is the woman who makes things happen. In one sense, this gives the woman force and agency, even though exerted through the man; but it also means that evil seems to enter the world most powerfully through her. Without Asaji, without the "evil spirit" in the forest, Washizu would remain at the North Castle in pastoral bliss. More so than Lady Macbeth, she is responsible for the dark web. At the same time, there is something weirdly admirable about women such as Kaede and Asaji, so single-minded, so passionate, so self-contained. The latter's face is a white blank, her eyebrows erased to a barely discernible lift, but for all that she has a fierce expression, a sense of irony as she mocks her husband's protestations of innocence, and a glittering, wary intelligence. (The whiteness derives from Noh masks and links her with the forest spirit, but unlike either she projects an individual personality.) And when Asaji rubs her hands together in madness we see her blank look in a new way, bereft now of all those hidden energies. The soundtrack, full of the screech of crows, staccato drums, high-pitched flutes, is mostly silent when she walks – except for the ominous squeaking of her slippers as she glides across the bare floor, spear in hand. That sound, at once soft and penetrating, innocuous and baleful, is her hallmark.

But perhaps also it registers a touch of weakness in the steely exterior. After Washizu leaves with the fatal spear, there is a brief scene in the blood-stained room where the previous occupant, the traitor Fujimaki, had committed suicide. Asaji, now alone, first sinks to her knees, then leaps up and moves wildly to the bloodied wall while percussion and flute beat a frenzied accompaniment. Incipient madness? Fear? We aren't sure, but it feels like a way of conveying the doubt implicit in Lady Macbeth's "Had he not resembled / My father as he slept, I had done't" (2.2.12–13). Once again we see Kurosawa reading Shakespeare closely. Like that of her counterpart, her hesitancy, if that is what it is, doesn't last long. When Washizu returns, his hands frozen around the bloodied spear, she does her job coolly, peeling his fingers back and taking away the spear to implicate the drugged guards. She briefly notes her own stained hands, hurries back and washes, while her husband sits transfixed, his posture and expression doing the work of Macbeth's famous lines about transforming the green sea into "one red."

Kurosawa seems ambivalent about how to represent the powerful woman and her role in the entropy of the world he has imagined. Who exactly is responsible? From one point of view, it is clear that the samurai code, with its hierarchies dependent upon one's skill at evisceration, its endless, though occluded, competition, and its elaborate but utterly untrustworthy courtliness, is both a cause of human evil and an effect of something embedded in human nature – the urge to dominate and kill (doomed though it is to lead to misery and desolation). So the men who are caught up in it, especially the supremely violent ones like Washizu and Hidetora, are to some extent pawns of the dark forces represented by the wood demon. But at the same time, we see them choose their paths. Asaji tempts Washizu to murder; Kaede drives Jiro to similar lengths. But neither of them has the power to *make* their men "do it" ("When you durst do it, then you were a man" [1.7.49]).

The women's force is at least partly, maybe almost completely, sexual. This is especially clear in *Ran* where Kaede seduces Jiro in a sequence that brilliantly combines indirection with the most overt sexuality: she lures him with sidelong moves, then, as they come to embrace, she threatens to cut his throat with a dagger, nicks him in a gesture that is half love-pinch, half assertion of dominance, and triumphs by licking the blood from his neck. Later, just before she is slashed to pieces and her blood spatters the wall, she is accused by Jiro's chief lieutenant of "female vanity"; but she turns the familiar sexist taunt back on him and her second husband, boasting of how she has accomplished her complex revenge. So Kurosawa's perspective remains ambivalent: men are at the (sexual) mercy of women they cannot do without, but at the same time, men do what they do because they are driven there by larger forces (cultural and "natural") that have little to do with women. They are both responsible for their own evil and fated to it.

168

One source of Asaji's power is her ability to reinterpret. Again, this is a feature of *Macbeth* that Kurosawa capitalizes on – and not only in the false prophecy sequence when Washizu, frustrated by what he sees as his "cowardly" council, dashes to the wood and is assured that he is in no danger until the Cobweb forest moves to the castle. The celebrated "amphibology" of *Macbeth* (see Mullaney and Booth) is moved into the center of the relationship between Washizu and Asaji. In Shakespeare, Lady Macbeth questions her husband's understanding of what it means to be a man: doing only what "may become a man" because of moral queasiness is not enough; rather, "When you durst do it, then you were a man." Asaji doesn't need to encourage an abstract notion of manliness – the samurai code does that for her. What she does instead is turn arguments around, redefine intention and motivation, provide an interpretation that makes sense in terms of that very code. And in so doing she highlights the unknowability of the human world, so deeply invested in the ambiguous gestures and glances of warrior life.

The film's plot turns on this skill of hers. Lord Tsuzuki comes to visit, and lays his martial intentions before Washizu: he will move against the enemy, Inui, taking over Washizu's North Castle for use as a base, sending Miki back to guard the main castle in the lord's absence, and appointing Washizu as head of his armies. Washizu sees this as a great honor, but a long holding shot on an immobile and thoughtful Asaji serves as a transition to the next scene – in the bedroom. Washizu laughs, mocking his wife for her fears that Tsuzuki, informed by Miki about the encounter in the forest, must now be suspicious of him. The laughter (ironically recalling that of the forest spirit heard just before Washizu's first encounter with her) echoes in the almost-empty room as Asaji sits in the same posture, with the same thoughtful expression, as in the previous shot. Her reinterpretation is masterful: Tsuzuki's project, she says, is all a ruse – Miki, given the responsibility of protecting the lord's castle, is poised to become second in command, while Tsuzuki, pretending to honor Washizu, is actually planning to double-cross him, using his secure position in the North Castle to take it over while Washizu is out naively fighting Inui, thus inadvertently strengthening his lord's position against himself. The very opacity of motive, the ever-present possibility that behind the bowing deference lies murderous intention, renders Asaji's version of events plausible. Her masked features are a mark of the world all the characters inhabit, and her identification of the precise epistemological problem is irresistible to Washizu, whose protests are ineffectual against the poison of doubt.

The pervasive sense of uncertainty sits uneasily with the film's overt moral about murderous ambition. If the world and other people are impossible to read fully and accurately, if the power of fate cannot be untangled from the intricacies of human motivation, how sure can we be about the moral positions we adopt? The question hovers around the edges of the film like the fog. Looking back from his position in mid-twentieth-century Japan, after the terrible devastation of World War II (which followed in the wake of a renewed militarism that sought to revivify samurai values), Kurosawa locates the evil he wants to probe but also allows a certain epistemological skepticism to pervade and partially undermine this world of apparent certainties. Influenced no doubt by the widespread philosophical doubt and emphasis on individual commitment that, in the West, found expression in existentialism, and immersed in the teachings of Zen, with its emphasis on the illusory nature of all things, Kurosawa shifts back and forth between personal responsibility and resignation. His work after the war (*Ikiru* and *Rashomon*, for example) manifests these opposing views. As Stephen Prince puts it, "one ·of the dialectics informing Kurosawa's works is a struggle between a belief in the materialist process – that human beings make their world and can change it – and an emphasis on dissolution, decay, and impermanence as fundamental truths of human life" (1999: 124). Reading his own cultural past, Kurosawa finds in Shakespeare a roughly similar model for his vision of impermanence, which highlights for him the very different ways in which the same problem can be instantiated in different periods and cultural contexts. That a similar skepticism, though with quite different cultural underpinnings, is discernible in *Macbeth* provides Kurosawa with philosophical leverage. His version of events is also a reading of Shakespeare: human beings, faced with the cryptic ambiguities of what they perceive, remain uncomprehending, lost in the very assertions they most definitively make (a perception which extends to the movie itself and its attempts at moral certitude). His heroes, Washizu and later Hidetora, are thus driven into a kind of epistemological solitude that matches their growing social isolation. Like Macbeth, Washizu opts for a chimerical certainty, but is brought up short as this certainty unravels like the thread on the spinning wheel turned inexorably by the spectral figure in the forest.

Nowhere in the film is this more brazenly illustrated than in the famous sequence that brings Washizu to his bitter and uncomprehending end. The arrows that surround, trap, and eventually penetrate him carry a message whose startling visual impact and bizarre humor cap the narrative of lost certitude and misplaced confidence. The final decline starts well before, when, reassured by the latest prophecy, Washizu climbs the wooden staircases inside the castle to observe the gathering army. We see the distant forest scene from his point of view, looking sharply down the curving roof-ridge of the castle, a precipitous falling line of vision that both mirrors and belies Washizu's overconfident perception. His commanding visual position above offers a delusive mastery: the castle, like the forest, *looks* stable, but the steeply dropping sightlines tell a different story. As he turns back to his restless troops, he laughs heartily; in a series of shots from below he looms large, seemingly in control. He recounts the story of the prophecy to the assembled troops down in the courtyard, and they cheer – but again the disorienting angles of the shots suggest the delusion in his self-assurance.

The same motif is continued in the night-time council scene that follows, when a flock of birds, driven from their boughs by the attackers' axes, invades the darkened room, ominous and foreboding – but not to Washizu. While his men see their wheeling presence as a portent, a dark omen, he reinterprets, having perhaps absorbed Asaji's skill in that art – for him, the birds are propitious, guaranteeing victory and success. Interpretation as desire is nowhere more starkly represented. But no sooner do his encouraging words emerge than he is interrupted by the women's shrieks, "My lady," and the film shifts to the handwashing scene, which is, in turn, interrupted by the impossible news that the forest is moving. The pace, for the most part slow and even repetitive, quickens and the emerging meaning is generated by this sharp, disturbing sequence of scenes: conceptual mastery – confidence in one's perceptions, even the very will to understand – is mocked at every turn.

Once Washizu gets word that the Cobweb forest is approaching, everything unravels. First he rushes to the window from which he confidently observed the attackers earlier: fronds wave in the mist, moving slowly forward, a seeming impossibility, but now a mental trap. The troops watch silently from below as Washizu keeps furiously checking the view; turning, he shouts down from the battlements, trying to command them into action. But they refuse to budge, their earlier cheers reduced to an ironic silence. They stand immobile as Washizu, the fly in the web, buzzes frantically. After a moment, a single arrow sings out, thudding into the wooden wall beside him.

Soon arrows are flying all around him, vibrating as they pierce the walls, some finding their mark in Washizu's body. He dances amid the explosion of arrows, stopping short as a dozen or so hit the wall in front of him so that we view him momentarily through a forest of criss-crossed lines, as we had when he first rode through the woods. The whole sequence is excessive and contrived, so many arrows, so few actually finding their mark. The idea is to keep Washizu moving, stopping and starting, staring wildly, caged by the quivers of arrows, caught in the web they weave. A few penetrate his armor, finding his flesh but barely slowing him down, until he begins to look like an archer's dummy or a particularly grotesque portrait of St. Sebastian. The climax finally comes in a moment of black comedy when an arrow, launched from an impossible angle, pierces his neck, sticking crazily out from each side as he staggers, bug-eyed, trying to hold on.[6] The arrows stop, the thudding and singing silenced, and we move to a slow, quiet ballet of collapse. There is hardly a sound, only the soft soughing of the wind as Washizu struggles to stay upright, pitches forward, and ends sprawled on the stairs. My initial reaction to all this was astonishment, mixed with laughter; it is an amazing sequence, but why the bizarre comedy, the extreme stylization, the excessive prolongation? Am I showing my cultural limitations here, not appreciating the Noh-like dance, the lack of concern for verisimilitude, the aims of a peculiarly Japanese artistic vision? Maybe – in fact probably. But it's still strangely comic, and I have a hunch that someone as canny as Kurosawa, immersed in Western as well as Japanese film, knows it. Perhaps, indeed, the darkly comic collapse only underlines Washizu's sense of separation, his distance from us and from his own past; perhaps the laughter, whether real or implied, is Beckettian, an acknowledgment of the absurd futility of human striving, funny to the last.

The film doesn't end there, however. We revert back to the victors, as in *Macbeth*, though again with a difference. There is no extended triumph, no sense of continuity. In Shakespeare, the monarchy prevails, Malcolm is reinstated, and life goes on, even up to the present king, James VI of Scotland and I of England. By contrast, Noriyasu's victory is as futile as Washizu's fall; it leads nowhere except to the dirge with which the film begins and ends, the silent monument in the mist, a piercing note on the flute, and a sharp percussive snap.

Kurosawa, it might be said, reads Shakespeare rather as Shakespeare read some of his authors, Plutarch, Ovid, Chaucer; that is, not just for stories as he did the chronicles or some of the pulp romances of his day, but from the inside, responding to the complex dynamics of the original work. At the same time, both filmmaker and playwright make their precursors' work their own, adapting it in relation to their own imaginative apprehensions as artists and linking it to contemporary cultural concerns. Thus Kurosawa's obsession with hierarchy and violence, and with social habitation and individual isolation, meshes with Shakespeare's but finds a unique expression not only in the images registering his understanding of tragic futility, but also in the darker, more bitterly sardonic attitude he develops towards his material. How this might relate to both the ancient and the recent Japanese past I leave to others, more qualified than I. But it seems to me that Kurosawa's reading of Shakespeare resembles that of Jan Kott, whose *Shakespeare Our Contemporary* (1964) was published not long after the filming of *Throne of Blood*. Parallel to Kurosawa's, Kott's understanding of Shakespeare was filtered through bitter wartime and Cold War experience and inflected by a reading of existentialist philosophy and absurdist drama. His interpretation (which strongly influenced a whole generation of critics and performers) was colored by a Beckettian vision of the abyss; it resembles that of Kurosawa in that both omit the hints of restoration that Shakespeare provides. Both emphasize instead the relentless destructiveness of human agency together with the malevolence of fate, motifs that are present in Shakespeare but in less vividly pure terms. Though Gloucester's despairing comment in *King Lear*, "As flies to wanton boys are we to th' gods, / They kill us for their sport" (4.1.36–7), has sometimes been taken as the play's most visionary statement, it is really only a single, though potent, voice and moment. If readers like Kott and Kurosawa seem to lean towards a view that favors a darker interpretation, the latter at least also recognizes the element of human responsibility and emphasizes the poignancy of loss entailed by a commitment to destructive warrior values.

I find it valuable to trace such filiations (cross-cultural, trans-historical), to be aware of sameness as well as otherness, to reach back in our interpretations of film to earlier ways of reading – aesthetic, author-centered, focused on the agency of the artist – without giving up the insights derived from more recent work in cultural studies. While acknowledging that authorial agency is constrained in multiple ways, I would still insist that it is a crucial consideration in our quest to understand works of art as products of both culture and individuals.

Anthony Dawson

Notes

1 While it is difficult to generalize, there are at least two broad currents in studies of Kurosawa's Shakespeare films, one that links them to the cinematic or metacinematic concerns of the filmmaker (e.g., Donaldson, Howlett), and another that sees them in relation to specifically Japanese styles of representation such as Noh (e.g., Parker, Hapgood); cutting across these, there is also often a concern with what might be called "universal" human characteristics, such as desire for power, "murderous ambition" and the like.
2 This issue has been much debated – many viewers see the film as only peripherally connected to Shakespeare's play, while others, such as Thompson, Parker, and Hapgood, have pointed out carefully etched connections.
3 Jiro, the ambitious second son, is seduced by and marries his slain brother's wife, Lady Kaede, whose revenge plot drives the film's second half.
4 Sué, Jiro's kind first wife, is later savagely murdered, becoming a kind of displaced Cordelia figure.
5 Donaldson (1990: 73ff.) comments astutely on the film's "feudal geometry" and its relation to "power [and] plenitude": "The social order is embodied throughout *Throne of Blood* in strict and uncluttered rectilinear compositions"; I would add that the deterioration of the same order is depicted in similar, though ironically refracted, images.
6 Donaldson (1990: 87) notes that the arrow comes across the plane of the screen, "perfectly horizontal," from a place where there are no archers; he suggests that this "hints at supernatural retribution, and completes the collapse of the illusory geometry of human violence that has been Kurosawa's subject."

References and Further Reading

Booth, Stephen (1983). *King Lear, Macbeth, Indefinition, and Tragedy*. New Haven: Yale University Press.
Dawson, Anthony (2002). "International Shakespeare." In Stanley Wells and Sarah Stanton (eds.), *Cambridge Companion to Shakespeare on Stage*. Cambridge: Cambridge University Press: 174–93.
Hapgood, Robert (1994). "Kurosawa's Shakespeare Films: *Throne of Blood, The Bad Sleep Well*, and *Ran*." In Davies and Wells, eds.: 234–49.
Mack, Maynard (1965). *King Lear in Our Time*. Berkeley: University of California Press.
Mullaney, Steven (1988). *The Place of the Stage: License, Play, and Power in Renaissance England*. Chicago: University of Chicago Press.
Parker, Brian (1986). "*Ran* and the Tragedy of History." *UTQ* 55.4: 412–23.

—— (1997). "Nature and Society in Kurosawa's *Throne of Blood*." *UTQ* 66.3: 508–25.

Prince, Stephen (1999). *The Warrior's Camera: The Cinema of Akira Kurosawa.* Princeton: Princeton University Press.

Ross, Alex (2003). "Rock 101." *New Yorker,* July 13 and 21: 87–93.

Strier, Richard (1988). "Faithful Servant: Shakespeare's Praise of Disobedience." In Richard Strier and Heather Dubrow (eds.), *The Historical Renaissance.* Chicago: University of Chicago Press: 104–31.

Thompson, Ann (1989). "Kurosawa's *Ran*: Reception and Interpretation." *East-West Film Journal* 3.2: 1–13.

Yong Li Lan (forthcoming). "*Romeos and Juliets,* Local/Global." In R. S. White (ed.), *Shakespeare's Local Habitations.* London: Palgrave.

Chapter 9

Will of the People: Recent Shakespeare Film Parody and the Politics of Popularization

Douglas Lanier

In *Shakespeare for the Modern Man, Lesson 2: Hamlet* (2003), playwright Scott Eckert offers two versions of Shakespeare's tragedy on the same stage at the same time. The first is a conventional performance in period language and, in the words of the introduction, "sissy costumes," the second a modern adaptation by "normal people in normal clothes" speaking in "language we can all understand." Though the simultaneous performances follow the Shakespearean narrative closely and mirror each other's blocking, the modern passages delight in finding irreverent pop analogies and allusions – Bernardo and Marcellus as dope-smoking Gen-Xers, Madonna films among the "slings and arrows" Hamlet must suffer – and contemporary slang they can set against the formal poetry and manner of "straight" Shakespeare. The effect of this juxtaposition is not as easy to locate as it might at first seem. Eckert denies that his intent is parodic; rather, he regards his play as a "comic deconstruction" which presents Shakespeare to modern audiences in terms that are entertaining and relevant while preserving the integrity of the original.[1] Nevertheless, there are reasons for placing the play within a tradition of Shakespearean parody stretching at least as far back as Victorian Shakespeare burlesques, where "high" Shakespeare was transposed into the "low" contexts of working-class characters, colloquial idioms, and popular tunes of the day. What makes *Shakespeare for the Modern Man* particularly illuminating is the undecidable object of the play's humor and thus the questions it raises about contemporary Shakespearean parody. Does the play principally target Shakespeare's dreary outmodedness in manner and language? The excessive reverence with which traditional Shakespeare is often presented onstage? Or does the play lampoon the terms by which Shakespeare has so often been modernized and popularized, particularly for a hip teen audience? Is the parody's effect finally transgressive, a popular riposte to a dominant voice of traditional high culture? Or is it in fact conservative, a humorous, finally self-consuming demonstration of the folly of popularizing Shakespeare? Or, most provocatively, does the parody target both Shakespeare and Shakespop at the same time (though not in the same way), leaving the viewer in a position of relative superiority to both? With its juxtaposition of Shakespop and Shakespeare, *Shakespeare for the Modern Man* makes explicit the vexed politics of cultural register that animates much contemporary performance, the oscillation between the drive to (re)popularize Shakespeare by "modernizing" him and the imperative to preserve those qualities that mark Shakespeare as a traditional icon of cultural authority.

Nowhere does the question of popularization loom larger than in Shakespearean parody on film, perhaps because film has long presented itself as a force both for making his works available to a wide, socially diverse audience and for adapting those works to pop cultural genres and idioms. Here I explore some dominant features of Shakespearean film parody in the last decade: first, its targeting of the specifically *cinematic* popularization of Shakespeare (as opposed to theatrical Shakespeare, the primary focus of earlier Shakespearean film parodies); second, its predominantly dark, violent tone, a quality which indicates forms of symbolic counter-violence; third, the extent to which these parodies problematize cinematic Shakespop hybridity even as they engage in it, in the process fashioning a knowing, yet strategically distant, relation of the viewer to screen Shakespeare; and fourth, the extent to which moments of cinematic parody are embedded in otherwise "serious" Shakespearean films. At the heart of my discussion are questions about the purposes of parody within what I regard as a distinctive cycle of Shakespearean film adaptation: are these parodies merely symptomatic of the postmodern practice of pop allusion with a self-congratulatory wink? Do they indicate the exhaustion of popular Shakespeare film as a genre almost before it gets established?

Do they betray a certain nervousness about Shakespeare's newly close affiliation with cinematic pop culture, allowing that affiliation to be pursued only under the veil of irony? Do they reveal the difficulties of finding suitably demotic, contemporary analogues for Shakespearean tragedy? Or do they function as a mechanism for regulating Shakespeare's relationship to the category of the popular?

Of course this is not the only strain of Shakespearean film parody produced during the period. *Shakespeare in Love* (1998), to take the most obvious example, situates Shakespeare very firmly in a theatrical, not cinematic, milieu and it certainly lacks the black humor and violence of other films I will be discussing. Even so, many of the film's best laughs spring from parodic parallels to contemporary Hollywood culture, particularly the overarching imperative to create a popular blockbuster with which the film begins. And even within the fiction of *Shakespeare in Love*, Shakespeare's popular success is accompanied by the loss of his artistic inspiration, Viola, who must obey the parallel, tragic commercial imperative of the marriage market. The film's coda in which he begins to write *Twelfth Night* suggests that the final triumph of Shakespearean art and love (the two become inseparable) over commerce can occur only in Shakespeare's fantasies, not in the "real" world of Elizabethan popular entertainment. My larger point is that the question of reconciling Shakespeare with the protocols of popular cinema is an overarching preoccupation in films of the period, which even so romantic and stage-struck a film as *Shakespeare in Love* pursues with ambivalence.

Before proceeding, it may be helpful to clarify the concept of parody. Stressing that parody is not a specific style but a transformational process, Don Harries defines it in terms of its oscillation between similarity to and difference from the distinctive formal characteristics of a target film or genre. Parody, he argues, replicates either the visual lexicon, syntax, or style of its target while manipulating the other components, creating a comic incongruity that is its signature feature (Harries 2000: 6, 9; for definitions, see also Jump 1972; Genette 1997; Rose 1993). Harries' definition usefully highlights two crucial issues. First, historically, Shakespearean parody has been most concerned with incongruities of stylistic register, that is, transposing Shakespeare's language to a lowbrow, colloquial, or contemporary style, or placing Shakespearean formal style in the mouths of mundane characters or in the service of trivial events. Built into the popularization of Shakespeare, then, is the ease with which it might shade into parody, a potential that each film under discussion here directly engages.

Second, parody is often distinguished from satire on the basis of its primary target. To lay out the distinction schematically, satire mocks social or political mores from the perspective of some implied ethical standard, whereas parody sets the formal qualities of a work, genre, or style against some implied standard of stylistic decorum. (Pastiche, to introduce a third distinction, offers parody's incongruous juxtaposition of formal components without the element of mockery or implied decorum.) This useful working distinction nevertheless may prevent us from considering (*à la* Bourdieu) the interrelationships between certain modes of decorum and processes of sociocultural stratification and marginalization, the ways in which regimes of style and register mark membership in and exclusion from social groups and thus are forms of power. It raises, in other words, the question of whether contemporary Shakespearean parody functions as a form of social satire once removed, as a means by which an erosion of stylistic boundaries elsewhere in the culture is policed and order reestablished (what Wes D. Gehring dubs "reaffirmative parody" [1999: 6–8]), or even as "conservative subversion" (Harries 2000: 129–30), routinized pseudo-transgression in which a stylistic defiling of Shakespeare substitutes for genuine oppositional politics.

One additional concept hovers over all my examples of Shakespearean parody: the quality of camp. Though camp sensibility typically involves elements of irony, aestheticism, theatricality, and humor (Babuscio 1993: 20–9), its essential quality is the value it places on stylistic excess as a means for redeeming cultural objects or performances that are outmoded, marginalized, or despised by the mainstream. As Andrew Ross observes, the camp effect is created when the work "of a much earlier mode of production, which has lost its power to produce and dominate cultural meanings, becomes available, in the present, for redefinition" (Ross 1993: 58), typically by celebrating that work's ironic or transgressive relationship to reigning stylistic norms. It shares with parody the element of exaggeration and humor, but it differs in several ways. First, camp is always a subcultural mode of taste, that is, it requires a special stylistic sophistication to appreciate, the possession of which marks one as a member of a particular cultural group. Second, camp involves an *ironized* appreciation for a cultural form. It is different from a naive attachment to or simple parodic mockery of some out-of-fashion or subartistic style; rather, camp requires that one acknowledge a form or style is unfashionable by conventional standards, but that one nevertheless values precisely those excesses or stylistic "failings" that make it culturally denigrated. Third, camp has long been closely identified with gay sub-culture and drag, within which, many commentators have noted, the camp sensibility has complex links to queer strategies for navigating an oppressive social system. Even so, camp cannot be reduced simply to an exclusively gay sensibility, for as a strategy of taste it allows various cultural coteries to recuperate through shared irony artistic styles that violate conventional canons of stylistic decorum. Recent cinematic Shakespeare parody often straddles the line between parody and camp. Camp becomes a means for redeeming the enterprise of Shakespop adaptation without sacrificing recognition that hybridizing Shakespeare with pop culture potentially produces kitsch. Camp, in other words, allows for the reinstatement of a form of cultural strati-fication, albeit one in which the traditional sociopolitical associations of high and low are (strategically) muted: where once there was low-brow pop culture and highbrow Shakespeare, now there is Shakespop and, for those few, those happy few capable of appreciating it, camp Shakespop.

Shakespearean parody is, of course, nothing new to the cinema. The silent adaptations of Shakespeare which appeared in the first decade of commercial filmmaking, many of which sought to establish film's artistic and social respectability, were followed in the 1920s by a spate of Shakespeare parodies. Those parodies, many of which took stage Shakespeare as their object, picked up elements of the Shake-speare burlesque and used them to distinguish the movies as a popu-lar performance form from the theater, which film increasingly treated as a province of the elite. The advent of sound extended this tradition. Pre-recorded Shakespearean dialogue first appeared in the movies with MGM's *Hollywood Revue of 1929*, which, in a portent of things to come, featured a traditional rendition of the balcony scene from *Romeo and Juliet* by Norma Shearer and John Gilbert, followed almost immediately by a jazz-age parody – ordered by studio executives, so the film claims – of the same passage performed by the same players. What distinguishes these and other earlier phases of Shakespeare film parody from the examples discussed below is the nature of late-century adaptation of Shakespeare to film. Whereas before the 1990s screen Shakespeare was predominantly an art film phenomenon, recent adaptations have by and large aimed to reach a mass market audience and recast Shakespeare as popular entertainment (see Crowl 2002: esp. 1–24). Crucial to that enterprise has been assimilating Shakespeare to popular film genres. That enterprise might be under-stood as part of the larger cultural phenomenon of postmodernism, with its problematizing of traditional boundaries between high and low culture, or as the mass media's decisive appropriation of a form of cultural capital traditionally associated with literature. Whatever the case, parody found this pop cinematizing of Shakespeare fertile material, and because Shakespeare films in the 1990s had the quality of a sustained film cycle, parody could engage not just individual plays and films but also the cycle's driving premises (see WALKER). A number of adaptations relocated the plays in contemporary settings, an approach new to screen Shakespeare, and some later films modernized or entirely replaced Shakespeare's language. The heightened, self-conscious engagement within the cycle with the problem of Shakespeare's relation to contemporaneity was ready-made for parodic (re)consideration.

One of the first salvos of Shakespearean parody in the 1990s, a wicked vignette in John McTiernan's *The Last Action Hero* (1993), addresses the relationship of Shakespearean art film to its cultural antitype, the action blockbuster. In it, a teacher, struggling to make Shakespeare interesting to bored middle-schoolers, claims that Hamlet is "one of the first action heroes," and to drive her point home, she shows the class a clip from Laurence Olivier's film adaptation. Hamlet's hesitation to kill Claudius prompts one student to imagine a fantasy trailer for a very different film *Hamlet*, one starring his favorite action star Jack Slater (Arnold Schwarzenegger) in which blockbuster-style Hamlet slashes, machine guns, and bombs everyone in sight. The absent middle term in this much discussed vignette (see Burt 1998: 141–2; and Mallin 1999) is one of the first major Shakespeare films of the 1990s, Franco Zeffirelli's *Hamlet* (1990), a film which (like Branagh's *Henry V* the year before) appropriated elements of the action blockbuster to produce Shakespearean cinema for a mainstream audience. Mel Gibson's star persona was central to Zeffirelli's film, for he brought well-established action-hero credentials from the *Lethal Weapon* franchise to the title role. Indeed, it was his performance as the melancholy, manic policeman Martin Riggs that reputedly convinced Zeffirelli to cast Gibson.

It is hardly incidental, then, that Shane Black, chief writer for the *Lethal Weapon* series, was also on the writing team for *The Last Action Hero*. Schwarzenegger's action Hamlet lampoons not only the conventions of the genre Black and others pioneered but also the very notion of an action-Shakespeare hybrid. Parodically recalled in the teacher's list of *Hamlet's* exciting adventure qualities – "treachery, conspiracy, sex, swordfights, madness, ghosts, and in the end everyone dies" – is the promotional campaign for Zeffirelli's film that included a button reading "murder, madness, lust, treachery, sword play, and a ghost . . . Hamlet." *The Last Action Hero* vignette establishes *Hamlet* as a generic fountainhead to which contemporary action blockbusters, with their anti-heroic smart-mouthed protagonists and themes of betrayal, institutionalized corruption, and avenging violence, might lay claim, but it does so only to demonstrate (with a spectacular example of its own violent excesses) the unbridgeable differences between first and last action heroes. Of course, it is Olivier's film adaptation, not Zeffirelli's, that emphasizes Hamlet's penchant for delay and excessive self-consciousness. In keeping with its action-adventure affiliation Zeffirelli's version cuts nearly half of Shakespeare's dialogue and stresses Hamlet's explosive temperament, active counter-plotting, and strategically feigned madness. Where Olivier's Hamlet hesitates, the corresponding scene in Zeffirelli's version becomes an occasion for Gibson's Hamlet to resolve to make his revenge upon Claudius apocalyptic in its fury, "to trip him that his heels may kick at heaven / And that his soul may be as damned and black / As hell whereto it goes" (3.3.93–5). My point is that *The Last Action Hero* deploys Olivier's much older film as a countertext to and substitute for its true parodic targets, Zeffirelli's adaptation in particular and action-Shakespeare hybrids in general. By doing so, *The Last Action Hero* can demonstrate a fundamental incompatibility between "classic" Shakespeare and pop cinematic genres to which he has been retrofitted, while at the same time it can offer an example of Shakespop hybridity under the veil of irony.

A number of Shakespearean film spinoffs from the mid-1990s onward veered in the direction of parody, a sign that the relative success of Zeffirelli's and Branagh's film adaptations had reignited debate about the relationship between Shakespeare and popular culture. The pivotal film in this history is Baz Luhrmann's *William Shakespeare's Romeo + Juliet* (1996), retaining the teen casting and lush neo-romanticism of Zeffirelli's 1968 film adaptation but jettisoning its period setting and costumes in favor of contemporary urban youth culture and a cinematically allusive, MTV-frantic style. Like *Clueless* (1995), *Romeo + Juliet* was a craftily marketed hit which demonstrated the commercial possibilities of adapting literary classics to teen-film genres. Accordingly it launched a series of youth pop Shakespeares – *10 Things I Hate About You* (1999), *Never Been Kissed* (1999), Almereyda's *Hamlet* (2000), *O* (2001), *Get Over It* (2001), *The Glass House* (2001), *Rave Macbeth* (2001), *The Street King* (2002), and *Deliver Us from Eva*

(2003) chief among them – that were to become a dominant adaptational strain. In the process this series fueled questions about the cultural consequences of reshaping Shakespeare to the contours of pop culture: did such adaptation lead to dumbed-down accessibility or travesty? Was Shakespeare's oppositional potential being blunted, his cultural authority appropriated by an omnivorous pop culture industry? Was pop adaptation merely a matter of dressing up traditional Shakespeare in a glossy pop veneer? *Romeo + Juliet* itself seems to anticipate some of these questions with its scenes preparing for Romeo and Juliet's entrance into the film, the gun battle at the gas station and the preparations for the costume ball at the Capulet mansion, both examples of cinematic self-parody which momentarily take the transpositional style of the film to comic extremes. Certainly these scenes establish the frenetic world of excess – of mindless violence and vapid wealth – from which Romeo and Juliet's romance offers refuge. But their very excessiveness, played largely for campy humor and filled with over-the-top allusions to kitsch genres like spaghetti Westerns, Hong Kong action films, and advertising, introduces an ironic, knowing distance from the act of contemporizing Shakespeare, even as the film engages – indeed revels – in it. These sequences function as a protective gesture, anticipating a critique of the film's approach to popularization by offering a passing parody of its own style in the act of introducing it to the viewer (compare WALKER).

If the function of parody in *Romeo + Juliet* is prophylactic, it functions rather differently in *Richard III* (1995) and *Titus* (1999), both of which punctuate their endings with moments of over-the-top cinematic parody. *Richard III* is peppered with allusions to the popular cinema of the 1930s, primary among them "the production values of the Hollywood musical, which rely on the ephemera of art deco styles and fashions, and the elusive, arbitrary signs that mark the matinée idol" (Buhler 2000: 41) and, one might add, the upbeat big band tunes that provide a sardonic soundtrack for Richard's rise to power. Indeed, the film seems obliquely to evoke elements of Hollywood fare like the musical and romance in order to suggest how their grand, escapist fantasies blinded viewers to the *Realpolitik* behind the scenes. Built into Shakespeare's play is a conception of Richard as a grotesque parodist of rituals of sincerity, civility, love, and piety, but much of this Richard's murderously parodic energy is also directed against images of the happy bourgeois family, an image first encoded in the film with the family snapshot (taken by Clarence) on the balcony. As the Yorks dance to a swing setting of Marlowe's "Come live with me and be my love," Richard contributes to the family's celebratory bash by offering what amounts to a victory toast (the first eleven lines of his "Now is the winter of our discontent" soliloquy), only abruptly to shift the scene to the men's urinal where in private he pisses all over the sentiment he has just uttered, adjusts his image in a mirror, and first begins to address the viewer directly. Family gatherings – holiday dinner around the table, or the court reconciliation engineered by the king, handled as a family seaside holiday at Brighton – become occasions for Richard to mime innocence and fidelity while strategically sowing distrust and guilt among the Yorks.

As noted, the film opens with a fleeting image of familial bliss. With a picture of adoring wife Anne at his side, his dog gnawing a bone hearthside in his country house, Prince Edward is the very picture of an Englishman's domestic contentment as he savors his roast dinner and wine, only to have that peace violated by Richard's tank turret bursting through the wall. The unmistakably phallic image hints that Richard's pursuit of political power is a compensation for sexual inadequacy, his inability by predilection or deformity to have a family of his own (see Buhler 2000: 47–9). The film presents Richard not just as a fascist tyrant but also as a gleeful parodist, a defiler of images of bourgeois familial concord. The final scenes of the film stress that it is Richard's escalating defilement of familial bonds, particularly his willingness to target children, that sets his downfall in motion. Tellingly, the words that wake him from his troubled sleep in the nightmare scene are Queen Elizabeth's anguished "where are my children?," a line which also opens the film's final sequence in Richard's camp. The compression of 4.4 emphasizes the parallel between Richard's designs on Princess Elizabeth, sealed with his horrifyingly lascivious kiss of her mother, and his taking of Stanley's son hostage. In both cases, Richard badly misjudges the parents' resolve, both of whom provide the crucial ingredients for his fall from power, Queen Elizabeth by engineering her daughter's marriage to Richmond, and Lord Stanley (portrayed as an RAF colonel) by providing decisive air support for the final battle.

This climactic sequence conspicuously lacks the sardonic edge of earlier sections of the film, especially during the battle scenes and final *mano a mano* between Richard and Richmond where "straight" borrowings from war films and film noir chase scenes pile up. For that reason the film's sudden turn back towards parody at the close is all the more startling. Piecing his way along a girder high in the power station, Richard, unarmed and cornered by Richmond, stretches out his hand to his nemesis in a last gesture of perverse partnership, uttering "Let us to't, pell mell– / If not to heaven, then hand in hand to hell" (5.6.42–3) as he begins to fall backwards, choosing to end his own life rather than be killed or captured. Richmond, taking just enough (ineffectual) shots at Richard to finish out his heroic role, then turns to look straight into the camera with a spreading smile. The final shot, surely one of the most savagely parodic in all of Shakespearean film, is of Richard laughing and waving in free fall as he plunges into the flames below, to the accompaniment of Al Jolson's jaunty "Sittin' on Top of the World." The image offers in updated form the descent of the damned into Hellmouth and thus evokes the providential scheme of the play's ending, where Richard's extermination is presented as the divinely ordained prelude to the peace of the Tudor dynasty. But this final sequence plays that conception of tragedy for camp. Even though he doesn't take Richard's hand, Richmond's gaze and smile links him to Richard and to the perverse pleasures of power. What has heretofore been presented to us as a clear moral opposition turns out to be an unsettling equivalence. And Richard's fall, with its wry parody of Cody Jarrett's fiery demise – "Made it, Ma! Top of the world!" – in *White Heat* (1949), locates him firmly in the genealogy of the cinematic anti-hero as he exits the film, with Richard actually outdoing Jarrett in his unrepentant amoral ambition and spectacular self-destruction. In the film's last seconds Loncraine deploys audaciously sardonic pop allusions to parody the culminating moral scheme of Shakespeare's tragedy while at the same time playing those allusions for campy excess, pushing them into the realm of self-parody. What this ending offers the viewer, in short, is the pleasure of gleeful cynicism, which may explain why the film ends with the image of a laughing hellbent Richard, his hand outstretched to the viewer (compare WALKER, HODGDON).

Taymor's *Titus* embraces the European art film as its primary cinematic forebear, with Fellini as its most important point of reference. Its allusions to popular culture tend to focus on examples of violence treated as play. In the film's prologue the boy engages in an increasingly berserk mock war with his food and toys at a stereotypical 1950s kitchen table as we hear a montage of sounds of violence from cartoons, film, and television, highlighting the escalating violence built into junk-food culture. This opening sequence leads directly to the arresting spectacle of Titus' marching legion – presented as if an army of giant toy soldiers has come frighteningly to life – through which the boy comes to confront the grim reality and aftermath of war.

Within the narrative proper, Demetrius and Chiron's predilection for video games and punk rock anaesthetizes them to the consequences of their horrific acts. Contemporary popular culture, particularly that directed towards boys, seems especially guilty of perpetuating cycles of violence. Taymor's critique is linked to the larger motif of murderous boys-as-men in the film. Saturninus is little more than a child-man who, given real political power, uses it to indulge his petulant whimsy. Just before he pursues his final revenges, Titus seems to regress to mad childhood, sitting in his tub like a boy in his bath (with a nod to David's *Death of Marat*) and drawing primitive portraits of his victims.

Given Taymor's critique of contemporary pop violence, it is striking that the film's penultimate sequence, Titus' revenge upon Tamora, her sons, and Saturninus, is underlaid with references to Anthony Hopkins' most famous role, the psychopathic cannibal Hannibal Lecter in *The Silence of the Lambs* (1991), another murderer and server of human flesh. The reference is announced at the climax of Titus' speech where he reveals his plan to kill the boys and "bid that strumpet, your unhallowed dam, / Like to the earth swallow her own increase" (5.3.189–90). Hopkins punctuates the line with the same grotesque slavering with which Lecter drives home his most famous line, the revelation that he once ate a victim's liver "with some fava beans and a nice Chianti." The icy horror of this moment Taymor sets against a saturated Technicolor shot of two giant meat pies cooling on a sunny windowsill, the image a savage parody of cheery bourgeois pop culture centered, as in the film's prologue, on a 1950s-style kitchen. This jarring shift in tone ushers in the banquet scene in which Hopkins' Titus oscillates between two oblique evocations of Lecter, one the quiet, chillingly deliberate murderer, the other an almost goofy parody that turns the revenger into a prancing, zany cannibalistic chef. Taymor uses black humor to magnify the viewer's horror when the scene finally erupts in a cascade of violence on the dinner table, a life-size version of what we witnessed in the prologue. But the oscillation of tone also suggests Taymor's discomfort with the subtext Hopkins brings and, more generally, with the affinities between *Titus'* climactic scene and the conventional bloody spectacles of the contemporary horror-thriller genre.

Elsewhere Taymor addresses her film's implication in the very re-presentations of violence she critiques by aestheticizing many of the play's horrifying moments. The mutilation of Lavinia, for instance, is revealed to us after the fact in a deeply disturbing yet eerily beautiful image of her in a white gown with tree branches as limbs. However, the banquet scene, with its long-awaited spectacles of revenge, simply cannot support such a strategy, so Taymor simultaneously acknowledges and parodies pop horror analogues, in the process frustrating our identification with the revenger or prurient satisfaction with the revenges, responses typically elicited by contemporary horror films. It is not that the film's arthouse style is unamenable to pop references (it certainly isn't) or that Taymor's penchant for artfully composed imagery and symbolic representation is fatally at odds with the material realities and traumatic consequences of violence with which she is concerned. Rather, Taymor's ambivalent treatment of cinematic horror at film's end reveals her fundamental unease with a pop culture she sees as perpetuating fantasies of violence and, perhaps just as important, her desire to preserve Shakespeare as a force for critique of that cultural system. Whether the utopian gesture closing the film – the boy carrying Aaron's son out of the historical arena of human violence – fulfills that desire, or merely dodges the problem of reproducing violence – through Shakespeare or mass media – remains open to debate (see Burt 2002a; compare AEBISCHER).

Two more thoroughgoing Shakespop parodies, bookending the raft of teen-market adaptations that dominated Shakespeare film from the mid-1990s on, provide illuminating commentary on the cycle of which they are a part: *Tromeo and Juliet* (1996) and *Scotland, PA* (2001). Appearing on the heels of Luhrmann's *Romeo + Juliet*, *Tromeo* is the contribution to the teen Shakespeare cycle by Troma Entertainment, a low-budget studio which specializes in exploitation films for the youth market. Troma films are campy pastiches of teen-oriented genres – horror, monster, and high school dramas predominating – spiced with plentiful nudity and sex, graphic violence, deliberately crude special effects, and gross-out or cruel humor, their gleefully adolescent will to violate good taste pursued very much tongue-in-cheek. Indeed, Troma productions evince a genuine (if perverse) affection for the American trash culture they lampoon; they even parody themselves with comically blatant product placements of Troma characters and videos within the films. As the brand name implies (a portmanteau of "trauma" and "home"), Troma combines grotesque caricatures of family and social dysfunction with surprising empathy for the social outcast protagonists of its films, a mix which may explain the studio's cult status among many alternative film and music fans.

Such is the formula for the film's Tromatizing of Shakespeare's *Romeo and Juliet*. Old Montague, here Monty Que, is recast as a loser drunk, "Cappy" Capulet as a sadistic, social climbing hypocrite, and the feud between them is treated as homicidal slapstick. The Capulet and Montague children and friends carry on the feud in a sleazy urban underworld in which incestuous sex and antisocial ultraviolence are regarded as normal. By contrast, Tromeo and Juliet are presented as innocents struggling to find love and bourgeois normalcy in an utterly dysfunctional world. Of course, in a Troma film "innocents" is a relative term. The couple's relationship is unabashedly lusty, and to gain their independence the two must brutalize "Cappy" in a battle that includes the *Yale Shakespeare* as one of the weapons. Both Tromeo and Juliet dream of middle-class "normality" which their oppressive circumstances deny them, even though, ironically, they pursue that dream of normalcy through phone and computer sex, violence against paternal authority, and finally incestuous marriage. True to the film's oppositionalism, the final scene substitutes a parodic "happy" ending for the tragic true-love-in-death that concludes Luhrmann's adaptation. *Tromeo*'s epilogue depicts a seemingly idyllic backyard barbeque in suburban New Jersey where Tromeo and Juliet (now revealed as brother and sister) and their family and friends celebrate the middle-class good life. In a sardonic touch, whether by incestuous genetics or Jersey pollution, two of Tromeo and Juliet's children are deformed mutants, while the third child in its playpen, as if to stress the utter randomness of fate, is revealed as physically normal. The film's oddly tender and tolerant final tableau presents father/brother, mother/sister, Monty the black grandfather, and three mutant and non-mutant siblings in the equivalent of a bizarre family snapshot, both evoking and mocking the bourgeois ideal that is so often the unstated ideological norm in teen dramas.

Though director Lloyd Kaufman claims that *Tromeo and Juliet* was inspired by George Cukor's 1936 film adaptation, in reality the antecedent is Luhrmann's film. *Tromeo* rarely alludes directly to *Romeo + Juliet*, but the two share distinctive features: teenaged lovers, a contemporary urban setting emphasizing alienated youth culture, a rock and pop soundtrack, an exaggerated cinematic style that violates conventions of filmic realism, use of Shakespearean dialogue (though *Tromeo* reserves that dialogue only for special moments), and a self-consciously hip sensibility. What *Tromeo* seeks to lampoon in Luhrmann's superficially daring update is its ultimately bourgeois idealization of love and teen alienation. That idealization operates not only through Luhrmann's obvious thematic emphases – most clearly glimpsed in his slowly ascending shot of the lovers dead in the church

– but also, Kaufman reveals, through an unconscious stylistic decorum that hovers over the adaptation and governs Luhrmann's
depiction of sexuality, violence, and class. This decorum of theme and
style risks reinstating a "high" romantic Shakespeare, dressed up with
a veneer of MTV-style cinematography and contemporary pop allusion.
Central to Kaufman's parodic strategy is his subjection of teen Shakespeare to the carnivalesque "body principle" – an insistence upon the
grotesque materiality of the physical body in the face of idealization,
spirituality, and social-discipline society, its capacity for being wounded,
pierced, tattooed, or deformed, its perverse desires, excretory functions, and unbeautiful appearance – one thematic sign of which is the
meat motif that runs throughout the film (see Kidnie 2000: 106–8).

Tromeo's carnivalized Shakespeare operates in several directions at
once: sex, violence, class. Whereas Luhrmann exercises great discre-
tion in picturing Romeo and Juliet's sexual consummation, offering
little more than point-of-view childlike play beneath the sheets, *Tromeo*
presents sexuality in all its unidealized, polymorphous glory. In a
cross-cut sequence early in the film, Juliet is comforted by a sexual
encounter with her lesbian nurse Ness, while in his bedroom Tromeo
masturbates to a Shakesporn CD-ROM, "As You Lick It"; Tromeo and
Juliet first consummate their relationship with a softcore tryst in a
glass torture chamber, and later when married, they publicly copulate
in the shadow of the New York Public Library. Kaufman's Capulet is
a leering tyrant obsessed with controlling his daughter's libido (while
at the same time being incestuously fixated on her); underlying his
brutal treatment of her is a sexual hypocrisy linked to his social
pretensions. Juliet's escape from bourgeois parental authority comes
not through spiritual transcendence (*à la* Luhrmann) but through
bodily indulgence: only when Juliet consummates her relationship
with Tromeo, in the very space where her psychotic father has
exercised his control, can she finally embrace "properly" lusty teen
(hetero)sexuality. Whereas Luhrmann filters much of the violence
through media allusions and the killings are handled as theatricalized
martyrdoms, Kaufman insists – to the point of discomfort and absurd-
ity – upon showing the wounded, mutilated body in all its gory,
vulnerable detail. Throughout *Tromeo and Juliet* the feud between the
Ques and Capulets leads to all manner of gleefully gratuitous bodily
abuse (animal killing, dismemberment, head and body wounds, de-
capitation, savage beating, disfigurement), presented in unflinchingly
ghastly if campily unrealistic detail, simultaneously satisfying and
mocking the viewer's assumed lowbrow taste for a good, bloody fight.

189

Whereas Luhrmann's Romeo and Juliet are children of upper-class privilege – Romeo's evident wealth and designer clothing making his attraction to the rundown Sycamore Grove seem like posh slumming – Tromeo and Juliet's disaffection springs from injuries of class oppression. For both lovers the indisputable villain is Cappy Capulet, who aspires to genteel respectability and economic power despite his working-class background; his double-dealings with Silky Films that plunge Tromeo's family into squalor, and his attempts to mold his daughter into a morally proper wife for upper-class London Arbuckle, underlie his cruel disciplining of Juliet.

One way to understand *Tromeo*'s carnivalization of Shakespeare is in terms of symbolic counter-violence. In analyzing cultural stratification, Pierre Bourdieu has traced the operation of "symbolic violence," the ways in which certain class-coded systems of meaning and symbolism are presented as exclusively legitimate and imposed upon social groups so as to create or preserve relations of power (Bourdieu and Passeron 1990: 1–68). Shakespeare, as an epitome of high art, often functions in just such a manner, as a bearer of notions about artistic and social propriety that tacitly reinforce (or at least authorize) certain forms of established class privilege. Extending Laura Kipnis' observation that pornography can be a deeply contradictory vehicle for expressing class *ressentiment* (Kipnis 1992: 373–91), we might observe that flaunting "low" or "trash" genres or the "uncivilized" responses they putatively court – titillation, raunchiness, cruelty, anti-intellectualism, bad taste, anarchy – can serve as symbolic counter-violence, a means of confronting or critiquing the power of bourgeois canons of propriety that undergird class distinctions. Interestingly enough, symbolic counter-violence also is often literalized in popular culture. This is the case with *Tromeo and Juliet*, which directs its exaggerated violence in two directions at once, literally against those who seek to subject the lovers' bodily desires to social or moral discipline, and symbolically against protocols of mainstream aesthetic taste represented both by Shakespeare and by mass market cinema (and thus the hybrid crafted by Luhrmann).

However, when it comes to language, one of the more sacred vessels for Shakespeare's cultural authority, *Tromeo and Juliet* is more ambivalent. Luhrmann's adoption of Shakespearean language rests upon his assertion that the Shakespearean idiom and contemporary youth culture can be seamlessly assimilated to one another. Though Luhrmann treats that assimilation with fleeting touches of irony when he (mis)uses Shakespearean tag-lines in billboards and advertising, those details only highlight the more "authentic" conjunction of Shakespearean verse and contemporary teen tragedy elsewhere in the film. (One small but important mark of that "authentic" conjunction is the full title of the film – *William Shakespeare's Romeo + Juliet* – a title that trumpets its Shakespearean credentials while changing Shakespeare's "and" to a contemporary post-verbal "+.") Indeed, Luhrmann presents Shakespeare and teen culture as mutually legitimating. His film uses the styles and images of contemporary youth culture to give Shakespeare a pop cultural cachet, while Shakespeare – in his guise as the eternal poet of love – is deployed to "classicize" the pop genre of the teen romance. The technique depends upon asserting a congruency of register, accompanied by a complicitously ironic wink to the audience early on that acknowledges the potential kitschiness of pop.

By contrast, *Tromeo and Juliet* insists upon (re)establishing the determinedly low nature of teen culture, stressing its stubborn resistance to being "classicized" and its incapacity to support Luhrmann's kind of tragic romanticism. Kaufman dismantles the process of reciprocal legitimation by suggesting that a Shakespop hybrid in fact operates only in one direction – the conversion of Shakespeare, a writer, in the words of the film's arch promotional campaign, made great by "body piercing, kinky sex, [and] dismemberment," into schlock. Accordingly, Kaufman's approach to Shakespearean language stresses its mismatch with contemporary teen culture. The prologue, epilogue, and revelation scene adopt a pseudo-Elizabethan doggerel that mocks the notion of a seamless Shakespop hybrid; long stretches of contemporary dialogue heavily laced with profanity (Murray's taunting of Tyrone with curses becomes an extended set-piece) are set against short patches of Shakespearean verse, slightly rewritten and offered only at "romantic" moments between the lovers. Wherever Tromeo and Juliet use Shakespeare's verse to celebrate their love, Kaufman is quick to undercut the mood. When the lovers share the "hands and pilgrims" sonnet, for example, a cheap "starry night" backdrop and silly spinning camera techniques undermine the surprisingly affecting delivery of the actors; when later Tromeo speaks lovingly of Juliet's hand upon her cheek, the camera cuts to his beloved's hand against her ass. Elsewhere, the yawning gap between Shakespearean high style and inarticulate teenspeak is played for laughs. After the revelation that the lovers are in fact brother and sister, for example, Juliet and Tromeo exchange Shakespearean passages about adversity and self-reliance (*As You Like It* 2.1.12–14 and *Much Ado About Nothing* 2.1.156–7), only to end with the "heroic" teen cliché, "Fuck it, we've come this far." Nevertheless, by adopting Shakespearean language for Tromeo and Juliet's declarations of love, the film endorses, almost despite itself, the emotional power of Shakespearean high style, utterly out of place though it may be in the dysfunctional, anarchic world of a Troma film. It may be that, as Richard Burt argues (1998: 230; but see also Kidnie 2000), *Tromeo and Juliet* has little to teach its audience about the meaning of Shakespeare's play (though that argument leaves aside the question of where that "real" meaning might reside – in the play's text or in the history of its performances). However, the final value of Kaufman's film lies in its dialectic relationship to the particular form of Shakespearean popularization of which it is a part. If Luhrmann's adaptation threatens to assimilate Shakespeare and pop culture into a vast middlebrow cultural mix, *Tromeo and Juliet* reasserts an incommensurability between high Shakespeare and pop trash in an effort to preserve a space for resistance to the bourgeois politics of mass market postmodernism.

Scotland, PA, a modernization of *Macbeth* filtered through the black comedy of twenty-something working-class life pioneered by *Clerks* (1994), would seem to mark the end of the teen Shakespeare cycle. Like nearly every teen Shakespeare adaptation that was to follow *Romeo + Juliet* (with the sole exception of Michael Almereyda's *Hamlet*), *Scotland, PA* almost entirely jettisons Shakespeare's language, which remains only in passing parodic reminiscences: a mangling of "Fair is foul, and foul is fair" in the film's opening scene, a distorted allusion to Macbeth's "Tomorrow and tomorrow" soliloquy on a vapid self-help tape. Unlike *Tromeo*, however, *Scotland, PA* follows its Shakespearean source relatively closely, transposing the basic plot and characters of *Macbeth* into that most archetypal of Gen-X loser milieus, the small-town fast-food restaurant, and the clichés of TV crime drama. King Duncan becomes Norm Duncan, manager of a dreary burger joint in 1970s America, murdered by his young employees, Joe McBeth and wife Pat; the two take over his restaurant and transform it into a prototype of a modern McDonald's. The couple is pursued throughout by Lieutenant McDuff, a Columbo-like vegetarian detective who confronts McBeth in a climactic fight on the roof of the restaurant. Key details are also slyly referenced: Birnam Wood becomes a local wildlife preserve where, in a passing riff on *The Deer Hunter* (1978), McBeth takes Banco and friends to hunt; later the wood motif resurfaces again with the tacky forest design on Pat McBeth's dress. For the bloodstain on Lady Macbeth's hand, director and writer Billy Morrissette substitutes a grease burn on Pat's hand which she receives when Duncan is dispatched in a fryolater.

In its (ironic) fidelity to its Shakespearean source, *Scotland, PA* might be fruitfully compared to another teen Shakespeare update, Tim Blake Nelson's *O*, filmed in 1999 but not released until 2001. Like *Scotland, PA* it remains faithful to the plot and characters of its Shakespearean source (*Othello*), even though it jettisons Shakespeare's language. For those familiar with their Shakespeare, one of the key pleasures of watching *O* is in charting how the screenwriters ingeniously transpose each Shakespearean event and motif into the milieu of high school sports. For many reviewers of *O*, the central questions were whether the fall of the black high school basketball star Odin James (an allusion to O. J. Simpson) was capable of achieving the tragic stature of Othello's downfall, and whether Hugo's motive – envy of his coach/father's affection for Odin – quite equaled the complexity or depth of malice of Shakespeare's Iago (see, for example, Barber 2002; Bradshaw 2002; Mitchell 2001; Taylor 2001). Throughout, *O* strains to make the analogy between the falls of Odin and Othello hold. It boosts Odin's stature, for example, by elevating the social class (setting the drama in private, not public school), and the presence of news media and police in its final shots seems designed to testify to the weight of the tragedy. (Both devices were also used in *Romeo + Juliet*.) *Scotland, PA* targets precisely the sort of "faithful" teen Shakespop hybridizing *O* exemplifies, with particular focus on the issue of tragedy. Considered in this context, it demonstrates the folly of assigning tragic significance to the downfall of teens and Gen-Xers, a *sine qua non* for adapting Shakespearean tragedy to contemporary youth market film. Such parody has added force when one notes that teen Shakespeare turned at century's end decisively in the direction of tragedy.

Scotland, PA rests upon two interlocking transpositional techniques. The first involves dressing up *Macbeth* in the style of 1970s small-town Americana. As is so often the case with postmodern versions of classics, the fun of the film turns on the pleasures of double recognition, in *Scotland, PA*'s case the identification of its ingenious transpositions of *Macbeth*, and camp nostalgia for the gauchery of 1970s fashion, its hairstyles, music, home decor, cars, and fast food. This parodic technique poses a rough equivalency: Morrissette presents Shakespeare and 1970s styling as equally archaic artifacts of the past. Notably, when one of the three hippy-witches suggests that McBeth kill McDuff's family (as of course Shakespeare intended), another retorts, "oh, that would work – about a thousand years ago! . . . These are modern times. You can't go around killing every body." *Scotland, PA* "redeems" *Macbeth* and middle-American kitsch from the superior perspective of camp, which can assign them ironic value only after first acknowledging their lapsed cultural currency.

Second, and more importantly, Morrissette shifts the social register of *Macbeth* sharply downward – from royalty to white trash. The parallel between the two murderous couples might have provided an opportunity for articulating the frustrated rage generated by the injuries of class and systems of grinding, demeaning subordination. But Morrissette's emphasis falls on the differences: the comparison with *Macbeth* only underscores the sordid and petty rather than heroic dimensions of the McBeths' small-town, working-class ambitions. That comparison is established as early as Joe's "courageous" rescue of Duncan's diner from food-tossing hooligans, the pale counterpart to Macbeth's victory on the battlefield of Fife. The McBeths' transgression never rises above the stuff of Jerry Springer and the local news: as Pat herself observes, "we're not bad people, Mac. We're just under-achievers that have to make up for lost time." And the McBeths' white-trash status renders them incapable of extended philosophical or moral reflection on their actions or the world they inhabit. Instead of offering soliloquies, they fall into marital funks and sullen silence. Lady Macbeth's sleepwalking scene is handled as a wordless drunk and unwitting suicide sardonically set to Three Dog Night's "Never Been to Heaven." The film's final moments, in which McBeth is replaced by McDuff, his successor in fast food who has converted the restaurant to vegetarian cuisine, savagely mocks the restoration of social order that Macduff's victory represents in Shakespeare's play. McDuff's culinary "sophistication," the empty parking lot makes clear, is destined to fail in what remains meat-eating small-town America. The point extends to Morrissette's own arch McDonaldization of Shakespeare, for that empty lot reminds us of the ineluctable power of the mainstream cultural marketplace, to whose dumbed-down values upmarket products like Shakespeare must conform or be abandoned. The difference is that, unlike McDuff, the film self-consciously recognizes and even highlights the dumbing-down of Shakespeare as it gleefully, ironically engages in it. By pointedly refusing any potential for genuine contemporary tragedy, it reasserts the gap in register between Shakespeare and pop culture that so much of recent screen Shakespeare has sought to efface (compare Burnett).

In discussions of the lifecycle of film genres, parody is often regarded as a symptom of a genre's senescence, a means for reviving what has become exhausted or irrelevant. The examples considered here suggest a more complex picture. These parodies indicate a fundamental instability in the pop Shakespeare hybrid that has persisted throughout the last decade, the ease with which it always might slide into camp or burlesque. They testify, that is, to a residual resistance to assimilating Shakespeare into the general postmodern cultural mix, even as, paradoxically, these films engage in exactly that. They also reveal how a traditional high–low cultural distinction is in the process of being recast in new terms, with "double access" – a facility, under a mask of irony, with both high and low culture, with an implied access to education and leisure time (Gripsrud 1998: 537–8) – as the defining quality of a cultural elite. In this sense, recent Shakespearean film parody is profoundly ambivalent in its transgression: it rearticulates principles of cultural decorum – Shakespeare's highness, pop's lowness – in the very act of temporarily violating them. This ambivalence highlights fundamentally contradictory goals in recent Shakespearean film as it moved from the art house to the multiplex: at once to "popularize" Shakespeare, and to preserve Shakespeare's cultural authority from the pernicious effects of mass culture (compare SHAUGHNESSY). It is useful, then, to reevaluate parody as a form of popular critique of the practices and premises of recent Shakespearean film, a critique symptomatic of postmodern culture's struggle to navigate and renegotiate the boundaries between high and low, traditional and modern, where film seeks to create a (new) space for Shakespeare in the empire of pop.

Note

1 Personal email communication with Scott Eckert, dated September 19, 2003. All citations from *Shakespeare for the Modern Man* are taken from script excerpts supplied by the author, whose help I gratefully acknowledge.

References and Further Reading

Babuscio, Jack (1993). "Camp and the Gay Sensibility." In David Bergman (ed.), *Camp Grounds*. Amherst: University of Massachusetts Press.
Barber, Nicholas (2002). Review of *O*. *Independent on Sunday*, September 15, Features section: 11.

Bourdieu, Pierre, and Jean-Claude Passeron (1990). "Foundations for a Theory of Symbolic Violence." In *Reproduction in Education, Society and Culture*. Trans. Richard Nice. London: Sage.

Bradshaw, Peter (2002). Review of *O. Guardian*, September 13, Friday pages: 13.

Buhler, Stephen (2000). "Camp *Richard III* and the Burdens of Stage/Film History." In Burnett and Wray, eds.: 40–57.

Burt, Richard (1998). *Unspeakable ShaXXXspeares: Queer Theory and American Kiddie Culture*. New York: St. Martin's Press.

Eckert, Scott (2003). *Shakespeare for the Modern Man, Lesson 2: Hamlet*. Unpublished play.

Gehring, Wes A. (1999). *Parody as Film Genre: "Never Give a Saga an Even Break."* Westport, CT: Greenwood Press.

Genette, Gerard (1997). *Palimpsests: Literature in the Second Degree*. Trans. Channa Newman and Claude Doubinsky. Lincoln: University of Nebraska Press.

Gripsrud, Jostein (1998). "'High Culture' Revisited." In John Storey (ed.), *Cultural Theory and Popular Culture: A Reader*, 2nd edn. Athens: University of Georgia Press.

Harries, Don (2000). *Film Parody*. London: BFI Publishing.

Hoffman, Adina (2001). Review of *O. Jerusalem Post*, December 10, Arts section: 15.

Jump, John (1972). *Burlesque*. London: Methuen.

Kidnie, Margaret Jane (2000). "'The Way the World is Now': Love in the Troma Zone." In Burnett and Wray, eds.: 102–20.

Kipnis, Laura (1992). "(Male) Desire and (Female) Disgust: Reading *Hustler*." In Laurence Grossberg, Cary Nelson, and Paula Treichler (eds.), *Cultural Studies*. New York: Routledge.

Malankowski, Jamie (2002). "A New 'Macbeth,' Droll and Deep-Fried." *New York Times*, February 3, section 2: 11.

Mallin, Eric (1999). "'You Kilt My Foddah': Arnold, Prince of Denmark." *Shakespeare Quarterly* 50.2: 127–51.

Mitchell, Elvis (2001). "The Moor Shoots Hoops." *New York Times*, August 31, Section E: 1.

Rose, Margaret A. (1993). *Parody: Ancient, Modern, and Post-Modern*. Cambridge: Cambridge University Press.

Ross, Andrew (1993). "Uses of Camp." In David Bergman (ed.), *Camp Grounds*. Amherst: University of Massachusetts Press.

Taylor Charles (2001). Review of *O. Salon.com*, August 31. dir.salon.com/ent/movies/review/2001/08/31/o/index.html?CP=IMD&DN=110.

Chapter 10

Brushing Up Shakespeare: Relevance and Televisual Form

Roberta E. Pearson and William Uricchio

Peter Brook, one of the leading theater directors of the age, has asserted: "the biography of Shakespeare doesn't matter one jot, it is only the plays that count" (Gardner 2003). We would assert that the representations of the man matter considerably, reinforcing Shakespeare's cultural relevance and implicitly underpinning the continuous and ubiquitous performance of the plays. Academics have addressed the mutability of Shakespeare's works at great length; few have so far addressed the mutability of Shakespeare's image, a topic that has great current relevance (Hodgdon 1998; Lanier 2002b; Taylor 1990). The shifting cultural values and multiculturalism characteristic of the twenty-first century render the meanings of Shakespeare more contested now than they have been since his establishment as the British national poet and icon in the eighteenth century.

In *Distinction* (1984), his landmark study of French culture, Pierre Bourdieu argued for a strong correlation between class and taste; the rich and powerful consume cultural forms universally recognized as aesthetically superior to those consumed by the poor and powerless. In the nineteenth and early twentieth centuries, legitimate art forms (literature, the theater, classical music, Western art) stood at the very top of stable cultural hierarchies to which all paid obeisance. But massively powerful and globalized culture industries such as

197

Hollywood have eroded rigid demarcations between elite and popular culture, both of which originate from the same producers, circulate in the same markets, and are often consumed by the same people. Multiculturalism has accelerated this leveling process. As Nick Stevenson says, "the attack on traditional divisions between high and low culture" poses "serious questions in terms of the common or national cultures that might be transmitted by public institutions. The diversification and fragmentation of public tastes and lifestyles have undermined a previously assumed 'cultural consensus'" (2001: 3). These trends can be seen in the erstwhile imperial powers of western Europe, as the descendents of former colonial subjects form an increasing percentage of the population and demand recognition of their own heritage and lifestyles. Greater recognition of regional heritage in such western European nations as Britain or Spain casts further doubt upon the notion of a unified national culture or heritage.

In Britain, the increasing legitimacy of both popular and non-Western culture threatens modern notions of Shakespeare's cultural centrality to such an extent that elite anxieties about the loss of cultural heritage or of "dumbing down" often find expression in debates over the national poet. Should a restructuring of the national curriculum be proposed, educators inevitably ask, "but what about Shakespeare?" Should Prince Charles have concerns about the training of Britain's youngsters, he asks, "but what about Shakespeare?" The Royal Shakespeare Company (RSC) must of course continually ask this same question, as it did most recently by commissioning a MORI (Market Opinion Research International) poll on the poet. The pollsters interviewed 647 young people aged between 15 and 35 and found that a third (34 percent) felt that Shakespeare was still relevant today, while 27 percent thought that Shakespeare's plays have had an important impact on the English language (MORI 2002). The RSC might take cold comfort from the fact that between a quarter and a third of young people acknowledge Shakespeare's importance, but what the poll reports is less interesting than the fact that it was commissioned at all. In the early 1960s, when Peter Hall founded the Company, it would simply have been assumed that young people bloody well better learn their Shakespeare – but now the argument for Shakespeare's relevance must be constantly reasserted.

This essay looks at two British television programs, which reassert the argument. In 2002, the BBC conducted a national poll to elect the "greatest Briton" of all time. The top ten candidates, including Winston Churchill (the eventual winner), the rather unlikely Isambard Kingdom Brunel (the Victorian engineer), and Shakespeare, each became the subject of an hour-long documentary meant to persuade the public of their qualifications for the number one spot. Actress Fiona Shaw served as Shakespeare's advocate in his *Great Britons* episode. In 2003, historian Michael Wood, well known to British television audiences through previous shows such as *In the Footsteps of Alexander the Great* and *Conquistadors*, presented the four-part BBC biography *In Search of Shakespeare*, released in conjunction with a book of the same name and shown on PBS in the United States in 2004.

Both *Great Britons* (GB) and *In Search of Shakespeare* (ISS) use the resources of the television medium to reconfigure Shakespeare for the twenty-first century by severing him from his quainter associations with "ye olde England" of the heritage industry. We use the phrase "heritage Shakespeare" to indicate a static and narrow conception of British history, national identity, and the national poet that has in the past lent unity to the diverse components of what some have dubbed the bardbiz, the constellation of institutions – tourism, education, and the theater – centered on the national poet (Samuel 1994; Higson 1997). In an earlier article Pearson examined the representation of Shakespeare in British silent newsreels and travelogues, beginning with the example of a 1926 travelogue titled *Shakespeare's Country*, an episode in the series *Wonderful Britain* (a Harry B. Parkinson Production for British Screen Classics; Pearson 2002). The film starts with an intertitle: "Shakespeare found success in London – but his heart, from his earliest days, was in his native Warwickshire. In the little village of Wilmcote, lived Mary Arden his mother." We see an exterior of a stone house, followed by a dissolve to a gate in a stone wall, then another intertitle: "And in the country around Stratford on Avon there breathes the very spirit of the Bard." A shot of a bridge over the River Avon is followed by a shot from one of the riverbanks. The rest of the film consists of similarly pretty "chocolate box" shots of an old-fashioned, cozy England composed of thatched houses, cottage gardens, and half-timbered buildings. This film, like other cinematic texts, travel books, biographies, and the like, constructed a Shakespeare who was strongly allied with a rural and idyllic Stratford. This Stratford, despite its Midlands location, was seen as synonymous with the rural south in which English national identity was heavily invested during the 1920s. Functioning as a marker of the stability of English national identity, this timeless and eternal heritage Shakespeare was enshrined in the tourist industry and embodied in the national curriculum.

During the last decades of the twentieth century, heritage Shakespeare came under attack from leading figures in both academia and the theater. The BBC World website publicizing the overseas transmission of *Great Britons* drew upon these attacks to sketch the case that Fiona Shaw had to rebut to remake Shakespeare into a suitable candidate for the greatest Briton of all time. "Shakespeare is only seen as great because he was adopted as an icon of Englishness by the political establishment during the Empire – he is a poodle of the establishment – he was disseminated by and used as a cultural justification for the British Empire." He represents the "archetypal Dead White European Man" whose "artistic supremacy has ceased to be debated: it is simply assumed. The Shakespeare industry ensures Shakespeare's greatness – he is a cozy choice made by lazy and complacent academics at the expense of contemporary writers and has dominated theatrical life in this country for too long." As a result, "Shakespeare's suffered for his greatness. He's been packaged as a symbol of Olde England, his lank figure stuck on banknotes and his work forced upon reluctant schoolchildren so that his words have become lost in a neat, clean Shakespeare brand, a trademark of British culture" (BBC World 2003).

To counter this critique, the two programs work to divorce Shakespeare from heritage and make him relevant to the present, although GB and ISS employ different means to the same end. GB uses what we dub an "analogy strategy," explicitly, as we have seen above, rejecting a heritage Shakespeare and replacing him with a hip, populist Shakespeare. The figure of Shakespeare links Elizabethan theater to rock concerts and Elizabethan plays to soap operas; his relevance stems from blurring the distinctions between past and present. ISS uses what we dub a "continuity strategy," asserting an uninterrupted flow from the past to the present and rejecting the frozen-in-amber commodity history of the heritage industry in favor of a living presence history that continues to shape our ends.

ISS shows the past manifested in the present – Stratford schoolboys performing Tudor plays and Stratford aldermen dressed in official regalia, pilgrims visiting ancient Catholic shrines, old roads and buildings, the English landscape. The figure of Shakespeare draws together his family's pre-Reformation England, his own early modern England, and the England of the present; he is relevant because no break with the past renders him irrelevant. GB uses the analogy strategy and ISS the continuity strategy to reject heritage and argue for relevance, but both programs construct their arguments through the specificities of the televisual medium: images, liveness, simultaneity, the everyday, intimacy, and familiar formats.

Great Britons

Toward the beginning of GB, Fiona Shaw tells us that Shakespeare is "possibly the most famous person in the English-speaking world. He symbolizes things, he's famous for being famous." The image track shows close-ups of Shakespeare items: a sign for the Bard's Walk; Shakespeare's blend English Breakfast tea; a Stratford souvenir plate with the famous First Folio portrait; the Hathaway Tea Rooms. Shaw continues, "He is also the most loathed writer, seen by many as irrelevant and old fashioned, an embarrassing symbol of ye olde England." Shaw then visits Shakespeare's Stratford birthplace, the holiest of holy Shakespeare shrines. As she walks from the bedroom to the kitchen, she says, "This unfortunate reputation is in part due to the Shakespeare industry. Shakespeare's imagination has little to do with this sanitized museum world." Shakespeare's imagination might not have depended upon this sanitized museum world, but television to some extent does, for the heritage Shakespeare embodied in the built environment and the tourism industry provides obvious points of visual reference – Stratford buildings, Shakespeare tearooms, souvenir plates – for a medium that cannot exist without images. Shaw continues her debunking of heritage by contrasting the sterility of the present-day birthplace with the earthiness of the Elizabethan past. Shaw: "If we're to begin in the beginning we must begin here." Image track (IT): close-ups of hides being tanned followed by a long shot of a tannery and tannery workers. Shaw: "His father was a glove maker, and also a tanner and a butcher." IT: more shots of the tannery. Shaw: "Shakespeare had a gruesomely precise knowledge of butchery." IT: shots of drying hides. Male voiceover: "Now could I drink hot blood and do such bitter business as the day would quake to look on." IT: the quotation from *Hamlet* (3.2) superimposed over the shots of drying hides.

Seeking visual equivalents of the poet's words is not specifically televisual; less inspired film as well as television adaptations of the plays do sometimes resort to this tactic, replacing or augmenting Shakespeare's vivid and evocative verbal descriptions with rather more pedestrian images. But, with such possible exceptions as the pyrotechnically dazzling *William Shakespeare's Romeo + Juliet* (dir.

Roberta E. Pearson and William Uricchio

Luhrmann, 1996) or the extended and spectacular battle scenes in *Henry V* (dir. Olivier, 1944), the verbal usually logically motivates and retains parity with, if not primacy over, the visual. Segments of GB retain the same word/image power relation, as when Shaw says that Shakespeare is famous for being famous and the image track substantiates her assertion with close-ups of souvenir plates and tearooms. Other segments seem to reverse the balance of power between the visual and the verbal, as when Shaw says, "If we're to begin in the beginning we must begin here." But why must we begin with Shakespeare's father's having been a glover, a tanner, and a butcher? The program uses the fact neither to locate Shakespeare's family within the class structure of Elizabethan England nor, despite the comment about "gruesomely precise knowledge of butchery," to establish a relationship between Shakespeare's childhood experiences and expertise exhibited in the plays. We begin here because John Shakespeare's occupation provides a compelling, but readily obtainable and inexpensive, image for a restricted-budget television documentary expected to entertain an easily distracted audience. The logic is a visual rather than a verbal one. In similar fashion, GB's analogy strategy often seems more motivated by the image than by the word, as it constructs visual associations between past and present in the bid to assert Shakespeare's relevance.

GB uses present-day relevance and utility to free Shakespeare from his fly-in-heritage-amber status. In rebutting heritage, Shaw says, "The problem about being a national icon means that he got trapped into a waxwork identity, where in fact his greatness and uniqueness lies in his ability to write about us as we are now." The RSC-commissioned MORI poll revealed that many respondents believed that Shakespeare was capable of writing "about us as we are now."

> Twice as many agree as disagree (40 percent versus 16 percent) that Shakespeare's history plays have some relevance to the politics of today. . . . In the same way, the poll reveals that Britain's staple soaps – *Coronation Street* and *EastEnders* – top the list of contemporary dramas likely to say something important about Britain in 2001. Among all respondents, 33 percent mentioned *EastEnders*, while 29 percent thought that *Coronation Street* was most likely to say something about Britain today. (MORI 2001)

Judging by their opening gambit, GB's producers might have been aware that the MORI respondents accorded Shakespeare the same lofty status as the nation's favorite soaps. The program begins with an intensely dramatic scene from *EastEnders*. A younger man with blood on his lip says, "I'm sorry, I'm really sorry," to an older man who responds, "Get out!" As two women look on in reaction shots, the older man says, "This isn't about you being illegitimate. It's about you being a bastard." Fiona Shaw then talks to camera, establishing the soap's populist credentials by saying that it is watched by over a quarter of the population everyday. She continues, "We see Shakespeare's legacy at work. This fiction is inspired by his great tragedy, *King Lear*." GB makes the Shakespeare/soap analogy visually as well as verbally, Shaw, and we with her, watching the soap scene projected onto a screen in an Elizabethan indoor theater, its historical period signified by its ornately painted and paneled ceiling. Later in the program, Shaw returns to the *EastEnders* set. Speaking once again to camera, she says, "Like soap writers today, Shakespeare realized that there are only a few good stories. The trick is how you tell it." The program then intercuts an excerpt from Edmund's 1.2 speech with the opening *EastEnders'* excerpt, making clear the parallels between soap and Shakespeare.

> As to the legitimate: fine word, – legitimate!
> Well, my legitimate, if this letter speed,
> And my invention thrive, Edmund the base
> Shall top the legitimate. I grow; I prosper:
> Now, gods, stand up for bastards!

A series of shots of *EastEnders* scripts, with *King Lear*, *Macbeth*, and *Romeo and Juliet* written on the covers, follows. Shaw says in voiceover, "*EastEnders* writers sometimes use the titles of Shakespeare's plays to describe the themes in their own scripts." The parallel between 1.2 of *King Lear* and the scene from *EastEnders* with which GB opens is quite explicitly a verbal one, with the latter's use of the words "illegitimate" and "bastard" deliberately echoing the former's. The parallel between other Shakespeare plays and other *EastEnders* scripts, however, is verbally asserted but visually verified. The audience can evaluate for itself the closeness of the relationship between Shakespeare's dialogue and the *EastEnders'* scriptwriters' dialogue but has no way to test the assertion that other *EastEnders* scripts similarly echo the Bard. The audience must accept that seeing is believing, as it must with the analogy argument employed in the rest of the program. Here are some examples. Shaw: "Shakespeare wrote for an audience that experienced his plays live – many couldn't read and write." IT: shots of exuberant crowd at an outdoor rock concert with supered-over First Folio title-pages from the early plays (*Richard III, Titus Andronicus*). Shaw: "This is what theater was like in Shakespeare's time – like a modern pop concert, raucous, lively, excited." IT: Shaw walks through crowd. Shaw: "Iambic pentameter – it's a horrible name for a beautiful thing. It's just a fancy word to describe the te tum te tum rhythm that's the sound of our beating heart." IT: soft-focus, dimly lit scene of people talking in a restaurant. Shaw: "He took the natural rhythms of English and turned them into poetry. He brilliantly captured the speech that people used in daily life." IT: men in pub discussing football. The image track repeatedly draws visual equivalencies for which the program provides little or no substantiating evidence. The rock concert crowd becomes the equivalent of the Elizabethan theater crowd; the restaurant diners become the equivalent of both a beating heart and iambic pentameter; the pub patrons become the equivalent of the Elizabethans speaking the speech of daily life.

GB's analogy argument depends upon the everydayness that some scholars see as television's primary defining characteristic; it is a familiar and intimate medium incorporated into and reflecting people's daily routines (Silverstone 1994; Mackay 1997). A housewife performs her household tasks to the accompaniment of the daytime programs; the family eats its evening meal to the accompaniment of the evening news; a nation's most popular programs, the evening soap operas, mirror in some respects the ordinariness of their viewers' lives. Making visual equivalencies between Shakespeare's plays and *EastEnders*, between the rhythm of his verse and restaurant patrons, between Elizabethan speech and pub chat about football, could be said to use the television medium to good effect, although the analogy strategy failed to persuade the critics. Paul Hoggart of *The Times* found it irritating, accusing Fiona Shaw of using "the old trendy vicar line." "Shaw mixed dewy-eyed assertions about his genius with comparisons to hip-hop and soap opera, which seemed both patronizing and irrelevant" (Hoggart 2003). Clearly a believer in traditional cultural hierarchies who sees no need to bang on about Shakespeare's relevance, Hoggart asserted, "But the whole point is that Shakespeare's language, imagination and psychological energy transcend what you would find in 99 percent of mass culture" (Hoggart 2002).

But it was a mass cultural form, specifically the televisual format of the reality show, that GB's producers decided would engage an audience that might be put off by dull history lessons. Asked in an online

chat whether GB was "dumbing-down" by concentrating on personality over historical events, producer Mark Harrison responded: "Quite
the reverse. By asking questions about why individuals have become
icons we are forced to ask very complex questions about historical
context and national character. In some sense *Great Britons* is a psychological history of Britain and the British people" ("Great Britons
Live"). The claims for historical complexity seem somewhat at variance with the program's hyperbolic publicity and presentational style.
The BBC World website trumpeted, "Each week, high-profile present-
ers each spend one hour passionately promoting their chosen Great
Briton in the hope of convincing you to vote for their choice."
Each of the ten episodes began with Peter Snow, the BBC journalist
famous for his energetic reporting of elections, urging viewers to vote
and giving the latest data on the relative standings of the contestants.
The following sequence played up the campaign analogy, with people
waving placards and cheering. The Shakespeare opening sequence
featured a placard with a Shakespeare portrait, then a hand holding
a skull, and then a man in an Elizabethan ruff holding a similarly
attired dog. The sequence's knowing irony aligned it less with the
serious political coverage intertextually referenced by Peter Snow and
more with popular interactive reality television – *Big Brother* or *Pop
Idol*. Which contestant would the nation take to its heart and which
contestant would it boot out of the competition? Perhaps in this sense
Harrison was right: *Great Britons'* complex questions about historical
context and national character were raised not by the selection of the
finalists but by the presentation of those finalists in a format mimick-
ing the most popular of its day. The producers' assumptions about the
BBC1 audience are revealed by their choice of format, just as the very
different format of ISS reveals its producers' view of a BBC2 audience
judged accustomed to viewing history programs. This essay looks not
only at the ways in which the argument for Shakespeare's relevance
is constantly reasserted, but how it is differently reasserted for different audiences.

In Search of Shakespeare

The *Guardian*'s Lyn Gardner liked ISS. "The style of *In Search of Shakespeare* may be lush and romantic, more *Shakespeare in Love* than *The
World at War*, but what makes it radical is the way it rescues Shakespeare from the heritage industry" (Gardner 2003). The reviewer

recognizes the program's primary goal, which Michael Wood articulates when speaking of the young Shakespeare at the beginning of his theatrical career.

> You have to think away that image of Shakespeare, the balding, middle-aged man in a ruff, the gentle bard, the icon of English heritage. This is a young blade in his mid-twenties. This is a young man, bold, ambitious in his art. He's funny, streetwise, sexy and, by all accounts, extremely good company.

Like the hero of the extremely successful *Shakespeare in Love* (1998), suffering from writer's block and visiting a shrink, this guy we recognize and might even want to have dinner with. Wood's strategy here bears similarities to that employed in GB. Let's update Shakespeare by making him relevant, by making him and his world like us and our world. But GB is so allied to the present that, bar a few fleeting shots of old buildings (the Elizabethan theater, the birthplace) and a few brief verbal references to Elizabethan theater or speech, history all but disappears. Wood takes his history very seriously, his argument for both ruptures and continuities between Shakespeare's time and our own buttressed by extensive analysis of Elizabethan society based on a selective representation of the latest scholarship (Duffy 1994, 2001; Haigh 1993). Wood begins his biography "once upon a time in the heart of old England." But the traditional phrase precedes not a fairytale but a dark story of spies, traitors, heresy, torture, betrayal, and social upheaval. As Paul Hoggart, much happier with Wood's program than with Shaw's, said, "Wood wants us to forget all that A. L. Rowse, dancing-round-the-maypole, Good Queen Bess, Merrie England nonsense. The reign of Elizabeth I, he explains, was a time of religious crisis and political and economic turmoil" (Hoggart 2003).

Wood refashions Shakespeare by locating him within the crucible of England's redefinition as a nation during the Reformation. Wood records the violent disruption resulting from the imposition of a new religion, grounding his recounting in the careful reading of period documents (wills, parish records, murals, and stained-glass windows), albeit augmenting it with great lashings of sheer speculation. He contends that Shakespeare and his family were caught between the pre- and post-Reformation world and argues that thinking of the poet as a Catholic or at least as of Catholic sympathies illuminates much about his life and his works. The argument is not new; Gary Taylor made the case in 1984 and consideration of Shakespeare's possible

206

Catholicism now regularly informs much scholarship (Taylor 2003). Park Honan devotes several pages of his biography to conjecture about the poet's religious affiliations and the "missing years" between the time he left Stratford and showed up in London (Honan 1998). Jonathan Bate looks for connections between Falstaff and "the old religion of Shakespeare's father and maternal grandfather" (Bate 1997). But the argument has not before been made in the popular medium of television to an audience perhaps more accustomed to a heritage Shakespeare than a Catholic one – it's Shakespeare, but not as we know him.[1] As Wood said,

> It's a series about England. Shakespeare is about Englishness and the national narrative, but in this case the narrative is not quite what we think it is. The cunning when making this kind of series is to make people feel warm and good and then take them somewhere unexpected, into a world that's different from the one they thought they were in. (Gardner 2003)

GB criticizes the heritage Shakespeare, which it locates in Stratford and souvenirs, but replaces him with a still reassuring figure associated with soap operas, pubs, and rock concerts. ISS criticizes but does not dwell upon the "icon of English heritage," substituting for the "gentle bard" a man caught up in what it presents as the fundamental controversy of his age. In the extended sequences set in and about Stratford, Wood uses television's visual power to deconstruct the heritage Shakespeare. Wood visits a key site on the heritage trail, the house of Mary Arden, Shakespeare's mother, telling us that "In his mother's village of Wilmcote is a revealing clue about her family." We see the interior of an Elizabethan country cottage, rendered shadowy and mysterious by the absence of all but the available light from the windows. Wood speaks in hushed tones, reading the will of Shakespeare's maternal grandfather. "It's a Catholic will." In the woods nearby he goes to the "ruined nunnery of Wroxhall, Shakespeare's family church before the Reformation." Again we see a dim interior with light coming only from the windows. Wood substitutes gloomy rooms and ruins for the cozy, fire-lit interiors and whitewashed, rose-gardened, sunlit exteriors of thatched cottages that would have constituted heritage Shakespeare in the 1920s. He also reveals unexpected aspects of heritage sites; workmen obeying the orders of the Stratford corporation to whitewash over the medieval murals in the guild chapel; the attic of the Shakespeare birthplace where, in 1757, John Shakespeare's putative Catholic testament of faith was discovered.

But Wood's avowed intent to reveal "the hidden landscapes of Elizabethan England and the secret archives of English history" takes him off the well-beaten heritage path. For example, we take a night-time drive with him to the village of Aynho, not exactly a well-known tourist destination. Here events occurred that would have "fateful results for all the Catholics in Warwickshire but especially for the Ardens." A young man named Somerville, a relative of the Ardens, had supposedly threatened to assassinate Elizabeth I. Edward Arden, the head of the family, was taken to the Tower, tortured, and eventually executed. Almost obligatory shots of the Tower, complete with patrolling beefeater as is common in historical documentaries (be they heritage or anti-heritage), accompany Wood's recounting – but they are not to be found in the book of the same name that accompanies the series, nor, of course, is the drive to Aynho, nor even any pictures of the village. Television permits us to see the "hidden landscapes of Elizabethan England" in a way that the book cannot, perhaps because, as Wood put it, "the goal was to excite and interest a general audience" (Wood 2003a).

Television's need for pictures and stories to entertain that general audience of which producers are ever mindful accounts for the differences between Wood's representation of the past on the page and on the screen. Comparing the treatment of the death of Christopher Marlowe in book and television program reveals the ways in which the latter, to borrow a recently current phrase, "sexes up" history. The book covers the death in three paragraphs on p. 155, with no accompanying illustrations (Wood 2003b).

The first paragraph sets the scene.

> On 30 May Marlowe went to a meeting at Deptford. . . . Disembarking at the Watergate – still there today, overgrown and sprouting weeds, washed by the greasy green swell – Marlowe would have walked down a narrow lane to a row of houses along the waterfront.

The second paragraph gives the names and backgrounds of the three men involved in the murder. The murder occurs in one sentence in the third paragraph. "The four men ate, walked in the garden and smoked, before tempers flared in the early evening and Marlowe was stabbed between the eyes by Frizer."

The television program devotes an extended sequence and several locations to the murder. It begins with a long shot of Tower Bridge at sunrise – grey/pink clouds, sun in speeded-up motion rising between the bridge's two towers. Over this atmospheric shot, enhanced with ominous music, Wood tells us that this was a dangerous time; two printers had been executed for publishing seditious books and the poet Thomas Kyd put to the rack. We see Wood standing on the deck of a motorboat on the Thames. Wood: "Marlowe's luck finally ran out." Shots of the boat are intercut with shots of industrial buildings on the shore. Wood: "In 1593 when the boatman took him down the river from the city to Deptford, he arrived here." Wood points towards a watergate parallel to the boat. The next shot shows an Elizabethan map of Deptford with a row of houses. Wood: "There was a row of houses with gardens going down to the river." The boat docks in the watergate. Wood steps onto the quay and then goes up the crumbling steps past the moss-encrusted stones of the structure. Telling us that it was not a tavern but a safe house for spies where Marlowe met his death, Wood walks to a row of dilapidated, boarded-up houses. The camera follows him into the front hall and then upstairs to the murder room while he tells us about the three men involved. The murder room has bare wooden floors, a leather arm-chair, a wooden chair, a wooden table (paper and candle on it), bare brick walls, two windows through which enters the gray London light, and a fire in the grate – not a tourist location, but rather a set decorated particularly for shooting the murder sequence. There's a cut to Wood walking in the garden down to the river, while he tells us about the four men eating, walking, and smoking. Then another cut back to the murder room. Wood: "Marlowe had been lying on the bed." Wood picks up a sheet of paper, which he tells us is the coroner's report. Standing behind the wooden chair at the table, Wood says, "Frizer was sitting with his back to Marlowe." He reenacts Marlowe's slashing Frizer's head with his dagger and concludes the sequence by reading the coroner's description of Frizer's stabbing Marlowe between the eyes.

To use an expression more frequently employed to describe the cinematic adaptation of a stage-play, the television show here and elsewhere "opens up" the book, seizing on opportunities to do what television does best: show things. The television program frequently elaborates upon dramatic incidents quickly recounted in the book. The phrase "Marlowe was stabbed between the eyes by Frizer" becomes Wood's reality television reenactment of the murder and reading of the coroner's report. The television program provides illus-trations, taking us to the locations that Wood only verbally evokes in the book. We can see for ourselves the watergate, "sprouting weeds, washed by the greasy green swell." Together with Wood we retrace Marlowe's footsteps to the row of houses by the waterfront and walk in the garden by the riverside where the three men smoked and argued. The book tells while the television program shows, although both use Marlowe's death, the incident in Aynho, and all the rackings, burnings, and disembowelings to the same end, reconfiguring Shakespeare by representing Elizabethan England as a dark and dangerous place or, as Wood often puts it, a police state. A Shakespeare living in a police state, caught up in the religious struggles of the Reformation, and perhaps even allied with the "losing" side, differs radically from the icon of English virtues constructed by the heritage industry.

The television program has an additional means of reconfiguration: the continuity strategy mentioned at the outset of this essay. It emphasizes the unbroken links between pre-Reformation England, post-Reformation England, and twenty-first-century England to make Shakespeare relevant by making his times relevant to and even manifest in our own. For Wood, an even deeper continuity underlies the apparent rupture with the past caused by the Reformation, a continuity manifested in Shakespeare's Catholicism or Catholic leanings. When Wood visits Shakespeare's ancestral church in the woods near Stratford he speaks of "that feeling for the English past that he grew up with and that later he conjures up in his plays. This is his deep roots." Wood makes Shakespeare a bridge between the rupture of pre- and post-Reformation England, as well as between both those periods and our own. Wood was quoted in a newspaper article as saying, "Through the real, living thing, we are trying to get to the past. Five hundred years is not a long time in history. What fascinates me most is the living connection with the past" (*Irish News* 2003). Television is particularly suited to the continuity strategy's construction of this living connection with the past. The medium's capacity for liveness and simultaneity distinguishes it from cinema, which delivers images but only on a delayed basis, and radio, which delivers events as they happen, but minus the image.

Wood uses television's visual power to connect the now and the then, taking us to the actual sites where events occurred and using images of the present to stand in for the past; here is where Marlowe disembarked; here is where the four men walked in the garden; here is where Marlowe met his death. Wood wants us to see it now as it happened then. The visual conflating of now/then asserts the uninterrupted flow from the past to the present central to the continuity strategy.

Wood begins his tale "once upon a time in the heart of old England." He strides down a sunlight-dappled, lush green-foliaged, wooded path, the very apotheosis of the English countryside. A young lad conveniently hanging about in front of a caravan hails him. "Where are you going?" "We're walking up an ancient road, one of the old roads of England." The next few shots abridge time and space. Wood in misty, autumnal woods; a close-up of Wood's legs and feet in the snow; Wood walking along the banks of the Avon in early spring, Holy Trinity Church in the background; a series of shots of the Stratford countryside complete with sunrise, mist, and cows, then an aerial shot of Stratford with the Holy Trinity spire prominently in the center. The visual rhetoric sutures past and present; it is still possible to walk down the same old road through the same changing seasons into the same sixteenth-century market town where Shakespeare was born. Wood stands on a hill in Gloucestershire and the camera replicates the view of Berkeley Castle that Henry Percy describes in *Richard II* ("There stands the castle, by yon tuft of trees"). Wood stands in the cellar of a London veneer shop on the site of James Burbage's Shoreditch theater and imagines "what it must have been like."

Wood argues for continuity of society as well as of place, images of the present again standing in for the past. A child called William is christened in the Holy Trinity Church, shots of the christening intercut with a shot of the parish register in which Shakespeare's birth was recorded. The current Stratford council takes a vote as Wood talks of their predecessors deciding to whitewash the medieval murals in the guild chapel. The mayor of Stratford proposes the loyal toast, followed by a shot of a portrait of Queen Elizabeth I. Uniformed schoolboys walk to the King Edward VI grammar school that Shakespeare attended and decline Latin verbs as Wood discusses Shakespeare's education. Actors from the Royal Shakespeare Company travel on a coach, eating, drinking, chatting, as Wood talks of Shakespeare and associates forming a new company under a new patron. ISS's visual rhetoric asserts that these places, these institutions, this way of living are all manifested in the present. ISS uses television's everydayness, its capacity for familiarity and intimacy, to render places and institutions normalized and quotidian, not merely nostalgic images as suitable for consumption as the chocolates in the boxes they so often adorn. Heritage's past is commodified, celebrated, fetishized; Wood's past is with us still.

Of course there may be some debate about the "us": about, that is, precisely the audience(s) for whom this program is intended. Wood himself spoke of exciting and entertaining a general audience, but the *New Statesman*'s Andrew Billen apparently sees the BBC2 audience somewhat differently, expressing surprise at Wood's occasionally hyperbolic tone. Billen quotes Wood's opening questions. "Can the life of a writer ever be as interesting or as exciting as that of an inventor, a conqueror, or an explorer?" "Who wouldn't want to know what made him tick?," then asks, "If this is how Wood addresses serious-minded BBC2 viewers on a summer's night, I want to be a fly on the wall when he pitches his next program to Sky" (the Rupert Murdoch-owned channel known as the antithesis of the serious minded; Billen 2003). But Wood's obligatory nods to a multicultural Britain did keep in mind the BBC's mandate to provide for the needs of minority populations. Discussing the scene that Shakespeare wrote for the multi-authored play *Sir Thomas More*, Wood says it "was about a race riot, anti-immigrant riot, anti-refugee and asylum seekers." The conservative tabloid the *Daily Mail* complained that Wood was "in danger of turning [Shakespeare] into a 21st-century New Labour figure," citing the poet as sexually ambiguous, "a fighter against racial prejudice," and "possibly in love with a Venetian Jewess" (Patterson 2003). We must admit that the sequences referred to smack a little of the imposition of twenty-first-century attitudes upon the past of which political correctness is so often guilty. At the same time, we wonder how non-whites and non-Christians might respond to Wood's claim to establish a living connection with a past that is so obviously not theirs. Some reviewers saw no difference between what we have dubbed the continuity strategy and heritage. Billen said that "all of the scenes of modern-day Stratford burghers, especially the cocktail party with the ex-mayors, were pretty off-putting" (Billen 2003), and Charles Saumarez Smith of BBC Newsnight Review "detested it. . . . I hated those shots of Stratford-on-Avon and schoolchildren dressed up in Tudor dress. It seemed like a travelogue [*sic*] of going to Shakespeare country" (BBC Newsnight 2003).

While Billen objected to Wood's hyperbolism as perhaps unsuitable for the serious BBC2 audience, the *Observer*'s Mike Bradley thought that the program was aimed at an entirely different audience. "[T]he dry style in which it is delivered is reminiscent of those educational programs you were occasionally made to watch at school. Wood's didactic tone seems directed at a young audience, presumed to know virtually nothing about the Bard" (Bradley 2003). The BBC website confirms Bradley's hypothesis, offering the seven-part question-and-answer educational series entitled "The Shakespeare Paper Trail:

Documenting the Later Years" and the five-part "Documenting the Early Years," both complete with dates, facts, links, and recommended books. It is not surprising that ISS, like the BBC's 1970s and 1980s versions of the complete Shakespeare plays, is an educational program; producing for the educational market guarantees a long shelf life and continuing profits. Indeed, we have written this essay on the assumption that the program will be readily available for years to come. Overseas markets, particularly the American one, also figure largely in producers' assumptions about their audiences, since sale to foreign broadcasters constitutes another profit point. The very shots of Stratford-upon-Avon that Saumarez Smith objected to may play well with the American Public Broadcasting Service's Anglophile audience.

But serious BBC audiences, multicultural audiences, young audiences, and American audiences alike would have recognized the televisual formats that ISS draws upon. ISS is one of numerous personality-driven factual programs held together by a celebrity presenter's talking to camera and narrating in voiceover – David Attenborough's nature documentaries, Michael Palin's travel documentaries, Simon Schama's, David Starkey's, and, of course, Michael Wood's history documentaries. Wood, in ISS and his previous programs, has built a relationship with the audience appropriate to the domestic medium, giving the impression that he is addressing the individual viewer rather than a scattered audience of millions of strangers, as, for example, when he says, "You have to think away that image of Shakespeare." ISS is also a celebrity biography, similar in some ways to those screened endlessly on the Biography Channel in the United States and the United Kingdom. Wood was defensive when charged with "representing the respectable face of our celebrity-obsessed culture": "The truth is that the average punter probably just wants to know whether Shakespeare loved his wife and whether he was gay or straight. To a certain extent, you have to go with that. I am the first person to accept that TV history is primarily entertainment" (Gardner 2003). ISS accords with the intimacy-establishing conventions of the celebrity bio, calling Shakespeare Will or William and pretending access to his thoughts and feelings: "Will loved this old world of the medieval kings and queens"; "Will was 18 and like any boy in his late teens his thoughts turned to love"; "Out there on that estuary William's world felt dark, lonely, and dangerous." Wood himself described the program as a "historical detective story, an Elizabethan whodunnit." His reenactment of the Marlowe murder resembles those seen in reality television shows such as *Crimewatch* or *America's Most Wanted*. ISS references several other familiar televisual formats: travel shows; garden shows; the royal pageantry of the evening news. As we argued at the outset, these familiar formats, coupled with other televisual characteristics (images, liveness, simultaneity, the everyday, intimacy) allow both *In Search of Shakespeare* and *Great Britons* to sever Shakespeare from heritage and to argue for his relevance to the twenty-first century. Shakespeare, not for an age but for all time?

Note

1 Compared to these scholars, however, Wood elides the Catholicism of Shakespeare's ancestors with the supposed Catholicism of the poet himself, as if memories of Catholicism haunting the culture (absolutely orthodox, undeniable, fascinating) lead logically to Shakespeare himself as Catholic/sympathizer. Some Shakespeareans, such as our editor, would argue that Wood's casual slippage from surmise to assertion, from one reasonable claim to some wild ones, distinguishes him from those who merely popularize standard positions.

References and Further Reading

Bate, J. (1997). *The Genius of Shakespeare*. London: Picador.

BBC Newsnight (2003). news.bbc.co.uk/1/hi/programs/newsnight/review/3032972.stm.

BBC World homepage (2003). July 10. www.bbcworld.com/content/template_clickpage.asp?pageid=2418.

Billen, A. (2003). "In Shakespeare's Footsteps." *New Statesman*, July 7.

Bourdieu, P. (1984). *Distinction: A Social Critique of the Judgement of Taste*. Trans. Richard Nice. Cambridge, MA: Harvard University Press.

Bradley, M. (2003). "OTV: Saturday." *Observer*, June 22: 37.

Duffy, E. (1994). *The Stripping of the Altars: Traditional Religion in England, 1400–1580*. New Haven: Yale University Press.

—— (2001). *The Voices of Morebath: Reformation and Rebellion in an English Village*. New Haven: Yale University Press.

Gardner, L. (2003). "Arts: Meet Mr. Shakespeare." *Guardian*, June 23: 17.

"Great Britons Live" chat (2002). November 12. db.bbc.co.uk/history/programs/greatbritons/chat_1.sthml.

Haigh, C. (1993). *English Reformations*. London: Clarendon Press.

Higson, A. (1997). *Waving the Flag: Constructing a National Cinema in Britain*. London: Clarendon Press.

Hoggart, P. (2002). "The Hugely Disappointing Project." *The Times* (London), November 11: 19.

—— (2003). "In Search of Shakespeare." *The Times* (London), June 30: 19.

Honan, P. (1998). *Shakespeare: A Life*. Oxford: Oxford University Press.

Irish News (2003). TV Choice. June 28: 53.

Lanier, D. (2002b). *Shakespeare and Modern Popular Culture*. Oxford: Oxford University Press.

Mackay, H. (1997). "Introduction." In H. Mackay (ed.), *Consumption and Everyday Life*. London: Sage.

MORI (2001). Shakespeare Still Relevant, Poll Reveals. April 23. www.mori.co/polls/2001/rsc.shtml.

—— (2002). Shakespeare Still Relevant to UK's Young People. June 12. www.mori.com/polls/2002/rsc.shtml.

Patterson, P. (2003). "French Disconnection." *Daily Mail* (London), July 14: 41.

Pearson, R. (2002). "Shakespeare's Country: The National Poet, English Identity and the Silent Cinema." In A. Higson (ed.), *Young and Innocent? The Cinema in Britain, 1896–1930*. Exeter: University of Exeter Press.

Samuel, R. (1994). *Theatres of Memory: Past and Present in Conceptualizing Culture*. New York: Verso.

Silverstone, R. (1994). *Television and Everyday Life*. London: Routledge.

Stevenson, N. (2001). "Introduction." In N. Stevenson (ed.), *Culture and Citizenship*. London: Sage.

Taylor, G. (1990). *Reinventing Shakespeare: A Cultural History from the Restoration to the Present*. London: Hogarth Press.

—— (2003). "The Heaven of Invention." *Guardian*, July 12.

Wood, M. (2003a). "False Impressions." *Guardian Literary Review*, August 2, Letters: 7.

—— (2003b). *In Search of Shakespeare*. London: BBC Consumer Publishing.

Chapter 11

REMEDIATION

Hamlet among the Pixelvisionaries: Video Art, Authenticity, and "Wisdom" in Almereyda's *Hamlet*

Peter S. Donaldson

Recent Shakespeare films, including Luhrmann's *William Shakespeare's Romeo + Juliet* (1996), Loncraine's *Richard III* (1995), and Michael Almereyda's *Hamlet* (2000), have presented a wide range of contemporary media on screen, reframing or "remediating" them as elements of cinema and thus creating a multi-leveled idiom that recalls Shakespeare's habit of drawing metaphors from book and manuscript production as well as from the theater. In the case of Almereyda's *Hamlet*, the media landscape is wide indeed – we hear recorded safety reminders in taxis, watch characters (including the ghost) on surveillance cameras, observe the use of miniature audio transmission devices (Ophelia wears a "wire" in the nunnery scene), see faxes, word processing documents, floppy discs, photographs (Ophelia's medium), recorded videocassettes, live news broadcast, a teleprompter, and, especially, amateur video. In this adaptation Hamlet is an amateur videographer, and *The Mousetrap* is not a play within a play, but, as the desktop-published flyer Hamlet sends Gertrude and Claudius to announce it proclaims, "A Film/Video by Hamlet."

Like other films in which remediation and Shakespearean adaptation join forces, Almereyda's *Hamlet* uses its complex array of media technologies, genres, and practices not merely to fill in the details of a contemporary setting in which media are ubiquitous, but in more nuanced ways that are central to the meaning of the film and to its interpretation of *Hamlet*. By creating a web of cross-media self-reference that has roots in Shakespearean metatheatricality as well as in postmodern media pastiche, Courtney Lehmann has recently argued, Almereyda reads Shakespeare's *Hamlet* as prefiguring cinematic and videographic ways of seeing, remembering, and constructing meaning (Lehmann 2002a).

Douglas Lanier (2002a) has offered a reading of the film's media landscape that emphasizes the opposition between Hamlet as an alternative or independent filmmaker and the corporate media system associated with "The Denmark Corporation." Lanier is persuasive concerning the "difficulty of imagining a specifically filmic mode of resistance" (2002a: 177) to corporate power, since both Hamlet's gestures of resistance and Almereyda's are entwined with the system they resist. The present essay is congruent with Lanier's account of the political double binds facing alternative cinema, but approaches the film's video forms and practices from a somewhat different perspective, focusing on the interplay of video art, authenticity, and "wisdom." I provide a short account of Pixelvision (Hamlet's own medium of expression in the film), offer a close reading of Buddhist monk Thich Nhat Hanh's videotaped discourse on "interbeing" (which plays on a monitor in Hamlet's room in a key scene), and discuss the relation between Almereyda's work and that of the video theorist and installation artist Bill Viola, whose "Slowly Turning Narrative" was to have been the setting for the "To be or not to be" soliloquy. While plans for the inclusion of this scene had to be canceled, the published screenplay offers evidence that it was central to Almereyda's original design, and the influence of Viola's career-long project of elevating video art to the status of a sacred text can be traced in the film as we have it.

Pixel This: Hamlet as Video Visionary

Before the credits, Ethan Hawke delivers an out-of-sequence version of Hamlet's speech to Rosencrantz and Guildenstern ("I have of late

... lost all my mirth ... and yet, to me, what is this quintessence of dust?" [2.2.296–309]), speaking directly to the camera, his image rendered in a grainy and distorted black-and-white close-up.[1] As the sequence proceeds, the camera pulls back to reveal that Hamlet, now seen sitting at his desk, is watching himself on the screen of a portable tape deck. Almereyda's version of the speech is more resolutely and literally depressive than Shakespeare's. He is alone in the image and faces the camera in direct address, with no Rosencrantz or Guildenstern present to make us wonder how much of his speech is an act put on for them. In the text his tribute to the beauty of the cosmos and the human species almost leads him away from the intended emphasis on his melancholy; in the film those lines are undercut by a montage of images of black batwing bombers hitting their targets in Bosnia, and, cued by the text's reference to man as "the paragon of animals," closely framed samplings of the malicious eyes and predatory teeth of a cartoon dragon. Hamlet's "mirth" vanishes like the empty glass he holds so close to the lens that its image breaks into shimmering reflections or the bright keys that disappear as he opens and closes his hand in a cheap cinematic version of a parlor trick, followed by video static. This brief snippet of Hamlet's black-and-white video diary contrasts with the brief vivid color sequence of New York at night just preceding (with Hamlet walking through a neon-lit square to the bright reflections in the lobby glass of "Hotel Elsinore") and with the sequence that follows, in which Claudius, the new "king and CEO" of the Denmark Corporation, brashly announces his succession in the glare of press conference lighting. Hamlet appears here too, in sunglasses (his "nighted color" accessorized here and associated with his mode of vision), "covering" the event with the help of a complex array of video gear, camera held high and miniature monitor/ recorder, cords and adapters at waist level.

The camera is a Fisher Price PXL 2000, made for several years in the late 1980s as a children's toy (see Revkin 2000). Its images were recorded not on standard videocassettes but on ordinary audiotape and could only be played back by using the camera as a player. The medium, which Fisher Price called "Pixelvision," was later adopted by alternative and experimental filmmakers precisely because of the special quality of its grainy image, its peculiar and unpredictable rendition of contrast, and its shimmering distortions of direct light or highly reflective surfaces. Hamlet, like Almereyda himself, is one of these advanced users, his PXL having been obviously "modded" or modified for recording directly onto videotape.

The double history of Pixelvision as both children's toy and avant-garde instrument offers a context for Almereyda's decision to "reveal the apparatus" by putting Hamlet's camera on screen. As a children's toy it is appropriate for Hamlet's family memories; at the center of a sophisticated suite of recording and editing tools it links Hamlet to the director's own work in alternative cinema. Michael Almereyda directed the first Pixelvision "near full-length featurette," *Another Girl, Another Planet*, in 1992, and Pixelvision sequences appear in his other films, including *Nadja* (1994) and *Eternal Kiss of the Mummy* (1998). Pixelvision was in fact an avant-garde instrument masquerading as a children's toy from the beginning. When its inventor, James Wickstead, a gifted and exceptionally idiosyncratic industrial designer, agreed to create a camera for children that would be inexpensive (about $100 in 1987) and easy to use, his reference point in cinematic tradition was Bergman rather than Disney:

> Mr. Wickstead said one of the biggest challenges was convincing his engineers and the toy company to keep the device simple and crude. He said he was determined that it should record stark monochrome images in the style of Ingmar Bergman by having each pixel – the tiniest, most basic piece of a video image – recorded as black, white or a few intervening shades of gray. In early prototypes, when the sensors detected an intermediate level of light, they would flicker back and forth between shades of gray, he said. "My people were spending all this overtime trying to solve that, and I was saying, 'No, this is great! Stop!'" (Revkin 2000)

Pixelvision films can indeed seem distant, kiddy cousins of the cinematography of the early work of Sven Nyqvist (*Persona*) or Gunnar Fischer (*Seventh Seal*). But if soul-searching visual ambiguities were latent in the technology, the marketing of the system largely ignored these subversive possibilities. For example, the manual for the system (see Pixelvision homepage: elvis.rowan.edu/~cassidy/pixel/manual) is illustrated with close-up photos of a singularly bright-eyed and unalienated young man and reads a bit like the *Boy Scout Manual*. Because the product was marketed in this way, it took several years for Pixelvision to be "discovered" as an artistic medium. In 1988 James Benning, himself an experimental filmmaker, gave his daughter Sadie, then 15, a PXL 2000 as a gift (Morris 1999). She ignored it for some months, then took it out of the box on New Year's Day 1989 and produced her historic first piece, a four-minute film entitled "A New Year." Benning's early work took the form of video diaries and autobiographical meditations, always narrated in the first person and centering at first on her somewhat confused sexual identity and gradually on her coming out, over the following two years, as a lesbian. Her work between 1989 and 1998 is now collected as volumes 1–3 of *The Work of Sadie Benning*, available from Video Data Bank at the Art Institute of Chicago. Within a year, Benning's films were at least partly supported by grants and in 1991 she won a Rockefeller Foundation fellowship. Her work is often featured at Pixelvision and other alternative film/video festivals such as Pixel This held annually in Venice, California (now past its thirteenth year), the multi-city Flicker events, as well as at gay, lesbian, and queer film series (including those at MIT), and her films are included in the syllabi of a number of video art courses around the country. Her work is hard-edged, gritty, dreamily surreal, and romantic by turns. She shares a stylistic vocabulary and, in large measure, an aesthetic of authenticity and rebellious self-disclosure with Almereyda and hence with his Hamlet. Aspects of this shared style may be regarded as a common inheritance of youth culture in the 1990s, and some can be traced to the stylistic "push" designed into the camera, but the link between Almereyda and Benning owes something, as well, to the emergence of conventions of representation within the Pixelvision community as it emerged in the 1990s.

Benning's work is insistently first person. Pixelvision makes it extremely easy to fall into video self-contemplation because of the inclusion of a well-designed "bipod" (a simple cradle to hold the camera still on a table) included as standard equipment. Young videomakers need not find either friend or tripod to get started, but can immediately set up the rig on a table, set the camera going, and, using the live video feed to the tiny television/monitor (also provided with the camera) as a viewfinder, experiment in real time with the interesting effects produced by the system. Indeed, given the limitations of the camera – only two light settings, no focus mechanism, unpredictable flare, pixelation, and loss of tonal range at close quarters – it is advisable to practice on yourself with the tiny monitor as a reference before trying out other subjects. Pixelvision could also provide an unusual degree of privacy because of its incompatibility with other media. Unless an adapter is used, playback is limited to your own equipment – audiotape won't yield a video image on any other player, so video diaries made in Pixelvision are likely to remain private and unlikely to cross over into network, cable, and VCR-dominated family viewing spaces.

The qualities of the image, discussed above, lend themselves to existential self-examination: narratives of identity are intensified by the sudden high contrast and other estrangement effects, as the image passes from crude-but-normal in tonal range to stark black on white or to pulsating reflection. In one film, as Benning ponders her self-worth and gender identity, she approaches the camera so closely that first one eye then another appears as a black spot against a white background before, gradually, a more graded image of her face re-appears. In another, she describes, in a bitter tone, how a neighbor, a boy of 7, pulled her hair out in clumps in a fight. The accompanying image is not of hair falling out but of a shimmering play of light, difficult to identify at first, which resolves itself into a stunning ultra close-up of a comb catching light as it passes through the (undamaged) hair of the narrator, now older and tougher. With such effects not "special" but unavoidable in Pixelvision, the medium is well suited to portray oscillations in identity and self-valuation. Benning also uses text in her work, handwritten on paper, glass, the knuckles of her hands, and other surfaces as counterpoint to image, and, like Hamlet, samples televised movies and animation (*The Bad Seed* is intercut with her story of running away with a lover in Benning's *It Wasn't Love* [1992]) as well as home movie and video footage (especially of childhood scenes) originally captured on other media.

In Benning's work as in Almereyda's *Hamlet*, the image and the processes of video self-portraiture are often eroticized, though in different ways. Ethan Hawke plays Hamlet as a young man who is notably isolated (even compared with other Hamlets) and as one who is compulsive in his solitary video-editing and viewing habits, replaying, for example, several short sequences in which Ophelia appears in seductive close-up. In Benning's work the narrating voice plays a larger role in the rehearsal of erotic or intimate moments and there is less compulsive looping of the image; but, filming her memories usually (like Hamlet) in solitude, she too finds ways of making video self-portraiture suggest self-and-other encounters.[2] Benning's work is also insistently media-referential, incorporating samples of recorded music, television, and other video media, displaying handwriting on paper, cardboard, or window glass as intertitles and transitions, showing print text, graphics, and photographs as part of the narration, and revealing (or at least registering traces of) the filming apparatus through self-conscious alienating and extreme close-up effects that make us aware of the process of filming and the presence of the camera.

I want to give one further example of such cross-media effects from the work of Kyle Cassidy, another Pixelvision videomaker. *Toy Soldiers* (1996) is, like Benning's work, one of the celebrated early pixel films. It is also a first-person narration, but the image track takes the form of autobiographical fiction rather than diary, with a child actor reenacting the scenes described from the narrator's childhood experience. It is a five-minute film about a boy who plays with toy soldiers on a hill behind his house during the Vietnam war. Some of the soldiers are maimed, damaged by the neighbor's lawnmower (we see them in close-up, in charge configuration, and afterward close-ups of those who have lost limbs to the mower). The narrator and his mother also receive letters from the soldier-father, on duty in Vietnam, and "have dinner with Walter Cronkite" every night, viewing battle footage on television. One day the father sends home a grenade pin – exactly like those seen on television held by soldiers who are afterward blown up. One of the toy soldiers is a grenade thrower in a stance precisely like those seen on television, and the boy takes this figure out of the action, out of the range of the lawnmower, and protects it by taking it to bed each night. In this simple, intentionally naive story, strong parallels link action-figure play, the realities of war (only just becoming comprehensible to the boy), and the coverage of those realities on television. This piece thus tells a story about the child's experience of the distant war that is also a story of its replay in several media, each of which is given added resonance by the fact that an adult has filmed this story in a child's medium. The implication is that the sorrows of the war – plainly audible in the narrator's adult but still childlike voice – remain painful, though partly managed in the past through play and television viewing, and in the present by representation in an artistic medium that retains a powerful link to childhood. In this work, as in Benning's, the ephemeral (and now obsolescing) character of the medium plays a role in enhancing a sense of poignant vulnerability. As one practitioner, Erik Saks (cited on the Pixelvision homepage), puts it, "Pixelvision is an aberrant art form, underscored by the fact that since the cameras wear out quickly, and are no longer being manufactured, it holds within itself authorized obsolescence. Each time an artist uses a PXL 2000, the whole form edges closer to extinction."

In addition to specific thematic and stylistic resonances of these works with Almereyda's *Hamlet*, there are more general lessons to be learned by placing Almereyda's film in the context of Pixelvision's mixed status as child's toy and avant-garde instrument. One of these concerns the way in which many contemporary filmmakers are, like Benning, Cassidy, and Almereyda, now making films that are more direct extensions and continuations of childhood and amateur media experiences. Spike Jonze (who was a skateboard videographer) and Peter Jackson (who was an action-figure horror and slasher filmmaker from age 12) fall into this category. In the work of such filmmakers, self-reflexive modes do not necessarily derive from New Wave precedent or film school aesthetics, but develop out of media practices going back to childhood. It may also sharpen our perception of Almereyda's intentions to note that Pixelvision as a subcultural practice balances isolation and community. In addition to festival and special event screenings, Pixelvision filmmakers are frequently part of an avant-garde art scene and/or alternative music community, or maintain a fitful online presence through various channels.[3] Almereyda's Hamlet may seem even more isolated against the slightly more sociable norm of the Pixelvision subculture, but in such a context his isolation will not seem a necessary consequence of making films in this medium.

This review may also support a reading of Hamlet's preoccupation with authenticity in the film that stresses its always-already sophisticated and artful character. Pixelvision was designed for authenticity effects and its history serves as one more reminder of the role of social and technological construction in narratives of artistic naiveté.

Hamlet's "grainy" medium, then, not only marks him as "independent," identifying with opposition to the corporate media spectacle; it also suggests that in "remembering" his father and his childhood by replaying video he has shot, he is continuing a childhood practice, cherishing a childhood toy, and rehearsing the unresolved and perhaps now unresolvable issues of childhood. Even his recent footage of his father and mother ("why she would hang on him") positions him as child voyeur, grabbing images of them on the fly as they walk along (and as, in voiceover, Hamlet celebrates their union and the superiority of his father to Claudius). Though these are images of what has been lost, and is now mourned for and even idealized, the sequence ends abruptly with Sam Shepard as Old Hamlet noticing the camera and covering the lens with his hand. The gesture will be closely echoed later in the film when Claudius, meditating on his guilt ("What if this hand were thicker than it is with brother's blood?") covers the image on the small-screen TV in his limousine.[4]

Michael Almereyda began to use Pixelvision as an adult filmmaker, but, like Benning and Kyle Cassidy, his adoption of this medium had a psychologically regressive side. He discovered Pixelvision in the aftermath of his failure to find a distributor for a "real" film, his 1990 35mm feature *Twister*, with Harry Dean Stanton in the lead role (Almereyda 1996, liner notes). Despite the critical acclaim for *Hamlet* and, to a lesser extent, for *Nadja* and *At Sundance* (1995), Almereyda's career is still oscillating between subculture and mainstream. His most recent film, *Happy Here and Now*, won the *Village Voice* award for best undistributed film of 2002. *Another Girl, Another Planet* is a fiction film shot entirely in Pixelvision, centering on a young East Village-dwelling semi-bohemian young man's failures in relationships with women. Almereyda, having apparently missed his "big chance" (if indeed he thought of it this way), reverts, in a sense, to a medium with associations to what Richard Burt calls "loserdom." The film's title conveys the main character's sense of estrangement, and in context suggests not so much that each woman he encounters is in fact or even metaphorically a different species of alien, but rather that women, in general and as individuals, are aliens *to him*. Ramona, the final "girl" in the series, makes this explicit, explaining with striking candor that the reason for the failure of Bill's relationships is his own emptiness.

While each of the protagonist's relationships do in fact fail, the film is poignant and painful, as if an early Woody Allen character suddenly forgot how to wisecrack, its gritty world suffused with unanswerable questions and a profound sense of unbelonging. The associations of this state with childhood are emphasized by Bill's ritual of screening Tex Avery's animated short *Dancing on the Moon* for new visitors. The title song celebrates "Dancing on the moon / With a girl in my arms," but the childish cartoon animal protagonist is so preoccupied with catching the moon rocket that he leaves his girlfriend behind. Though it is permeated with a sense of the incapacity for "adjustment to adult life," the world Almereyda constructs in the film out of East Village staircases and rooftops, candles, bare electric bulbs, and reflections in the polished wood of the local bar, is also touched by an occasional sense of wonder and beauty rendered in the shimmering, out of focus light-show effects of the Pixelvision medium.

The characters, especially the main character, keep looking: not only for partners but also for the radiance that is momentarily present in the world, for some grounding in their lives. This aspect of the film – in which a quest for meaning and connectedness on the narrative level and abstract visual shimmer on the visual level combine – finds a center in the scenes of meandering talk in the local bar about a seer and healer (who never appears on screen) called Mother Mira. She is first mentioned as someone to consult when one of Bill's girlfriends talks about wanting "more spirituality in her life." Mother Mira can answer difficult questions such as "which is true, that God is eternal presence or the Buddhist awareness of God as emptiness." Mother Mira is said to have answered (somewhat predictably) that "both are true: God is everything and nothing." In addition to her vatic utterances and ability to heal her visitors spiritually, Mother Mira is a transfigured, literally refulgent being: "suddenly light starts streaming from her face and whole body; lights dripping from the ceiling like a waterfall" (Almereyda 1996, sequence beginning 00:10:30 [my transcription]). A bit later, Ramona herself (though she has not visited the seer) is seen combing her hair with a fork with the ceiling light behind her, and in Pixelvision distortion we see what may be taken as a replay of one of Sadie Benning's *motifs* as well as a pale, perhaps mocking, analogue of Mother Mira's transfiguration. As the film unfolds, the inability of the characters to sustain more than a momentary contact with such fleeting images of radiance becomes clear, and it ends with Bill accepting the fact by recalling a film seen in childhood, *Nabu*, in which a visitor to India admires a maharaja's elephant and on his return home finds an elephant in his apartment, sent as a gift – one that doesn't quite fit in with the furniture. Both the philosophical/spiritual vocabulary of *Another Girl*, its sense of missed contact with sources of spiritual fulfillment or wisdom, and the uneasy mingling of credible anguish and sophomoric intellectual meandering are present in Almereyda's *Hamlet* as well. Indeed, these elements are not entirely absent in Shakespeare's text.

Being and Interbeing: Hamlet's Multitasking Medi(t)ation

Sophomoric or not, the posing of ontological and metaphysical questions in drama is certainly Hamletic. Philosophical language occurs in many places in the text, with "To be or not to be" only the most notable instance. "To be or not to be" is "the question" in the Folio and Second Quarto, while in the First Quarto reading it is "the point" – perhaps registering an actor-reporter's impatient hankering after certainty. But even in Q1, metaphysical questions abound in the soliloquy, and shape our hearing of the rest of the play, inviting us to listen for possible answers and to wonder when and if Hamlet has found them. Later passages take on a metaphysical shading from their echoing of "to be or not to be": "let be" and "let it be" may be heard as responses to "the question" that is posed so abstractly and starkly in Q2 and F. Hamlet's words to Horatio in response to the invitation to fence with Laertes hazard, in addition, a direct citation of the Sermon on the Mount, suggesting the possibility that with the words "let be" Hamlet has come into possession of a specifically scriptural Christian wisdom in regard to "being."

Almereyda's *Hamlet* extends this echoing pattern beyond the text. The soliloquy itself is anticipated by Hamlet's recitation of the first lines several times on the Pixelvision monitor: during this scene he holds a gun to his head, experiments with various positions for pulling the trigger – with the barrel in his mouth, at the side of his head, etc. It is also anticipated by a sequence that seems to offer a kind of answer (before the question is asked), when Thich Nhat Hanh's videotaped discourse on being and interbeing plays on one of the video monitors in Hamlet's room while he watches his own pixel footage of Ophelia on another. I will cite the screenplay version and then fill in additional details of the sequence as it appears on film.

THICH NHAT HANH

We have the word to "be," but what I propose is the word to "interbe." Because it's not possible to be alone, to be by yourself. You need other people in order to be.

Hamlet, holding the clamshell monitor, crosses to his unmade bed.

Not only do you need mother, father, but also uncle, brother, sister, society. But you also need sunshine, river, air, birds, trees, birds, elephants, and so on.

Hamlet studies the monitor: a repeated pixel image of Ophelia in bed, a book covering her face. She lifts the book, looks into the camera.

So it is impossible to be by yourself; alone. You have to interbe with every one and every thing else. And therefore "to be" means "to interbe." (Almereyda 2000: 37)[5]

The screenplay makes it clear that Hamlet's attention is divided and that he processes Thich Nhat Hanh's words in counterpoint with his "study" of Ophelia's image (an equivalent in the text might be Ophelia's description of Hamlet's distracted visit to her chamber, and his "perusal" of her face). The sequence is preceded by a lingering shot of Ophelia waiting for Hamlet at the fountain, and followed by a sequence in which he feverishly composes poetry for her in a nearby diner ("Doubt that the stars are fire"). What he takes from the discourse of "interbeing," then, is a sense of the importance, indeed the urgency, of breaking out of his solitude and "interbeing" with one person, whereas Thich Nhat Hanh speaks of relationship to immediate family, society, "elephants" (a touch of Buddhist humor that might provoke Goneril's objection, "what need one?"), and, indeed, with "everything and everyone else."

If Hamlet responds to this teaching in the sequence, he narrows its context to romantic/erotic relationships. The interplay of videotaped wisdom and Hamlet's reaction to it is precise. Our attention is directed to Thich Nhat Hanh's image through a slow camera movement that closes in on the monitor until the video image is literally reframed by the 35mm film frame. Hamlet sits in his chair, listening to (but not watching) the tape. Then a shift of attention is cued by the voiceover's inclusion of "mother . . . father . . . *uncle*" among the beings with whom one has to interbe, and Hamlet crosses to the bed and focuses intently on the pixel monitor. As he does so, that image too is reframed for our close attention by a slow movement of Almereyda's camera. Ophelia is seen on the small screen, her face at first hidden behind a book on whose cover we can see a photograph of an elderly man while the voice of Thich Nhat Hanh – "It is impossible to be by YOURSELF, alone . . . you have to interbe with other people" – continues, now heard as if Hamlet were considering it as a possible soundtrack to his video diary. As Ophelia "unmasks" to his camera's gaze, the sequence suggests that she is the "other person" Hamlet needs to relate to; but her appearing from behind the face of another relates the shot to other moments in the film and play in which Hamlet has doubts concerning the doubleness of female self-presentation. Indeed, his replaying of the sequence suggests continuing hesitation. Yet Ophelia is shown here not only as an object of Hamlet's gaze but also as herself, one for whom "being" is a question, even a subject of inquiry. The portion of the book's title (. . . *Living/. . . Dying*) that is visible in the Pixelvision frame connects her to Hamlet's persistent meditations on mortality, and, if one recognizes the book's cover portrait as that of Jiddu Krishnamurti (1895–1986), to this Hamlet's interest in Eastern spirituality.

Ophelia's time-shifted, virtual interaction with Hamlet in the sequence also instances the shading of memory into autoeroticism. The footage of Ophelia records an intimate moment (a prelude to lovemaking may be suggested) in which two people took part, though only one appears on screen since Hamlet was holding the camera. In a double movement, Almereyda's camera moves in for a closer framing of the pixel monitor as Hamlet's shot moves closer to Ophelia's face, drawing the film audience into the dynamics of foreplay and replay. If it is impossible to "be" by yourself, ontologically, as the Buddhist teachings insist, it is now almost impossible to "be by yourself" in another way, since one is surrounded by hypermediated simulacra (see Lehmann 2000a: 96–100). Read along this axis, both the reframing of a romantic and sexual moment as video replay and the remediation of ancient wisdom as videotape background noise may be taken as instances of the fragmenting effects of contemporary media.

But Hamlet's half-heeding of the doctrine of interbeing does produce a change in him: hearing it in the context of reviewing his memories of Ophelia, he foregoes the isolation of his video-suffused bedroom/editing suite and moves towards sociability, abandoning for the moment the simulacra of electronic media for pen, paper, and a solitary table in an all-night diner where he writes poetry intended to be delivered to Ophelia face to face. This suggests a more positive reading of the now common practice of splitting attention among several media forms: the combined effect of the Buddhist discourse and the revival of Hamlet's memories of Ophelia is to make the project of reconnecting with her look like Hamlet's first step towards "interbeing." However, this project fails when Polonius interrupts Hamlet's visit to Ophelia's apartment, intercepts the poem, and later brings it to Gertrude and Claudius, and its failure cues the sequence in which the words "to be or not to be" are first heard in the film as the soundtrack to Hamlet's anguished, replayed suicide gesture. Thich Nhat Hanh's gentle and expansive teaching first narrows in Hamlet's mind to Ophelia as a kind of test case, and then, when the test fails dismally, produces the starker opposition in which not being rather than interbeing is the alternative to being. Hamlet has misheard, misrecognized the message.

"Slowly Turning Narrative": Video Art versus Action Blockbuster

If the two video monitors in Hamlet's room signal an opposition between meditative equilibrium and media as distraction and fetish, the screenplay of Almereyda's *Hamlet* suggests a more powerful fusion of ancient wisdom and contemporary media by counterpointing the full version of "To be or not to be" with the Bill Viola retrospective at the Whitney Museum.

In the film as released, "To be or not to be" takes place in the "Action" aisles of a Blockbuster video rental store. This setting – along with the ghost's disappearance into a Pepsi machine in the opening sequences – was widely criticized, despite Amereyda's ironic intentions, as inappropriately commercial and even a betrayal of the claims the film seems to make to authenticity as an "independent" production (see Lanier 2002a: 175–7). But, as the screenplay makes clear, the speech was intended to be divided between locations, beginning at the Whitney Museum, where Hamlet wanders into the Bill Viola retrospective and begins the soliloquy in counterpoint to the sound-track of one of Viola's most ambitious installations, "Slowly Turning Narrative." Then the location shifts: "the idea was to then balance the Viola video with its nemesis, a Blockbuster store with mass-market images flooding in from the store's monitors" (Almereyda 2000: 137). A conflict arose when Ethan Hawke and Uma Thurman's wedding was set for the day scheduled for shooting the sequence and another opportunity could not be found before the exhibition moved on. Plans for following the Viola show to Amsterdam were discussed but there were insufficient funds to move the crew to the Netherlands. As a result, Blockbuster became the setting for the whole speech. While Almereyda claims to have gradually become satisfied with this unavoidable change, the omission of "Slowly Turning Narrative" leaves frayed edges. The structure and meaning of the film were changed in major ways by the substitution. The sequence of scenes had to be altered; the metastory of Hamlet as a video artist is compromised; the range of media references is drastically narrowed, leaving video as surveillance, mass medium, and amateur practice, but eliminating the potentially powerful presence of video as fine art. Examining how Almereyda recoups, accepts, and rationalizes this breach in his design may not repair the damage, but perhaps it can provide a useful context for understanding the several ways in which the film as we have it engages the question of Hamlet's catastrophic loss.

"Slowly Turning Narrative," the centerpiece of the Whitney Viola retrospective of 1998 (see online excerpt at www.sfmoma.org/espace/viola/dhtml/content/viola_gallery/BV07.html) is a major piece in Viola's career-long project, which might be described as turning video art into a sacred text on themes congruent with Thich Nhat Hanh's discourse on "interbeing": the ephemerality of the self, its connectedness to the world, its persistence as a center of meaning. The exhibition was installed in a large room, most of which was filled by a large revolving screen in the center, on which were projected images of birth, accident, celebration, amusement parks, fire, accompanied by a voiceover mantra-like chant: "The one who lives, the one who strives, the one who despairs, the one who sees, the one who enjoys, the one who feels." The catalogue for an earlier exhibition describes the piece:

> A large screen (9 × 12 feet wide) is slowly rotating on a central axis in the center of a large dark room. Two video projectors are facing it from opposite sides of the space. One side of the screen is a mirrored surface, the other side a normal projection screen. One projector shows a constant black-and-white image of a man's face in close-up, in harsh light, appearing distracted and at times straining. The other projector shows a series of changing color images (young children moving by on a carousel, a house on fire, people at a carnival at night, kids playing with fireworks, etc.) characterized by continuous motion and swirling light and color. On the black-and-white side, a voice can be heard reciting a rhythmic repetitive chant of a long list of phrases descriptive of states of being and individual actions. On the color image side, the ambient sounds associated with each image are heard. The beams from the two projectors distort and spill out images across the shifting screen surfaces and onto the walls as the angle of the screen alternately widens and narrows during the course of its rotations. The mirrored side sends distorted reflections continually cascading across the surrounding walls – indistinct gossamer forms that travel around the perimeter of the room. In addition, viewers in the space see themselves and the space around them reflected in the mirror as it slowly moves past.
>
> The work is concerned with the enclosing nature of self-image and the external circulation of potentially infinite (and therefore unattainable) states of being, all revolving around the still point of the central self. The room and all persons within it become a continually shifting projection screen, enclosing the image and its reflections, all locked into the regular cadence of the chanting voice and the rotating screen. The entire space becomes an interior for the revelations of a constantly turning mind absorbed with itself. The confluences and conflicts of image, intent, content, and emotion perpetually circulate as the screen slowly turns in the space. (Rose and Sellars, 1997: 106–7)

Caught up – as many viewers are – by being at once in the midst of the spectacle and apart from it, Hamlet begins the soliloquy, "To be or not to be," blending with and counterpointing "The one who finds, the one who meets, the who waits, the one who dives" mantra (Almereyda 2000: 49–50). His voice joins the chant for the first eight lines of "To be," ending with "and by a sleep to say we end / The heartache and the thousand natural shocks / That flesh is heir to." At this point the screenplay indicates that here "Hamlet stops following the mirror, letting his reflection slide away, consumed in video flame" (Almereyda 2000: 50).

Like the Thich Nhat Hanh sequence, this moment can be read as both quest for and misrecognition of a source of wisdom. Bill Viola's own description of "Slowly Turning Narrative" is worth citing as it makes clear the origins of the piece in Buddhist meditative practices as well as affording insight into the convergence of the themes of this work with Shakespeare's *Hamlet* and Almereyda's adaptation. He begins: "The work concerns the enclosing nature of self-image and the external circulation of potentially infinite (and therefore unattainable) states of being all revolving around the still point of the central self" (Viola 1995: 226). By reflecting the observer's image in a revolving mirrored surface that also displays and scatters video images of birth, disaster, and celebration, and alternately presenting and scattering both, Viola's work evokes ("evokes" is a weak word for the startling experience of being in the midst of this remarkable piece) Buddhist notions of the ephemeral nature of self (that is, self as self-image) and world, while the observer's body and gaze are made to enact the idea of "self" in Viola's second sense, that of a detached but aware meditating consciousness. As Viola explains, charting the interplay of self and its reflection, projection and its image in the turning mirror, and the spinning image of the room itself in which the installation is set, "the entire space becomes an interior for the revelations of a constantly turning mind absorbed with itself."

Viola began his career in video art in the early 1970s as assistant to Peter Campus and Nam June Paik. By 1980, his work had become (and remains) closely connected to the serious study of Asian religious art and ritual. He traveled to Indonesia, Java, and Bali in the late 1970s to record traditional music, studied with Zen masters in Japan, and began a long-term artistic partnership with Zen painter and priest Daien Tanaka in 1980. Extended trips to study at Tibetan Buddhist monasteries in Ladakh (1982) and to observe and record the Hindu firewalk ritual in Fiji (1984) and Native American art (1987) followed (Viola 1995: 288–9). Viola's interest in non-Western religion and ritual has been especially focused on the connections between spirituality and memory systems, which he sees as posing questions concerning time and experience that provide insight into the nature of modern technologies of record and memory such as video. In his formative period in the late 1970s and early 1980s he also became interested in the writings of Christian visionaries such as St. John of the Cross, Hildegarde von Bingen, and Meister Eckhart. Many of Viola's major works are influenced by and even "versions" of Christian religious painting, including *Room for St. John of the Cross* (1983); *The Nantes Triptych* (1992); *The Greeting* (1995; a monumental ultra-slow motion video based on Pontormo's *Visitation* [1529]); *Five Angels for the Millennium* (2001), recently purchased jointly by the Pompidou, the Whitney, and the Tate Modern for the highest price ever paid for a work of video art (Vogel 2002); *Going Forth By Day* (inspired by Giotto's frescoes in the Scrovegni Chapel in Padua; Viola 2002); and *The Passions* (2003).

While religious themes are not infrequent in contemporary art, they are often presented (for example by Serrano) in an idiom that can seem provocative or inappropriate to the uninitiated, generating controversy. Viola's work is sometimes misconstrued in an opposite way, his reach towards the status of sacred art being so direct that new viewers look in vain for postmodern irony. Viola is also a major theorist of video. As might be expected given the nature of his work, many of his writings concern video and time, video and the sacred, and related themes. His best known theoretical piece, "Video Black: The Mortality of the Image" (Viola 1994, repr. Viola 1995: 197–209), understands video as the most recent development in a movement of the arts away from "timelessness" towards expression of temporal limitation that he sees as beginning with Brunelleschi and Renaissance perspective. Video, in this scheme, is one of the most ephemeral of the arts, and, as such, offers possibilities for representing mortality. In "Video Black" Viola is interested in subject matter – a video camera can be on hand to record the most impromptu of events and, unlike still photography, does so by means of images that move through time themselves – but also in video's dependence on equipment, electric current, freedom from electrical interference or static, vicissitudes of the image in a medium that can bring about one of the three stages of video fatality: a static-filled screen, a blank "on" one, or a "dead" black one.

When Hamlet stands in the midst of "Slowly Turning Narrative" and begins his soliloquy, then, he does so in a different mood and in a different context from his first "rehearsals" of the lines in his Pixelvision suicide attempts. As media allegory, the Whitney sequence relates Almereyda's search for a philosophical video idiom to that of the major, now canonical artist working in that vein, and does so at an exhibition of historic importance – one at which Viola's work, already successful, achieved enhanced status in the art world.[6] "The piece," Almereyda writes, "seemed almost ready made for Hamlet's state of mind, for Shakespeare's hypnotic words" (Almereyda 2000: 137). The metanarrative changes substantially if the traces, survivals, and renewals of ancient "wisdom" traditions in Viola's work are felt as reinforcements of Almereyda's attempt to replay *Hamlet* in the mixed medium of Pixelvision and 35mm.

The scene in the Whitney was to have been followed by a continuation of the soliloquy in the video store: as indicated above, the idea was to "balance the Viola video with its nemesis, a Blockbuster store with mass-market images flooding in from the store's monitors" (Almereyda 2000: 137). But Blockbuster also provides, in the screenplay, raw material for Hamlet's renewed filmmaking, as the scene shifts to his apartment/editing studio where he finishes the last words of the speech while feverishly juxtaposing images of "sex and death," including footage from an Elizabethan-dress Shakespeare porn and from a silent *Hamlet*. In the release version the entire speech takes place in Blockbuster, the nemesis environment, and we do not see Hamlet renting tapes at the end of the sequence.[7] The "To be or not to be" speech is therefore more bitter, less connected to his own filmmaking, and unconnected to video installation art. Instead, Hamlet is more despairingly absorbed in lamenting the injustices of the world (of which our Blockbuster-inflected culture is one, no doubt, along with the law's delay and the whips and scorns of time).

Perhaps for a Hamlet to make a film (or put on a play) is just another evasion, another failure to act effectively in opposition to the corrupt court of Denmark or the corporate-media system. Indeed, the planned editing sequence ended, like Shakespeare's text, with the reflection that "enterprises of great pith and moment / With this regard their currents turn awry / And lose the name of action" (Almereyda 2000: 52). But at least in the screenplay we see that Hamlet's work on his film/video, however little it may accomplish in the realm of "action," has been inspired by a major work of art and is connected to a tradition.

The Whitney sequence is – or rather could have been – central not only to the media allegory of Almereyda's *Hamlet*, but also to the story it tells about Hamlet and the ghost of his father. The ghost is present on screen at several key moments at the end of the film as released. I suggest that these moments, which define the film's take on Hamlet's acceptance of death and his hopes for the telling of his story, would have a slightly different effect in a narrative that included the Viola exhibition.

The first of these moments occurs before the fencing match. Somewhat unaccountably, the ghost appears here first seated by the bedside of Horatio's sleeping girlfriend ("Marcella"), in an attitude of concern, more guardian angel, perhaps, than ghost, or like a parent worried over a child's illness. Hamlet spots him and turns away, rejoining Horatio for the exchange concerning the hazard of the proposed fencing match. Hamlet's delivery of the lines is anxious and hurried until, at "the readiness is all," he looks up, sees the ghost again, acknowledges his presence with a nod, and offers the words "let be" in a calmer tone of settled acceptance, looking up once more to his father as he concludes on a fade to black followed by a close-up of the poison being put into the cup.

The final return of the ghost comes during Hamlet's dying request to Horatio to "tell my story." The camera tracks in to Hamlet, from medium shot to close-up as he stands bloodied in combat in his fencing whites. The "story" he imagines is shown in Pixelvision, and is a complex reprise (with a difference) of several moments previously seen. There is Ophelia at intimate distance, recalling the shots of her in the Thich Nhat Hanh sequence – but now, in a shot divided into three short sequences separated by other material, the intended kiss is completed. The intercut shots include one of Gertrude, her hands to her face in grief; then a return to the main color sequence, which is now an extreme close-up of Hamlet's bloodied eye "watching" the imagined video story; and then replays of Hamlet being punched by Laertes and by Claudius' thugs. But the ghost is present too, virtually and briefly, moving left and out of the image after the shot of Gertrude, turning away from the sequence in which Hamlet is beaten ("more in sorrow than in anger") to look into the Pixelvision camera. The camera point of view is third person, no longer that of the intimate self-address of Pixelvision autobiography, but is nonetheless closely associated with Hamlet's "mind's eye" and with the ghost's presence as witness to the events of Hamlet's life (see Lehmann 2002a: 99 on the convergence of the cinematic "mind's eye" and Shakespeare's; see also Viola's theorization of the video as "mind's eye" [1995: 101]).

The final moments of the film also resonate with the structure marked out by the intertwining of Hamlet's videomaking and his efforts to find release from the anguished question of "being." Here Robert MacNeil reports on the carnage at Elsinore as if in a public television news report, borrowing Fortinbras' words and concluding with the First Ambassador's half-line: "The sight is dismal." But MacNeil then continues with lines from the player king:

Our wills and fates do so contrary run
That our devices still are overthrown;
Our thoughts are ours, their ends none of our own. (3.3.209–11)

The effort to "restore" the film by imagining it as originally planned may perhaps only help us to see what is already there: Almereyda himself was at first distraught at having to leave out the Whitney scene, then slowly came to the conclusion that "the lonely Block-buster aisles, with their in-house 'action' signs and 'Go home happy' wall placards, just might be sufficient" (Almereyda 2000: 127). But as we watch his Hamlet struggle in the last moments of the film to "let it be," to come to terms with the collapse of his hopes and his failure to alter through action or through art, it would have been good to be able to remember the beginning of the "To be or not to be" sequence as it stands in the screenplay where Hamlet, having joined his voice, reciting the first eight lines of the soliloquy, to the recorded chant that accompanies the surge of images that fill the screen and spill out over the walls of the room, *"stops following the mirror, letting his image slide away, consumed in video flame"* (Almereyda 2000: 50).

Notes

1 Shakespeare citations refer to David Bevington (ed.), *The Complete Works of Shakespeare*, 4th edn (New York: Longman, 1997).
2 Through devices as diverse as playing to the camera and suggesting sexual activities through out-of-focus thumbsucking (all but unidentifiable as such at close range), Benning's more recent fictional work contains some "hardcore" scenes. At the outer edge of Pixelvision eroticism, one website reviews a no-longer-online "pixelporn" competition on the "Art is Dead" website. The reviewer (Amzen 1997) confides that "what I liked about the films is that most of the time you couldn't tell exactly what was going on, due to the poor resolution and framerate of the medium."
3 See, for example, the Flicker New York City at oakshire.ionestudios.com/~flickernyc/PastFlickerPixel.htm; Indiespace at indiespace.com/pxlthis/.
4 The father's interdiction of the son as voyeur or competitor is of course a part of the normative resolution of the Oedipus complex in Freud's read-ing. In Almereyda's film there is an implication that, with his father gone, Hamlet's filming and his viewing and reviewing of what he has filmed may become unhealthy and compulsive, his poignant reveries shading into "unmanly grief."
5 Versions of this speech occur throughout Thich Nhat Hanh's voluminous writings (e.g., 1999: 6), where the first words the Buddha utters after

235

achieving enlightenment are said to have been "Dear friends, I have seen that nothing can be by itself alone, that everything has to interbe with everything else." Hanh's words are so apt as one answer to Hamlet's famous question that one might think that they were written and spoken with *Hamlet* in mind, but of course they are core Buddhist teachings. Hamlet's "to be" vocabulary corresponds to the Buddhist terms *Brava* (being) and *abhava* (not being).

6 Viola had received one honorary doctorate before, from his alma mater, four afterward, in rapid succession.

7 We do see Hamlet piling tapes onto the Blockbuster counter ten minutes earlier in the film, where the shot plays as just one more index of Hamlet's obsession with video.

References and Further Reading

Almereyda, Michael (1996). *Another Girl, Another Planet*. Pixelvision video. Published in PAL by Screen Edge (UK).

Amzen, Monica (1997). "Pixelporn: The First Annual Pixelvision Pornography Film Festival." *Sur Review*, online. wwwcgi.cs.cmu.edu/afs/cs/ user/ jthomas/SurReview/reviews-html/pixelporn.html. Consulted October 31, 2004.

Cassidy, Kyle (1996). *Toy Soldiers*. Pixelvision video. Digital copy supplied by author.

Hanh, Thich Nhat (1999). *The Heart of the Buddha's Teaching*. New York: Broadway Books.

Krishnamurti, J. [Jiddu] (1992). *On Living and Dying*. San Francisco: HarperSanFrancisco.

Lehmann, Courtney (2002a). "The Machine in the Ghost: Hamlet's Cinematographic Kingdom." In Lehmann: 89–129.

Morris, Garry (1999). "Sadie Benning's Pixel Pleasures." *Bright Lights Film Journal* 24 (April), online. www.brightlightsfilm.com/24/benning.html. Consulted October 31, 2004.

Pixelvision homepage. elvis.rowan.edu/~cassidy/pixel/manual, online. Consulted October 31, 2004.

Revkin, Andrew C. (2000). "As Simple as Black and White: Children's Toy is Reborn as an Avant-Garder Filmmaking Tool." *New York Times*, January 22.

Rose, David A., and Peter Sellars (1997). *Bill Viola*. New York: Whitney Museum of American Art and Flammarion Press.

Viola, Bill (1994). "Video Black: The Mortality of the Image." In Doug Hall and Sally Joe Fifer (eds.), *Illuminating Video: An Essential Guide to Video Art*. New York: Aperture: 46–86.

—— (1995). *Reasons for Knocking at an Empty House: Writing 1973–1994*. Cambridge, MA: MIT Press and London: Anthony D'Offay Gallery.

—— (2002). *Going Forth by Day*. New York: Guggenheim Museum and Harry F. Abrams and Berlin: Deutsche Guggenheim.

Vogel, Carol (2002). "Museums Team up to Foot the Bill and Find the Space." *New York Times*, October 17, ArtSection: 17.

Unending Revels: Visual Pleasure and Compulsory Shakespeare

Kathleen McLuskie

In his contemporary biography of David Garrick, Arthur Murphy recounts a curious episode that summed up Garrick's art as a performer of Shakespeare. The player apparently received a poem written on behalf of a deaf-mute who insisted that he understood all passions from Garrick's acting even though he could not hear the words:

> What need of sound? When plainly I descry
> Th'expressive features, and the speaking eye;
> That eye, whose bright and penetrating ray
> Does Shakespeare's meaning to my soul convey.
> Blest commentator on great Shakespeare's text!
> When Garrick acts, no passage seems perplext.
> (Murphy 1969, 2: 183)

In the subsequent discussion, the deaf man explained that Garrick's power of communication was perfect because "his face was a language" (Murphy 1969, 2: 185).

It may seem curious to use this, possibly apocryphal,[1] story in the afterword to a collection of essays on screen Shakespeare. The events it records took place more than a century before the development of film as a technology of representation and it concerns a figure whose fame in the history of Shakespeare's afterlife lies in his restoration of Shakespeare's *text* in the theater. Nevertheless, it signals the beginning of a set of metaphors for the communication of Shakespeare that transcend the primary relationship of text to reader. "That eye, whose bright and penetrating ray / Does Shakespeare's meaning to my soul convey" is a vivid image for the film camera, while the idea of a language, only metaphorically related to the lexis and syntax of speech, is now a commonplace in the description of filmic effect.

These shared metaphors, like the anecdote, assume that there is some kind of Shakespearean essence, a mix of ethical transformation and emotional affect, that is only metaphorically related to the words in the seventeenth-century copies of his plays. They are also critical to the central fantasy, embodied in the story of the deaf-mute, that there can be a direct communication between the artist and the spectator, unmediated by the technologies of scenography or the even more complex work of camera, film stock, or *mise-en-scène*.

The establishment of this metaphoric relationship between the Shakespeare text, theatrical performance, and an effect on an audience required considerable discursive effort on the part of Garrick and his admirers. Murphy recounts the miracle of the deaf-mute as further evidence of Garrick's ability to give bodily form to the feelings in his art (see Murphy 1969, 2: 177). This articulation of the relationship between the senses, the emotions, and the ethical capacity of human beings drew on the contemporary science of physiognomy, the idea that facial expressions and bodily action provided a route into understanding the character and even the ethical tendencies of individuals.[2] In applying these scientific ideas to acting, Garrick and Murphy gave the profession a standing that elevated it above mere pleasure and also forged a link between the emotional pleasure of theater and physical action on the stage.

Garrick's varied accounts of his work in the theater present an interesting paradox. On the one hand, by restoring Shakespeare's text and debating readings with bibliographers such as Dr. Johnson, he engaged with the new editorial controversies to deepen the sense of complexity that he brought to the performance of character (see, for example, Murphy 1969, 1: 83). On the other, he insisted on the connection between his particular style of physical performance and the manifestation of Shakespeare's genius.

The epitaph on Garrick's tomb reads

> Though sunk in death the forms the poet drew,
> The actor's genius bade them breathe anew.
> (Murphy 1969, 2: 337)

The poetic sleight of hand substitutes Garrick's genius for Shake-speare's and leaves no space for all the other commercial and artistic relations that connected the two. In fact, the words that Shakespeare wrote were anything but "sunk in death." There was intense commercial competition to reproduce them for new and controversial editions both from the monopoly publishers and from the pirate publishers who wanted a share of the backlist of earlier literature to launch their own companies (see St. Clair 2004: 122–40). Performance, too, was subject to commercial pressures and Garrick was perfectly open about using his attachment to Shakespeare to establish a particular market for his productions at Drury Lane.

By driving a wedge between old texts and new performances, high-minded poetic drama and commercial necessity, Garrick established the terms of engagement for the future reception of Shakespeare. It would involve the pleasures of mastery over old texts together with the immediate and constantly renewed pleasures of non-verbal communication of emotional and ethical truths; it would acknowledge the commercial constraints of its existence but would strive for the higher pleasures of poetry as against physical display.

These overlapping oppositions between old words and new performances, artistry and commerce had circumscribed the arena of contested cultural values since Shakespeare's own time. (Their classic early modern discussions are to be found in Ben Jonson's Induction to *Bartholomew Fair* and Dekker's *Gull's Hornbook*.) As the essays in this volume show, they inform the discourses of criticism with which filmmakers[3] and critics in the twentieth century established their claims to cultural value. The creative tension that Garrick established between text, performance, and the essence of Shakespeare is reiterated in modern times. Kenneth Branagh's often-quoted claim to be using the full text of *Hamlet* (a gesture that has no bibliographical or historical rationale) is used to mitigate the innovation of his setting the film in an imagined nineteenth-century Blenheim Palace. In contrast, *The Times'* review of Beerbohm Tree's *King John* (1899), where the whole text was not used, was felt to "accelerate the action of the play without impairing anything of its truth and spirit" (see GUNERATNE). The "truth and spirit" of a Shakespeare play is so nebulous and immaterial a concept that it can be invoked in a variety of different critical strategies without recourse to formal and historical analysis.

These discursive continuities between Shakespeare's historical afterlives and his representation in film, however, disguise the fundamental innovation occasioned by the development of film as a mode of Shakespearean representation. Shakespeare provided a valuable and ready-made cultural capital for the new industry in the form of a backlist of well-known narratives, but the form of his plays also embodied a set of representational problems that could be solved by the developing technologies of film form. The tension that Garrick experienced between the work of carpenters and poets, or that the Prologue to *King Henry V* articulated in his account of the limitations of the Wooden O, was eliminated by the visual pleasure of the new form.[4] The film camera's capacity to control point of view, whether in the tight close-up of intimate human exchange or the wide-angled shot that encompassed epic action, created a powerful illusion of immediate and personal communication. It could, in effect, directly convey Shakespeare's meaning to the souls of individualized spectators, through its bright and penetrating ray. This effect, of course, occluded the economic basis of film production in the studio system, the profitability of a technology of representation that allowed multiple performances at marginal additional cost. It also left no space for reflection on the political implications of the dislocation between the epic aspiration of battle narratives and the comic reality of the "four or five ragged foils" with which they had previously been performed.

This powerful combination of a technology of affect and an economics of widespread distribution also intersected with new anxieties about the role of film in public culture. By the early twentieth century, Garrick's engaging deaf-mute had been replaced as the paradigm spectator by the alternately threatening and needy urban working class. In the famous Newbolt report of 1921, its author articulated the rationale for public education in the humanities:

> Deny to working-class children any common share in the immaterial, and presently they will grow into men who demand with menaces a communism of the material. (Newbolt 1921: 200)

One of Newbolt's recommendations was that English literature, including Shakespeare, should be the foundation of education in English schools.

Newbolt's call for access to the "immaterial" as a bulwark against the demand for "a communism of the material" has generated a certain cynicism about the role of Shakespeare in progressive education,[5] and Will Hays' vision, discussed here by Guneratne, that the Warner Brothers/Reinhardt *Midsummer Night's Dream* film "would inaugurate 'a new epoch in the popular and universal appreciation of Shakespeare'" is similarly tainted by Hays' association with film censorship. Nonetheless, in insisting on public education that was not merely functional, Newbolt laid the foundations for universal access to Shakespeare and the Hays accolade signaled the cultural capital that could potentially be invested in film. The fact that Newbolt and Hays could be accused of false consciousness or misrecognition of the underlying reality of the culture they envisioned only indicates the complex power of the myth of Shakespeare in mediating the effects of the new form.

Film's enormous potential to combine a technology of affect with an economics of universal access did not need to be linked to Shakespeare, as the history of film in other European contexts shows.[6] Nevertheless, "compulsory Shakespeare" had an important mediating role to play in constructing the discourses through which film is received in Anglo-American culture. It extended the brand recognition that was an important feature of the growing Shakespeare market, but its association both with schooling and the state mitigated the positive effects of that brand. Orson Welles, who had a perfectly jolly time producing Shakespeare at Todd School for boys, nonetheless constantly opposed "school Shakespeare" to his creative experiments with Shakespeare at Mercury records, on radio and film (Anderegg 1999: 21). In spite of the creativity of generations of gifted schoolteachers, "school Shakespeare" has been used by adapters and commentators on filmed Shakespeare as the shorthand for the residue of the spent capital of the old technologies of reading print. Invoking "school Shakespeare" occludes the role of the technologies of affect in creating the pleasure of filmed Shakespeare and it valorizes the role of innovation, essential to the continued creation of film in a capitalist market.

This discursive handling of "compulsory Shakespeare" creates a number of contradictions in the usual binaries of value that structure the cultural role of filmed Shakespeare. Its provision of universal access leaves it on the valorized "popular" side of the popular/elite distinction, but its association with culture that is imposed by the state positions it problematically at the opposite pole. Similarly, in the parallel binary opposition between old and new, Shakespeare is both denigrated as the last Dead White Male and at the same moment rescued with the lifeline of enduring culture and the potential for these values to be continually renewed (see PEARSON AND URICCHIO).

The process of resolving those binaries requires considerable discursive agility. For example, Jonathan Bate concludes his account of *The Genius of Shakespeare* by drawing attention to Shakespeare's presentation of "The oldest and most enduring stories – children coming to terms with their parents; men and women falling in love, fearing infidelity, seeking power, renouncing power, growing old, dying well" (1997: 327). Bate's list abstracts the narratives of Shakespeare's plays from their moment-by-moment effects of verse, prose, and stage directions to a generalized litany of essential human narratives. The rest of his book reveals the extent to which these narratives may be recognized as essential because of their constant reiteration in Shakespeare reproduction.[7]

This strategy of abstraction is used by many advocates of Shakespeare's eternal relevance, and its association with "school Shakespeare" is comically rendered in John McTiernan's *Last Action Hero* (1993). McTiernan is able to engage his spectator by invoking the familiar scene of the tedious high school Shakespeare class in which a sad, if enthusiastic, teacher insists that Hamlet will appeal to her ungrateful charges because it includes "treachery, conspiracy, sex, swordfights, madness, ghosts, and in the end everyone dies." As Lanier points out, a similar strategy had been used three years earlier by Franco Zeffirelli in his marketing campaign for another *Hamlet* film. The list of abstracted narrative elements is used by Zeffirelli as well as by McTiernan's schoolmistress to condescend to a recalcitrant audience. It tries to bridge the gap between old, high-culture Shakespeare and the narratives supposedly attractive to youthful taste. What she, and perhaps Zeffirelli, misses is the fact that narrative itself has been marginalized by the new culture in favor of a piling up of immediate and violent special effects. The alternative version of *Hamlet* dreamt up by the bored schoolboy is similar to parodies of Shakespeare since Duffett in the 1670s and of other high-culture texts before that. It retains the bare narrative structure and reverses or explodes the key markers of affect. Duffett's witches in his anti-Macbeth are turned into foul-mouthed prostitutes and the last action hero comically reduces Hamlet's ethically and dramatically complex poetry to "You killed my foddah": "four or five ragged foils," indeed.

Whether we admire or deplore the postmodern turn to parody, the tendency that Robert Shaughnessy notes of the past's "potential to be recycled, fairly indiscriminately, as kitsch," it is important to return this cultural effect to the institutional structures of compulsory Shakespeare. Shakespeare in schools may have been the abandoned starting point for innovation in Shakespeare, but it was also the place that turned Shakespeare into the abstract packages in which it could be transported into the new. Schoolrooms provided the locus in which the Shakespeare narratives were first learned and became the common culture of the nation; they were also, as McTiernan's film dramatizes, the paradigm site of contest between young (often male) students and older (often female) teachers.[8] However, while school Shakespeare offered the possibility of reading and rereading the humanist "enduring stories," outside the schoolroom those same stories were being transformed into different and new forms of entertainment. Romantic and emotional stories of "children coming to terms with their parents; men and women falling in love, fearing infidelity, seeking power, renouncing power, growing old, dying well" moved into the realm of the "women's weepie" and, in time, into television soap-opera while, as McTiernan's film shows, the "action" elements moved into the male narratives of the Mafia movie and the crime film.[9]

The repetitive quality of these "enduring stories," together with their scope for reworking in new film forms, opened a gap between "school Shakespeare" and the more sophisticated methodologies of academic film criticism in the later twentieth century. The repeatability of the film and the continued existence of copies protected the film reader from the subjectivism of theater criticism and allowed the use of familiar historiographical techniques for recovery of lost artifacts (see GUNERATNE). The innovation of the new film criticism, celebrated in this collection, however, lay in deploying the analytical discourses of *Cahiers du Cinema* and *Screen* to inform a new critical attention to "the specific qualities of Shakespeare film *as film*" (SHAUGHNESSY). These new forms of reading have some continuity with older practices. They often deal with individual films, reading them as Dawson claims Shakespeare did with Ovid and Plutarch, "from the inside, responding to the complex dynamics of the original work" (p. 173).[10] Their effect has been to create a canon of Shakespeare films, transformed by those very readings into "readable" texts that will respond to a more complex hermeneutics of abstraction. The earlier abstraction of Shakespeare's narratives into "enduring stories" was replaced by an abstraction of larger themes that connect the Shakespeare film to the pressures of modern existence, not least through the technology and forms of representation that they share with advertising and the multiple modalities of technologized entertainment (see AEBISCHER). The resulting analogies between the motifs of Shakespeare films and the treatment of similar motifs in the culture at large generalize their significance, reinstating their universality and insisting, once again, on their relevance for the wider audience of mass culture.

Mark Thornton Burnett, for example, shows how "high-security culture" in Denmark can be invoked in Cavanagh's film by using a setting in the Irish city of Derry. Physical location can be read as establishing a connection with Shakespeare's narrative and both the present crisis of the Northern Irish struggles and their originating seventeenth-century conflict between the apprentice boys and Catholic James II. Burnett acknowledges that the effect of this use of *mise-en-scène* in both Cavanagh's and Branagh's *Hamlet* "could work finally to suggest that one global conflict may be indistinguishable from the next." That simple (and dangerous) analogizing is avoided by the sheer density and excess of possible readings that the films discussed in this collection provoke. All of them acknowledge that "the moment of a film's production cannot be privileged as an arbiter of how it is to be read," but they nonetheless assume that the film can be *read*, preferably by a knowing educated reader who can tease out the full range of referents, even if they are hidden from the very multiplex viewer assumed to be their intended recipient (compare LANIER).

As Diana Henderson points out in her essay, this process of reading can turn the film into a "commodity fetish, rather than the product of complex, contingent relationships and transactions" (compare Barbara Hodgdon's account of the way that filmic processes can marginalize the actor as the source of signification). Henderson's analysis of the process of filmmaking, her discussions with designers and performers, highlights the gap between the knowing academic reader and the intractability of the process of making the filmic object (what shall we do about the coachman's clothes?). Her account of Blair Brown's search for a psychological "through-line" to underpin her performance as Gertrude also offers a reminder of the continuities with interpretive processes associated with "school Shakespeare." Those processes remained dominant in the theater via the long tradition of a Stanislavski/ Method approach to acting training. In that tradition, the individual actor was responsible for interpretation, a process that is the antithesis of the postmodern play of signification informing current critical discourse. For Blair Brown, the play is less to do with abstracted "privatized relationships" (as described in Burnett's reading of Almereyda's *Hamlet*) or even the story of a man who cannot make up his mind. It deals with the more immediate motivating narrative of a mother with an absent husband and a distressingly recalcitrant son. Blair Brown's psychologized account of Gertrude's "character" represents a return to the resonant "enduring stories" that lie behind the form of a Shakespeare play. It may well strike more of a chord with a (feminized) mass audience, but its echo of motifs that have transferred to the realm of soap-opera also indicates the irrepressible resurgence of feminized popular discourses[11] in the face of consistent attempts at exclusion from academic criticism of Shakespeare in the twentieth century.

The same modernist moment that saw the establishment of the feature film as the dominant mode of popular entertainment and the publication of the Newbolt report also produced anxious accounts by the critics of the "dissociation of sensibility" (see Mulhern 1979; Halpern 1997). Like Garrick before them and many writers since, these critics fantasized a kind of immediate communication that attempted to identify the historical break in poetry's potential for immediate communication penetrating, as T. S. Eliot puts it, "the cerebral cortex, the nervous system and the digestive tracts" (1963: 290). For the proponents of this desired symbiosis between poetry and its readers, film, for all its ability to achieve this communication via the technology of affect, was altogether too populist a medium. They sought instead, through the educational medium of "practical criticism," to create an exclusive intellectual cadre who would be able to "read" the culture of the past in a way that might link the ethical and the emotional through language. An important part of this endeavor was to distance "readers" from "all the irrelevant moral and realistic canons that have been applied to Shakespeare's plays, for the sentimentalizing of his heroes . . . and his heroines."[12] Instead they emphasized the humanizing values of an attention to the language defined in terms of connecting strands of imagery that identified the core values of the play and required an abstracting critical process to give them meaning.

These refined critical strategies have, of course, proved to be completely impotent in the face of film's development, and in terms of the culture as a whole seem increasingly marginal. The *auteurs* of Shakespeare film and video have been able to use the infinite creative potential of the form to encompass the excluded areas that critics attempted to reserve for themselves. Film could link images through coherent visual style far more effectively than in critical prose: consider, for example, the glowing renaissance colors of Zeffirelli's *Romeo and Juliet* (1968). As Pearson and Uricchio have described, the screen could both make the "chocolate box" image of rural Stratford available to urban audiences and equally, fifty years on, present the gritty, urban version of Shakespeare's life to a different generation. Critical connections made between the politics of Shakespeare's time and the pressures of the modern world were both preempted in Orson Welles' presentation of "the old dumb-show of monarchy" (Denning 1996: 380) and echoed in the sexual politics of the Polanski *Macbeth* (1971). The recent return to a critical emphasis on the commercial nature of Shakespeare's theater is gently mocked in *Shakespeare in Love* (1998), and even the use of new technologies to create individualized works of art can be absorbed, as Peter Donaldson shows, into the effects of a feature film.

The trajectories of criticism that translate visual experience into academic prose and the experiential into the analytical are reversed in film. In film the address to the spectator via camera-work and high production values is all-encompassing and, unlike theater, cannot, once the film is made, respond to the audience's reception. It makes no difference to the film whether that reception is articulated in an immediate emotional response of tears or laughter, in the "school Shakespeare" abstractions of character analysis, or the academic Shakespeare analogies with global or local or gender politics. As the ultimate commodified cultural product, a film of a Shakespeare play (or any other subject) has a commercial relationship to its audience that (give or take the cost of a ticket) renders it uniquely democratic. Individual *auteurs* may, like Garrick, engage in the discourses of criticism or cultural policy, but if those moves are not explicitly obfuscatory, they are marginal to the activity of making films.

Some recent directors have generously acknowledged historical criticism by explicitly stratifying the pleasures that their films offer according to assumptions about the range of different critical niches that their audiences might inhabit. Both Baz Luhrmann's *William Shakespeare's Romeo + Juliet* (1996) and John Madden's *Shakespeare in Love* drew on historical scholarship to place clever academic jokes in the midst of their films. The academic-critic's lifetime activity of historical knowledge brought to bear on exegetical or hermeneutic problems is endorsed by the simple pleasure of recognition: "Ooh, look, it's John Taylor the water-poet." That recognition might lead on to the complex and enlightening articulations of cultural analysis and social policy, but that analysis occurs in another place. The dialogue between Garrick and the deaf-mute continues as before.

Notes

1 Murphy's account of the unlettered but eloquent mute is a little too close for comfort to Thomas Gray's almost contemporary "mute inglorious

Milton" in "Elegy Written in a Country Churchyard" and the style of his poem suspiciously akin to that of Garrick's own prologues.

2 See Hartley's introduction (Hartley 2001) for an account of the codification of facial expression as a route into the mind and character of individuals.

3 I am referring here, as do many of the essays in this collection, only to feature films. Other arenas of art informed by reproductive technology (such as those addressed in Peter Donaldson's chapter) are fascinating, but the differences in funding, production, and distribution are so different as to make comparisons impossible.

4 See Shaughnessy's discussion of these technologies of reproduction in this volume.

5 See Baldick (1983: 89–107 and passim); he is particularly interesting on the role of famous Shakespeareans in the Newbolt report.

6 Similar debates about state-funded high culture and the role of artistic innovation were played out in France, as Guneratne notes.

7 The material process of publishing that made these narratives available in print is discussed in St. Clair (2004: 135–9).

8 It might be instructive to read *Last Action Hero* against the mythologies of films such as *Dead Poets Society* or *Mona Lisa Smile* as well as against Shakespeare.

9 Note Mulvey (1989: 29–80) on women's films; consider the influence of *The Godfather* on *Richard III* and *Macbeth* in films such as Pacino's *Looking for Richard* (1996) and *Men of Respect* (1991).

10 Dawson insists that Kurosawa's films "are not just adaptations of *King Lear* and *Macbeth*, but readings of them" (p. 160).

11 See Rose (1991: ch. 5, 165–204) on the feminization of romance and its critical exclusion from the body of Plath's writing.

12 Knights (1946: 1); compare Rutter (2004: 38–53).

References and Further Reading

Baldick, Chris (1983). *The Social Mission of English Criticism 1848–1932*. Oxford: Clarendon Press.

Bate, Jonathan (1997). *The Genius of Shakespeare*. London: Picador.

Denning, Michael (1996). *The Cultural Front: The Labouring of American Culture in the Twentieth Century*. London and New York: Verso.

Eliot, T. S. (1963). "The Metaphysical Poets." In *Selected Essays*. London.

Halpern, Richard (1997). *Shakespeare among the Moderns*. Ithaca and London: Cornell University Press.

Hartley, Lucy (2001). *Physiognomy and the Meaning of Expression in Nineteenth-Century Culture*. Cambridge: Cambridge University Press.

Knights, L. C. (1946). "How Many Children had Lady Macbeth? An Essay on the Theory and Practice of Shakespeare Criticism." In *Explorations*. London: Chatto and Windus: 1–39.

Mulhern, Francis (1979). *The Moment of Scrutiny*. London: New Left Books.

Mulvey, Laura (1989). *Visual and Other Pleasures*. Basingstoke: Macmillan.

Murphy, Arthur (1969). *The Life of David Garrick*, 2 vols. New York and London: Benjamin Blom. First published London 1801.

Newbolt, Sir Henry (1921). *The Teaching of English in England*. Government Report. London: HMSO.

Rose, Jacqueline (1991). *The Haunting of Sylvia Plath*. London: Virago.

Rutter, Carol Chillington (2004). "Remind Me: How Many Children had Lady Macbeth?" *Shakespeare Survey* 57: 38–53.

St. Clair, William (2004). *The Reading Nation in the Romantic Period*. Cambridge: Cambridge University Press.

Select Bibliography

Almereyda, Michael (2000). *William Shakespeare's "Hamlet": A Screenplay Adaptation*. London: Faber and Faber.

Anderegg, Michael (1999). *Orson Welles, Shakespeare, and Popular Culture*. New York: Columbia University Press.

—— (2003). *Cinematic Shakespeare*. Lanham, MD: Rowman and Littlefield.

Ball, Robert Hamilton (1968). *Shakespeare on Silent Film: A Strange Eventful History*. London: Allen and Unwin.

Boose, Lynda E., and Richard Burt, eds. (1997). *Shakespeare, The Movie: Popularizing the Plays on Film, TV, and Video*. London/New York: Routledge.

——, eds. (2003). *Shakespeare, The Movie, II: Popularizing the Plays on Film, TV, Video, and DVD*. London and New York: Routledge.

Branagh, Kenneth (1989a). *Beginning*. New York: St. Martin's Press/London: Chatto and Windus.

—— (1989b). *Henry V by William Shakespeare: A Screen Adaptation by Kenneth Branagh*. London: Chatto and Windus.

—— (1996). *"Hamlet" by William Shakespeare: Screenplay, Introduction, and Film Diary by Russell Jackson*. London: Chatto and Windus.

Buhler, Stephen (2002). *Shakespeare in the Cinema: Ocular Proof*. Albany: State University of New York Press.

Bulman, James C., ed. (1996). *Shakespeare, Theory, and Performance*. New York: Routledge.

——, and H. R. Coursen, eds. (1988). *Shakespeare on Television: An Anthology*. Hanover, NH: University Press of New England.

Burnett, Mark Thornton, and Ramona Wray, eds. (2000). *Shakespeare, Film, Fin de Siècle*. London: Macmillan.

Burt, Richard (2002a). "Shakespeare and the Holocaust: Julie Taymor's Titus is Beautiful, or Shakesploi Meets (the) Camp." In Burt, ed.: 295–329.

——, ed. (2002b). *Shakespeare After Mass Media*. New York: Palgrave.

Cartmell, Deborah (2000). *Interpreting Shakespeare on Screen*. New York: St. Martin's.

Collick, John (1989). *Shakespeare, Cinema and Society*. Manchester: Manchester University Press.

Crowl, Samuel (1992). *Shakespeare Observed: Studies in Performance on Stage and Screen*. Athens: Ohio University Press.

—— (2002). *Shakespeare at the Cineplex: The Kenneth Branagh Era*. Miami: Ohio University Press.

Davies, Anthony (1988). *Filming Shakespeare's Plays: The Adaptations of Laurence Olivier, Orson Welles, Peter Brook, Akira Kurosawa*. Cambridge: Cambridge University Press.

——, and Stanley Wells, eds. (1994). *Shakespeare and the Moving Image: The Plays on Film and Television*. Cambridge: Cambridge University Press.

Díaz Fernández, José Ramón (1997). "Shakespeare on Screen: A Bibliography of Critical Studies." *Post Script: Essays in Film and the Humanities* 17.1: 91–146.

Donaldson, Peter S. (1990). *Shakespearean Films/Shakespearean Directors*. Boston: Unwin Hyman.

Hatchuel, Sarah (2004). *Shakespeare, from Stage to Screen*. Cambridge: Cambridge University Press.

Hodgdon, Barbara (1998). *The Shakespeare Trade: Performances and Appropriations*. Philadelphia: University of Pennsylvania Press.

——, special editor (2002). *Shakespeare Quarterly* 53.2.

Holderness, Graham (2002). *Visual Shakespeare: Essays in Film and Television*. Hatfield: University of Hertfordshire Press.

Howlett, Kathy M. (2000). *Framing Shakespeare on Film*. Athens: Ohio University Press.

Jackson, Russell, ed. (2000). *The Cambridge Companion to Shakespeare on Film*. Cambridge: Cambridge University Press.

Jorgens, Jack J. (1977). *Shakespeare on Film*. Bloomington: Indiana University Press.

Kliman, Bernice W. (1988). *Hamlet: Film, Television and Audio Performance*. London and Toronto: Associated University Presses.

Kott, Jan (1964). *Shakespeare Our Contemporary*. New York: Doubleday.

Kozintsev, Grigori (1967). *Shakespeare, Time and Conscience*. Trans. Joyce Vining. London: Dennis Dobson.

Lanier, Douglas (2002a). "Shakescorp *Noir*." *Shakespeare Quarterly* 53.2: 157–80.

Lehmann, Courtney (2002b). *Shakespeare Remains*. Ithaca, NY: Cornell University Press.

——, and Lisa S. Starks (2002). *Spectacular Shakespeare: Critical Theory and Popular Cinema*. London: Associated University Presses.

Loehlin, James N. (1997). "'Top of the World, Ma': *Richard III* and Cinematic Convention." In Boose and Burt, eds.: 67–79.

McKellen, Ian, and Richard Loncraine (1996). *William Shakespeare's "Richard III": A Screenplay written by Ian McKellen and Richard Loncraine.* New York: Overlook Press.

McKernan, Luke, and Olwen Terris (1994). *Walking Shadows: Shakespeare in the National Film and Television Archive.* London: BFI Publishing.

McMurtry, Jo (1994). *Shakespeare Films in the Classroom: A Descriptive Guide.* Hamden: Archon Books.

Manvell, Roger (1971). *Shakespeare and the Film.* London: Dent/New York: Praeger.

Rothwell, Kenneth (1999). *A History of Shakespeare on Screen: A Century of Film and Television.* Cambridge: Cambridge University Press (new edition 2004).

——, and Annabelle Meltzer (1990). *Shakespeare on Screen: An International Filmography and Videography.* New York: Neal-Schuman.

Shaughnessy, Robert, ed. (1998). *Shakespeare on Film: Contemporary Critical Essays.* London: Macmillan.

—— (2002). *The Shakespeare Effect: A History of Twentieth-Century Performance.* Basingstoke and New York: Palgrave Macmillan.

Taymor, Julie (2000a). *Titus: The Illustrated Screenplay, Adapted from the Play by William Shakespeare.* Introduction by Jonathan Bate. New York: Newmarket Press.

Willson, Robert F., Jr. (2000). *Shakespeare in Hollywood, 1929–1956.* Madison and Teaneck: Fairleigh Dickinson University Press/London: Associated University Presses.

Worthen, W. B. (1997). *Shakespeare and the Authority of Performance.* Cambridge: Cambridge University Press.

—— (2003). *Shakespeare and the Force of Modern Performance.* Cambridge: Cambridge University Press.

Index